DOCUMENTARY ACROSS PLATFORMS

DOCUMENTARY ACROSS PLATFORMS

Reverse Engineering Media, Place, and Politics

Patricia R. Zimmermann
Foreword by Gina Marchetti

INDIANA UNIVERSITY PRESS

This book is a publication of

Indiana University Press
Office of Scholarly Publishing
Herman B Wells Library 350
1320 East 10th Street
Bloomington, Indiana 47405 USA

iupress.indiana.edu

© 2019 by Patricia R. Zimmermann

All rights reserved
No part of this book may be reproduced or utilized in any form or by any means, electronic or mechanical, including photocopying and recording, or by any information storage and retrieval system, without permission in writing from the publisher. The paper used in this publication meets the minimum requirements of the American National Standard for Information Sciences—Permanence of Paper for Printed Library Materials, ANSI Z39.48-1992.

Cataloging information is available from the Library of Congress.

ISBN 978-0-253-04346-7 (hdbk.)
ISBN 978-0-253-04347-4 (pbk.)
ISBN 978-0-253-04349-8 (web PDF)

1 2 3 4 5   23 22 21 20 19

*For Sean Zimmermann Auyash
and Stewart Auyash*

CONTENTS

Foreword by Gina Marchetti ix

Introduction 1

Part I Platforms

1 Reverse Engineering: Taking Things Apart for the New Global Media Ecology 15

2 Ardent Spaces, Formidable Environments 29

3 Precious Places: Scribe Video Center, Philadelphia 37

4 The Hand That Holds Up All This Falling: The Works of Daniel Reeves 43

5 Cartographies of Impossible and Possible Worlds: The Photography of Michael Kienitz 59

6 Black Soil: *Chernozem* and *Tusit* in Ukraine 71

Part II Reversals

7 Matrices of War 83

8 Blasting War 105

9 Digital Deployments 115

10 Public Domains: Engaging Iraq through Experimental Digitalities 135

11 Cambodian Digital Imaginary Archive:
    Genocide, Lara Croft, and Crafts *151*

Part III Histories

12 The Home Movie Archive Live *165*

13 Throbs and Pulsations:
    Les LeVeque and the Digitizing of Desire *179*

14 Just Say No: Negativland's *No Business* *189*

15 Remixed and Revisited Black Cinema:
    Oscar Micheaux's *Within Our Gates* Live Project *199*

16 Live!: Reconnecting the Histories of Live Multimedia
    Performance *213*

17 Toward a Theory of Participatory
    New Media Documentary *231*

Part IV Speculative Engineering

18 Home Movie Axioms *241*

19 Speculations on Environmental Sensualities and
    Eco-Documentaries *245*

20 Speculations on Reverse Engineering: Algorithms for
    Recombinant Documentaries across Platforms *249*

Acknowledgments *253*

Index *259*

FOREWORD

JOHN GRIERSON FAMOUSLY DEFINED DOCUMENTARY AS THE "CREATIVE treatment of actuality" in 1926.[1] However, he certainly did not have the final word on the matter, and the critical engagement of media practitioners with the technologies, aesthetics, politics, and cultural dynamics of nonfiction continues. As a collection of key essays by Patricia Zimmermann, a towering figure in documentary theory, new media, film history, and social critique, *Documentary across Platforms: Reverse Engineering Media, Place, and Politics* makes an intervention in an evolving field at a critical juncture in its own history. Twitter rants, fake news, alternative facts, and mockumentaries have thrown what Gilles Deleuze in *Cinema 2: The Time-Image* calls our "faith in the real" into crisis.[2] Zimmermann, however, has the rare ability to wade into this morass and shed a light on the vital role documentary plays in effecting social change. While news comes and goes, documentaries endure by providing us with a more capacious picture in which quotidian concerns become part of greater social patterns responsive to political action. Citizen activists, radical artists, and media guerrillas search for ways to speak truth to power, produce meaningful change, and challenge orthodoxies. Ripping through propaganda and pointing to enlightened engagement, documentaries, at their progressive best, offer hope that images can, indeed, transform lives for the better.

Zimmermann's essays span continents and decades, and her critical concerns range from home movies to environmental agitprop. In this book, she calls for an ecology of nonfiction practices to provide a critical platform for thinking beyond more conventional feature-length documentaries aired on public television or screened on the festival circuit. Ecology has its roots in the Greek word *oikos*, which refers to home as a dwelling place. Although ecology as an interdisciplinary science deals with the relationship of organisms to their environments, the term also has a social dimension. Human ecology concerns the ways in which people interact with institutions within a socially constructed setting. Zimmermann's focus on new documentary ecologies draws on all the rich significations of that term from its link to the domestic in amateur filmmaking to its political engagement with environmentalism and the emerging discipline of ecocriticism. Documentary ecologies, moreover, speak to a deep and sustained critique of human institutions predicated on injustices stemming from capitalist exploitation, sexual and racial inequalities, and imperialist profiteering. As Zimmermann points out, the progressive documentary goes beyond conventional screens and the false dichotomy between art and action by speaking to the need for practitioners to be intimately engaged with their communities as the environments that sustain them.

The digital revolution spawned a plethora of new nonfiction organisms. This burgeoning ecology of installation, performance, new media, and participatory arts defies easy categorization. Zimmermann steps in as a perspicacious guide to an environment that sustains a burgeoning diversity of forms, from YouTube intermediations to hybrid autobiographical installations. With an emphasis on exhibition as well as production, she offers a primer on how documentaries work concretely in local venues such as museums, galleries, concert halls, and community centers as well as globally through transnational digital networks connected to NGOs, trade unions, and political movements around the world. Onscreen and off these documentaries provide alternatives to skewed propaganda and mainstream pablum. Zimmermann, to her considerable credit, does them justice.

Her role as an essayist, in fact, parallels the work of the documentarists she researches.[3] It is certainly no coincidence that the seminal theorist of realism, Hungarian Marxist Georg Lukács, should also write eloquently about the essay as a literary form. For Lukács, it is not the essayist's verdict that holds the greatest significance; rather it is the "process of judging."[4] The joy of reading this collection rests with following Zimmermann's critical process as it weaves through chapters written over the span of more than twenty years. Theodor Adorno sees the essay as heresy offering a challenge to the conventional modes of thought: "By transgressing the orthodoxy of thought, something becomes visible in the object which it is orthodoxy's secret purpose to keep invisible."[5] Indeed, these essays bring issues of concern to women, minorities, the disenfranchised, and the dispossessed into clear view.

As *Documentary across Platforms* demonstrates, the essay allows the writer to take risks, experiment, speculate, and explore in ways that more conventional histories of nonfiction film cannot. Her robust and lively conversations with marginalized works make these essays particularly engaging. Her ideas spring from the scintillating cross-fertilization of arts and activism. Each essay collected here represents a particular moment of engagement with a work as part of a festival, installation, exhibition, or collaboration. However, taken together, they function as far more than the sum of each part. They speak to the preoccupations, insights, and commitments of a scholar who sees documentary inside and outside of institutions such as colleges, universities, museums, and film festivals and who can spotlight the contribution these various works make to the larger tapestry of engaged media arts and progressive public discourse.

Zimmermann blesses documentary film criticism, theory, and history with her heretical views on the subject. She takes her readers away from the feature film and television journalism to show us the world on small screens, in unconventional exhibition spaces, and from people neglected by commercial media outlets. Lukács celebrates minutia as essential to the essayist's vision of the world, which he calls "the eternal smallness of the most profound work of the intellect in face of life."[6] This does not mean seeing the world in miniature, but rather the opposite, encountering the world's depths in the details of daily life. Zimmermann captures this *smallness* in her essays in a way that brings the bigger picture into sharp focus, highlighting the relations of power that prompt the documentarist to take action by taking up the camera. She provides us with what Fredric Jameson in *The Geopolitical Aesthetic: Cinema and Space in the World System* calls a *cognitive mapping* of geopolitical points of contact invisible within the ideological haze favored by for-profit mainstream media.[7]

Through mapping the world of the documentary, Zimmermann takes us on an intellectual journey she characterizes as reverse engineering in the volume's opening chapter. She invites us to dismantle these documentaries in order to give us the tools needed to make critical and practical use of them—expanding the nonfiction canon, inspiring new production, and nurturing alternative possibilities for screen activists. When I think of reverse engineering, I imagine a cheeky tinkerer trying to get around patent restrictions by dismantling an overpriced piece of machinery and copying its constituent parts with just enough variation to avoid litigation. This same spirit of righteous piracy animates alternative documentaries that reverse engineer the aesthetic norms and practices of commercial media. Zimmermann, too, reverse engineers screen criticism to put it in the service of underappreciated works by artists who stand outside of the established methods used to analyze nonfiction. Through these essays, she manufactures her own methodological toolkit that merges theory and history to reassemble the discipline to accommodate the marginal, the radical, and the neglected. Inspired by the works she showcases, Zimmermann shows us how the "stuff" of film scholarship "gets made" and initiates her readers into the delights of documentary criticism.

These essays not only rewrite the putative history of nonfiction filmmaking in the late twentieth and early twenty-first century, they force us to confront the ideological underpinnings of media historiography by extending the borders defining the documentary as a form. Gender, race, ethnicity, class, sexual orientation, and other markers of bodies lacking social, economic, and political power come back as actors on the historical stage rather than mute and marginalized objects of oppression. As the protagonists of the revised history found in these documentaries, Zimmermann reconfigures the media archive and gives the public sphere a more inclusive and dynamic cultural force.

Zimmermann developed her scholarly perspective during a time of enormous change in the academy. Civil rights agitation, antiwar protests, and the rise of feminism's second wave coincided with the growth of cinema and media studies in American universities, and these essays speak to the intellectual maturity of a scholar rooted in that tradition. Although some feminists claim women's traditional role as nurturers makes them natural peacemakers, the existence of women warriors who take up arms around the world testifies to the fact that war crosses gender categorizations. However, as victims in equal measure with males and subject in larger numbers to sexual torture, genocidal rape, and sexist intimidation, women emerge as protagonists against the landscape of military conflict in a decidedly gendered fashion. The fact that the essays collected here link Zimmermann's feminist scholarship with her intense critical scrutiny of imperialism and war on screen seems apt. Anti-imperial feminism critiques the predominantly male power of the military, and Zimmermann weaves a seamless tapestry in this volume in which antiwar and antipatriarchal sentiments serve to ground her perceptive analyses of the role technology plays in warfare and in domestic life. The same digital technology gamifies military operations in the battlefield and chronicles the everyday life of the family. Drones assassinate military leaders by remote control, but the antiwar movement also happens online, and feminism pops up as flash mobs formed through social media. Undeniably, Zimmermann's scholarship speaks to the contradictory nature of the digital present without losing sight of its potential for substantive and sustainable social change.

In fact, the essays offer a scholarly autobiography by highlighting Zimmermann's love affair with nonfiction through her personal involvement with Women Direct, the Finger Lakes Environmental Film Festival, the Robert Flaherty Film Seminars, and many other curatorial endeavors. The chapter on her own contribution to innovative forms of film exhibition including commissioning music and spoken-word accompaniment for a screening of pioneering African American Oscar Micheaux's *Within Our Gates* (1920) takes the book beyond conventional film criticism and into the realm of the academic memoir. Her chronicles of her travels to the Ukraine and Cambodia speak to her personal engagement with the documents, art objects, and artifacts she analyzes.

As engineer and archeologist of the documentary, Zimmermann mines the home movie and digs into the film archive. In fact, like the author, many of the filmmakers featured in the book have a form of what could be called *archive fever*, but not necessarily in the sense meant by Jacques Derrida in *Archive Fever: A Freudian Impression*.[8] Les LeVeque, Craig Baldwin, Art Jones, Negativland, and Code Pink, among others, raid the archive, expand the canon, and give the concept of the public domain a new significance. Montage, bricolage, the compilation film, and the cut-up aesthetic play a key role in the agitprop works Zimmermann favors. At several points, she shares her love for early Soviet nonfiction film with tributes to Sergei Eisenstein, Dziga Vertov, and Alexander Dovzhenko, as well as the long tradition of left-wing documentary from the Workers' Film and Photo Leagues of the Great Depression to Latin American third cinema, Newsreel, Paper

Tiger TV, Scribe Video, and the other politically engaged media groups discussed throughout the book.

Sergei Eisenstein trained as a civil engineer before turning to theater and film. However, he never completely turned his back on his early schooling, but used these skills to create films in which the aesthetic tension of conflicting forces generated new meanings through montage. Similarly, Zimmermann puts her reverse engineering skills to use to construct critical approaches apposite to the emerging documentary ecologies of the digital age. In *The Long Revolution*, Raymond Williams speaks of the importance of a society's *structure of feeling* as *practical consciousness* that describes an era's lived experience rather than the official ideology of the time.[9] For Zimmermann, the organization of this book into four sections parallels the emergence of the structure of feeling that characterizes the dawn of the new media age. The initial focus on *platforms* foregrounds the breakdown of the lines between production and exhibition in the new documentary ecology. Rather than focusing on a single feature film in each chapter, Zimmermann considers the role of the collective (Not Channel Zero), the curator *(Fierce)*, the community (Scribe Video), and the nation (America, Vietnam, Cambodia, El Salvador, Northern Ireland, Pakistan, and the Ukraine, among others). The section on *reversals* flips these platforms over to discover how the digital contributes to war but also opens up possibilities for resistance just as the photographs documenting the Khmer Rouge's extermination of Cambodia's citizenry becomes Rithy Panh's memento mori *S21: The Khmer Rouge Killing Machine* (2003). The national and the personal archive merge in the third section on *histories* as Zimmermann demonstrates the importance of expanding the canon as well as repurposing commercial images for social critique. Classical Hollywood provides images for experimentation that uncovers the zeitgeist of the digital age. The book builds, then, to its climax in *speculative engineering*, which spreads the participatory impulse at the heart of reverse engineering into the theoretical domain by extending an invitation to engage in DIY screen criticism and documentary practice. The book's structure maps a new theory of the documentary suitable across media platforms, personal styles, aesthetic strategies, and geographic borders.

In the first section of the book, on *platforms*, Zimmermann does a superb job of showing how documentaries not only operate across various media technologies but also serve as platforms for debate and arenas for democracy. The initial section sets the stage for Zimmermann's advocacy of participatory documentary as a move away from the "personal, individualistic, and idiosyncratic" to a direct engagement with the community. This theme runs throughout the book as Zimmermann draws on Nicolas Bourriaud's *Relational Aesthetics* to celebrate the ways in which digital technology and new forms of media exhibition provide participatory and collaborative opportunities that blur the line between media artist and spectator.[10]

In a dialectical turn, the next section, on *reversals*, looks at the way in which media arts intervene when democracy breaks down during war. Zimmermann begins with conventional warfare (Vietnam), pointing out the ways in which aerial footage from downed B-52s was reversed engineered into material for antiwar compilation films. Daniel Reeves reworks the trauma of the war through still photographs and museum installations. Still images testify to the terror of the American bombing as well as the horrors of the killing fields in Cambodia. Satellite technology (Gulf War; Kosovo) creates digital "warfare without bodies." However, Michael Kienitz returns these bodies to our gaze through photos of children in warzones. The society of surveillance and drone warfare (post-9/11) meets its critical cinematic match in Mohsen Makhmalbaf's *Kandahar* (2001), in which a female journalist's physical point of view from behind her burqa speaks to the gendered nature of the military gaze. War becomes *history* as the third section of the book shows how documentary practices reanimate the archive by reworking the facts of the past in the service of present struggles.

In *Keywords*, Raymond Williams notes that, linguistically and historically, the word *theory* shares common roots with words related to the senses, particularly to sight.[11] For Zimmermann, the spectacle at the heart of all images invites theoretical speculation on their utility in enabling us to see new worlds, unexpected connections, and networks of struggle. The final section moves, therefore, from historical evidence to speculation on the future, and Zimmermann excels at putting her finger on the documentary's role as instigator of progressive political action. The concluding chapters invite us to participate in the author's project and push the boundaries of the documentary practice in our own way and on our own terms. Zimmermann's work speaks to moments of crisis and states of emergency; however, it also exhibits tremendous hope. With these exquisite essays, we take off into a future of digital interconnection in order to live rather than simply imagine a more just, inclusive, and peaceful world.

—Gina Marchetti,
University of Hong Kong

GINA MARCHETTI is Professor of Comparative Literature at the University of Hong Kong. She is author of *Romance and the "Yellow Peril": Race, Sex and Discursive Strategies in Hollywood Fiction*; *From Tian'anmen to Times Square: Transnational China and the Chinese Diaspora on Global Screens*; *The Chinese Diaspora on American Screens: Race, Sex, and Cinema*; *Andrew Lau and Alan Mak's Infernal Affairs—The Trilogy*; and *Citing China: Politics, Postmodernism, and World Cinema*.

Notes

1. John Grierson, *Grierson on Documentary* (London: Collins, 1946), 147.
2. Gilles Deleuze, *Cinema 2: The Time-Image*, trans. Hugh Tomlinson and Robert Galeta (Minneapolis: University of Minnesota Press, 1997).
3. See Timothy Corrigan, *The Essay Film: From Montaigne, After Marker* (New York: Oxford University Press, 2011).
4. Georg Lukács, "On the Nature and Form of the Essay," *Soul & Form*, trans. Anna Bostock (London: Merlin, 1974), 1–18.
5. Theodor Adorno, "The Essay as Form," *New German Critique*, no. 32 (Spring-Summer, 1984): 151–171, 171.
6. Lukács, "On the Nature," 9.
7. Fredric Jameson, *The Geopolitical Aesthetic: Cinema and Space in the World System* (Bloomington: Indiana University Press, 1992).
8. Jacques Derrida, *Archive Fever: A Freudian Impression*, trans. Eric Prenowitz (Chicago: University of Chicago Press, 199).
9. Raymond Williams, *The Long Revolution* (London: Chatto & Windus, 1961).
10. See Nicolas Bourriaud, *Relational Aesthetics* (Paris: Les Presse du Reel, 1998).
11. Raymond Williams, *Keywords: A Vocabulary of Culture and Society* (London: Croom Helm, 1976).

DOCUMENTARY ACROSS PLATFORMS

INTRODUCTION

Why This Book

Documentary is not simply a genre.

Documentary cannot be reduced to one form or set of practices. Rather, it may be more productively thought of as a continually evolving constellation of practices across many different technologies that investigate, engage, and interrogate the historical world.

Documentary, then, represents a conceptual practice presenting us with strategies to think through how the world is organized and to imagine ways that it might be reorganized with ideas, communities, and actions. Documentary practices are multiple, diverse, and urgent. Documentary, then, can be seen as a historiographic method, a way to consider evidence, explanation, and context.

This book is a collection of essays and speculations about documentary and experimental media work written over the last twenty years and published in anthologies, journals, magazines, museum catalogs, and other venues beyond more traditional scholarly journals in the fields of screen and documentary studies. These essays share a similar set of concerns. They envision documentary as a complex ecology composed of different technologies, sets of practices, and specific relationships to politics, communities, social struggles, and engagement. I use the term ecology to suggest a diversity of practices and a heterogeneous documentary culture, rather than a monoculture.

In documentary studies, whether in the United States or elsewhere, much of our work has focused solely on long-form documentaries in the modes of art cinema or televisual styles. These practices are often identified with what is sometimes referred to as the documentary industry, whether the projects are realist direct cinema, are deductive interviews with archival evidence, or use more art cinema strategies of aesthetic complexities and ambiguities. Instead of the monoculture of feature-length works, the notion of a heterogeneous documentary ecology could expand the terrains of documentary into a more variegated landscape comprised of dynamic interrelationships among different layers of practices and economics.

Thinking of documentary as an ecological system also provides a way to bypass unproductive binaries between documentary and experimental practices, between highly resourced feature films and low-resourced community media, between film and photography, between the moving image in a theater and the art installation in the gallery. These essays map vibrant and emerging documentary ecologies beyond larger-budget feature-length festival or television projects. Both of these have attracted significant scholarly as well as exhibition attention in film festivals, theaters, and in broadcast venues. In contrast, the essays assembled here engage alternative documentary practices marked by their scalability and sustainability, projects that are small rather than large in scope.

In this diverse new documentary ecology, many of the projects I have written about are low budget or no budget, produced with more modest resources. Quite a few of these projects are short. None of the projects were produced by major media outlets, and most did not garner major support from foundation or government grants. These essays probe a different landscape of documentary practice, one that is more modest, on a smaller scale, and often in a liminal zone between arts practices and political engagement, between a documentary vision and communication. Many are modular, adaptive to their context, and unfixed. They exploit both sophisticated high-end professional and amateur, consumer-grade technologies. They are marked by movement and migrations through different political terrains, different platforms, and different exhibition contexts.

In this context, we might posit a documentary octagon, composed of eight panels: technologies/platforms, form/aesthetics, structure, sound, historiography, context, community, and spaces/exhibition. The essays in *Documentary across Platforms* engage different parts of this octagon, arranging and rearranging its parts in different combinations.

Reverse Engineering and Historiography

The term *reverse engineering* in the subtitle of this book suggests a conceptual model of documentary—not simply as a representation or argument about the historical world, but also as a dismantling and rebuilding of the world through conceptual redesign.

My argument advocating the notion of a documentary ecology is not located in the realm of the pastoral or idealized. Instead, I consider ecology a dynamic interaction among nature, social relations, and the built environment. In looking for an alternative to the artificially imposed binaries of mainstream and oppositional, commercial and independent, documentary and experimental, I encountered the idea of reverse engineering after hearing some graduate students in information science critique the positioning of new media as immaterial at a symposium in the mid-2000s at Cornell University.

The notion of reverse engineering posits that ideas as well as things can be regarded as material and therefore be taken apart. Reverse engineering is a process whereby something is disassembled in order to understand how it works, and then rebuilt into something new and better. It is an idea derived from software and technology, but one that can offer some new ways of conceptualizing the work of documentary across platforms.

Reverse engineering suggests materiality, the historical world, and agency, refusing to consider any construct as insurmountable or fixed. It means taking a concept or an object apart in order to enhance it, to disassemble and analyze it to discover notions of form, function, operation, and structure. Reverse engineering is a strategy employed by those who are not resource rich: it is less glamorous and immersed in popular culture than hacking and less full-stop confrontational than piracy. Instead, reverse engineering is a strategy that can unleash invention and imagination to change the environment.

Reverse engineering also alludes to the assumption that everything can be continually reconfigured, reimagined, and remade to work better. This strategy seemed to explain many of the documentary projects I was exploring in these essays. These projects appeared to be about much more than just the image. Rather, they operated in the nexus of places, politics, spaces, systems, and technologies.

Evoking a reverse engineering model, the projects I write about in the essays in this collection present multiple strategies of intervention into power structures: adaptations, infiltrations, recalibrations, reinventions, summonings. They move not only against but through, around, behind, and beneath power structures. These images, projects, and sounds live not solely as representations, but also as an archive to be reanimated through reversals and reengineered spaces.

The essays in *Documentary across Platforms* vary in the kinds of documentary practices and platforms they analyze, but they share some common themes of marginalized practices, political engagements, polyvocal stories, scalable low-cost strategies, and war. Each of these essays either directly or indirectly raises questions of historiography. They probe both straightforwardly and obliquely how documentary in its many iterations engages in deliberate acts of historiography. Through excavation, exhumations, and archaeologies, these various documentary practices posit history not as laden with artifacts of the past, but as a series of active renegotiations to create new imaginaries of possible futures.

Invoked, inferred, and interrogated, the historical in these essays presents itself as polyphonic, with multiple routes through the terrains of documentary. A critical historiographic orientation expands the kinds of evidence marshaled and deploys analytical models to explain and interpret patterns. Many of the essays suggest that documentary operates as a practice of creating new relations between context, place, and representation. The historiographic in documentary, then, generates multiple pathways, gestures, and inflections rather than pronouncements on the past. These projects often work with or create a distributed archive of image and sound, configuring it as a mobile, constantly changing interface.

The works addressed in these essays operate in a different social and political milieu than a festival film: their vectors may be within communities of place or online, or within political and social struggles. They chart a world of documentary engagements within different systems of circulation and in different kinds of institutional infrastructures beyond the festival and the television broadcast, such as activist groups, the art world, colleges and universities, concert halls, media centers, museums, online communities, political groups, and specific local communities. These essays also chart a documentary ecology that migrates across a variety of different interfaces and platforms. The ecology is comprised of forms (algorithms, new media, film, video art, photography, live performance), locations (archives, apps, installations, websites, social media, community media), and practices (amateurs, remixes, gaming, user-generated projects). Together, these essays form a kind of symbiotic ecosystem of alternative ways of thinking about and practicing documentary.

One way to categorize the works that *Documentary across Platforms* analyzes is to identify them as more marginalized micropractices in contrast to bigger-budget, long-form documentaries. All the projects I write about share an orientation toward and a practice of generating dialogue and conversation. They operate in constant movement against dominant forms such as character-driven structures and traditional narrative arcs in order to dislodge their powers through dispersal and decentralization. This is not to argue against long-form documentaries, which we all teach and program, but to argue against their domination of our discourse, our disciplines of screen and documentary studies, our writing, and our programming. This is essential so that we may carve out conceptual space to consider a more heterogeneous documentary ecology. The works discussed in these essays share an interest in opening up ways to think about documentary that are in and of themselves a practice of historiography, asking questions we should ask of all documentary forms: What is evidence, what are useful analytical models, what is significant, and how can we understand the world better?

The essays and speculations in this volume also explore a different approach to writing and organization than my more traditionally conceived scholarly projects. They are intended to be more poetic and lyrical than academic and tradition bound. Some utilize a structure outside the deductive model of argument or the application of a particular theoretical model for analysis. Some emerged out of writing for the art world, the museum, or a general audience rather than for a specialized scholarly readership. Some were written as literary nonfiction, employing a more exploratory, meandering, personal style. The speculations that make up the last section of this book were inspired by activist media makers, archivists, museum programmers, students, and audiences for invited lectures who asked me for some form of concrete takeaway from these exploratory theoretical ideas, something that could be referenced and read more easily and quickly than a scholarly book or article.

Theoretical models of critical historiography together with documentary, feminist, new media, poststructuralist, and postcolonial theory inform and locate all of these essays. Each provides a close analysis of form, structure, style, approach, context, and exhibition to show how documentary functions as a form of historiographic inquiry. Across all these essays, an argument coalesces around thinking about documentary as multivalent and polyphonic, a system of contiguity rather than continuity where placing works in juxtaposition and collage can move us to understand documentary as a complex of form, meaning, structure, argument, technology, and community.

The Origin Story of *Documentary across Platforms*

The essays and speculations gathered in this book emerge out of the specific historical context of my own trajectory as a scholar and writer as well as my location in upstate New York. As a scholar, my research over the last thirty-five years has focused on the areas of documentary history and theory, with a heavy emphasis on primary research in archives in order to tell the story of more marginalized practices in amateur film, documentary, experimental work, institutional histories of nonprofit media, new media, and photography. These projects have been labyrinthine, long term, overlarge, and often overwhelming as I tried to organize an argument out of the chaos of documents and practices. The research and writing process involved in these projects has been slow, inching forward incrementally as I figured out how the pieces of these puzzles might cohere into a pattern, a history, an argument. My engagement in these writing projects has been a process of immersion and investigation.

Simultaneously, I have been intrigued by emerging practices, projects, and tactics developing from media ecologies beyond the scope of more traditionally academic projects. These new documentary works provoked questions and rattled my accustomed theories and methodologies. I am a screen studies scholar trained in the late 1970s and early 1980s at the University of Iowa, and then for graduate school at the University of Wisconsin—places in the middle of the country with no major media industries and few art cinemas or independent media scenes. I believe this context heightened my interest in alternative media practices linked to specific marginalized communities and radical politics.

During this period our field was trying to define and legitimate itself as an area of academic study. It was a time of conflict between different theoretical schools. Psychoanalysis and Marxism fought for dominion over the field, and new approaches like cultural studies, feminism, industry studies, and the new film history pushed their way into film and media academic research—and recalibrated it. My own experience of this time was that people thinking about film and media in intellectual and political ways defined themselves not so much as members of the academic discipline of film studies, but as part of an expansive, diverse film culture, which extended far beyond the universities and libraries we worked in.

To think intellectually about cinema, one needed also to be part of cinema culture in as many ways as possible, to be in the world, to consider theory and practice and cinema and politics as continually paired and intertwined. It demanded looking at how cinema engaged politics and people. This experience of film and media culture was formative. To me, it was a volcanic terrain populated with community media, emerging technologies, independent features, international cinemas, and video art offering both hope and despair and generating constant debate about what cinema could be and what it could do politically. As a young scholar, I found film culture broad and perplexing, and because film culture inspired so many unanswered questions, also exhilarating and full of opportunity. In that period, film and media culture functioned as a nodal point to bring together communities, debates, dialogues, ideas, and works.

Looking back, I probably idealize this period, perhaps erasing the difficulties and ruptures so that I can fortify myself and my work for an increasingly challenging political landscape where the amateur, the contentious, the democratic, and the critical discourses of gender, nation, race, and sexuality are attacked and muzzled. Still, part of what I learned during those years has stayed with me, fertilizing all that I did in the subsequent years.

In that period and throughout the decades that followed, I thought of myself as part of screen cultures, rather than screen studies, as part of documentary rather than documentary studies, a term that developed as it was legitimated and professionalized in conferences and books in the early 1990s. As a result, I have always inhabited and worked in multiple screen worlds, as a film programmer; as someone who collaborated with museums and archives; as a film and new media festival codirector; as a member of boards of independent media organizations both local and national; as a presenter at community organizations, festivals, and museums; and as a speaker at events both inside the academy and outside of it in what might be termed third spaces beyond the corporate world and academia.

I experienced screen cultures not as a career, but as a calling, a place to help create discourse and space for engagement about politics, a place for making things public apart from commercial media practices. In the archival world, my interest has been directed toward expanding what is collected to include the amateur and all forms of documentary and to figure out conceptual categories of organizing these materials to make sense of them in a wider way. I also have thought extensively about how to configure these materials so that they would not be seen as inert artifacts but as some active form of history making.

Inspired by the energies of these particular historical moments, I found myself always operating in kind of helix that doubled back on itself, as you will see. With my colleague from the Writing Department, Barbara Adams, I programmed the Women Direct Film and Video Series at Ithaca College, inaugurated in 1981 and continuing for nearly twenty-five years. Observing this series, I saw how audiences engaged feminist political cinema. I saw how programming came alive through a model of heterogeneity when audiences and makers realized that in an open space, anything was possible when an experimental video work was juxtaposed against an activist, community-based project. I moved between historical and theoretical scholarly research and working as a film, media, and new media programmer and as a board member for independent media arts organizations like Cinemapolis (the local nonprofit arts cinema in Ithaca, New York), Northeast Historic Film, the Robert Flaherty Film Seminars, and Women Make Movies.

I also shuttled between working in the long, slow process of historical archival research, often years in the writing with boxes and boxes of documents and notes, and writing shorter pieces on documentary and experimental practices that intrigued me because they represented disjunctures, new openings with the past, paradigm shifts, or unresolved questions. Across the years, the short form of the essay for an audience often outside academia yet frequently including it offered something different than these longer projects: an outlet to experiment with new theories, a way to think about emerging rather than historical practices, a road to travel into the unknown and undertheorized, and a structure where argument, ideas, and language could be the subject of experimentation. These are the essays included in this volume. Although they represent a range of literary strategies, structures, and styles, they are all explorations into unknown territory. In these essays, I often started with a media practice or a topic or a set of concerns that baffled me but which felt like it was reversing how we thought about existing power relations and political systems. Scientists, for example, refer to a subject that captures their interest as an anomaly. An anomaly is a phenomenon that should not occur given prior knowledge systems but appears anyway, leading to new concepts and ways of thinking.

The other context that frames where these essays come from is my specific geographical context of living and working at a small comprehensive college in upstate New York. The degree programs I teach courses in at Ithaca College are mostly professionally oriented toward the commercial film industries and production and do not include many screen studies courses. What could have become the chilling effect of marginalization, where what I loved the most was not considered sufficiently worthy to be taught as a main part of the curriculum, transformed itself into the blessing of community: to circumvent despair and isolation, I had no choice but to build my independent media and documentary networks elsewhere, beyond my particular institution, colleagues, and students.

I was lucky—I lived in upstate New York, a vibrant region for independent media arts in documentary, experimental work, and new media, partly propelled by the generous, field-changing arts funding of the New York State Council on the Arts (NYSCA), and partly nurtured by the many colleges and universities that sprouted out of the hills almost everywhere, each with a different historical contribution to the world of independent screen cultures. Beginning in experimental film in Rochester in the 1920s with the *Fall of the House of Usher* (1928) and in 1949 with the opening of the George Eastman House Museum and Archive, it continued in the 1960s with innovations in the media arts and technology in places like the Experimental Television Center in Owego. The history of cinema production in upstate New York included few feature-length documentary films. Most of the work was short, whether it emerged from activist collectives or from video artists. The NYSCA operated with an explicitly decentralized public arts policy into the geographies of New York, which ensured that media arts funding was distributed beyond New York City to the regions upstate.

In Owego, the Experimental Television Center served as a center for technological innovation, video artist residencies, and support for the exhibition of film, video, and new media from 1971 to 2011. One of the first exhibitions of video art in a museum in the United States was mounted by the Everson Museum at Syracuse University in 1972, featuring the work of Nam June Paik and Charlotte Moorman, and the first video art festivals, curated by Philip Mallory Jones, were held at the Herbert F. Johnson Museum of Art at Cornell University from 1975 to 1984. Organizations such as the Central New York Programmers Group, Cornell Cinema, the Everson Museum of Art at Syracuse University, the Experimental TV Center, the George Eastman House, the Johnson Museum of Art at Cornell University, Media Buffalo, the Robert Flaherty Film Seminar, the Rose Goldsen Archive of New Media Art, and Squeaky Wheel, as well as the journal *Afterimage*, convened people, mounted programs, screened cutting-edge work, and spurred gatherings. For more than three decades, the programming that I saw at Binghamton University, Cornell University, Ithaca College, the Robert Flaherty Film Seminars, SUNY Buffalo, Syracuse University, and the University of Rochester, and the festivals, gatherings, screenings, symposia, and talks I took part in felt alive, alluring, necessary, and urgent, and often confusing, ephemeral, and inexplicable.

Film and media culture—not just studies—thrives in upstate New York, part of our region of gray skies, hiking trails, hills, lakes, rain, snow, and waterfalls. Most of my colleagues in critical studies who live or have lived in this region combine the two worlds of screen studies and screen cultures. They are scholars who research and write and also programmers who bring emerging media cultures to audiences and create space for public interaction with this work: some of these are Tula Goenka (Syracuse University), Roger Hallas (Syracuse University), Dale Hudson (Ithaca College and now New York University Abu Dhabi), Scott MacDonald (Hamilton College, formerly at Utica College and Bard College), Laura U. Marks (a former graduate student at the University of Rochester and assistant editor at *Afterimage*), Tim Murray (Cornell University), and Claudia Pederson (Ithaca College and now Wichita State University). In 1997, with Michelle Materre, I programmed a four-day Flaherty Seminar at Ithaca College entitled "Explorations in Memory and Modernity," one of my initial forays into programming and thinking about new media, especially about all the work percolating across the upstate New York region from Buffalo to Albany and Rochester to Binghamton.

These years saw a fortuitous confluence of factors: my own institution that positioned screen studies as ancillary to production courses and extracurricular hands-on engagement, the upstate New York region as a thriving media scene, the many academic colleagues at other institutions who migrated between scholarly work and public programming, and encountering work that unsettled my preconceptions. This assembly generated a desire in me to contribute to the dialogues and debates in a faster, shorter form of writing. In fact, my regional colleagues all seemed to write scholarly books but also articles for journals, magazines, and museum catalogs as a way to stay on the front lines. So, to come clean in this personal narrative, I copied them.

The Structure of the Book

Documentary across Platforms is composed of twenty essays and speculations, written over the last twenty years. This is the first time these essays have been brought together. They were originally published in *Afterimage, Framework, The Moving Image*, the National Association for Media Arts and Culture publications, museum catalogs, special issues of journals, and some anthologies. They are not arranged chronologically. Instead, they are divided into four conceptual categories that progress from the material to the strategic, the archival, and the speculative: Platforms, Reversals, Histories, and Speculative Engineering. Each of these sections works with what I have begun to identify as a documentary octagon, a fluid schematic foregrounding different aspects of technologies/platforms, form/aesthetics, structure, sound, historiography, context, community, and exhibition spaces.

The first section, Platforms, features essays that consider documentary across different interfaces and technologies, including community-based collaborative media, experimental shorts, installations, photography, new media art, and social media. These different platforms engage the historiographic as an active process of communities, context, reception, spaces, and structure. Documentary as probed in this section occupies multiple decentralized zones. This section looks at the documentary project as dispersed across many different technologies and interfaces. Projects often move across interfaces in fluid ways, layering plural temporalities through new imaginary zones composed of networks, public places, and technologies. The projects analyzed in this section consider the function of documentary to be an exploration of microterritories, microhistories, and microplaces, a historiography moving from the macro to the particular.

The projects in this section operate as transversals, positing documentary as a historiographic enterprise focused on reconfigurations of places, politics, and technologies. To open up the documentary project beyond the theatrical and broadcast industry models, this section explores its diverse platforms: collaborative projects, community media, digital paintings, film, games, installations, loops, new media, photography, robots, shorts, video, and web-based work. These multiple platforms suggest a shift in documentary to the modular and the small, so documentary can be seen as an ideological constellation of discourses about power and conflict. The essays in this section probe the relationships between conflict zones and documentary in Cambodia, El Salvador, India, Malaysia, Nicaragua, Pakistan, Ukraine, and the United States.

The second section, Reversals, groups together essays that deal with documentary historiographies of wars in Cambodia and Iraq. These essays look to how documentaries of state-sponsored wars utilize argumentative structures, context, form/aesthetics, and technology as a reverse engineering strategy, asking audiences to engage in critical opposition to dominant power relations. This section functions on two levels. First, it seeks to explore how documentary works to reverse the power of hegemony and dominance. Second, it looks at how documentary practices reverse the occupation of discourse by mainstream commercial media to create space and place. The term *reversal* suggests a different strategy than oppositional or against, one that presents a new domain rather than a negativity.

This section explores how the documentary project across platforms engages questions of war and political trauma. These essays argue against unproductive binaries of mainstream versus indie film; analog versus digital; features versus shorts; embodied versus ephemeral; transnational versus local; and material versus immaterial. They look at conflict zones in Afghanistan, Cambodia, Indonesia, Iraq, and Kosovo and how documentary across platforms has operated to reverse their existence as illusions by locating them firmly in the material. The essays assembled here share an interest in resisting this disembodiment. They propose a strategy of reversal to circumvent unproductive binaries. They probe interstitial zones, attempting to uncover where engaged publics and democratic places can emerge.

In Reversals, different technologies and platforms such as activist documentary, cable television, Flash animation, handicrafts, networks, new media art, and short-form works mobilize reversals. The projects analyzed in this section work with ideas of sedimentary and plural pasts, multiple in their complexity. The historical and the political in documentary are investigated as transformative acts to reconsider and recalibrate how we think about conflict zones.

The essays in the third section, Histories, investigate how documentary practices operate in conversation with historiography, either through communities, exhibitions, images, or soundscapes. The essays in this section position the documentary archive as a site for active engagement to generate new historiographic formulations in different exhibition contexts and platforms. This section considers different ways in which a diverse set of documentary practices engage the archive, artifacts, history, and the historiographic as dialectical and dialogical processes. Taken as a group, the essays in this section conceptualize history as spatialized rather than linear, mobilizing contiguity rather than continuity. Constructing history through collage, the projects analyzed in this section align with postcolonial and poststructural concepts of multiplicity, mutability, performativity, and polyvocality.

Many of the documentary projects unpacked in this section move from the image to the interface, from the archive as static to the archive as dynamic. The projects interpreted here all share an interest in collaborative, contingent, participatory, and reanimated zones that work to disrupt received wisdom. They consider the materiality of the archive as functioning in a state of constant transformation. The essays in this section explore ambient media, audio projects, collage, live performance, locative media, new media art, remixes, and short films. They ask how the documentary project's multiplication of formats, places, and spaces have engaged in a reanimation and reconfiguration of the archive and its artifacts. All of these essays ask how the documentary project engages mutation as a tactic to disrupt our notions of what constitutes an archive, what is evidence, and what is documentary.

The final section, Speculative Engineering, ends the book on a more utopian, open-ended, and imaginary note. It features three axioms and speculations about home movies, environmental documentary, reverse engineering, and recombinant documentary practices. These speculations were developed through collaborations with archives, artists, colleagues, museums, musicians, and programmers who asked for condensed versions of ideas in my books, essays, and talks that could be used for creative projects, grant writing, live performance remixes, or teaching.

This final section does not include analytical essays. Instead, these speculations move in two dialectical directions. Informed by critical historiographic theories, these speculations serve as a coda for ideas traversed throughout this volume, a kind of summary of the processes of collage, contiguity, dispersals, polyphony, and transversals. These three sets of speculations also operate in the reverse direction as an opening and loosening up of documentary, considering interconnections, moving vectors, multiple temporalities, and recombinant theories as a way to create imaginary places in interstitial zones.

These speculations were created to be deployed as malleable documents for handouts for students and audiences, live performances, takeaways from lectures, and nonprofits looking for language for grants and projects. They are presented in numbered lists so that they can be utilized in a modular way, rearranged and reconfigured by the user. The numbering is arbitrary; the concepts can be used in different ways, in different combinations, for different purposes. Operating as a coda, they also offer a more utopian view of documentary and its theoretical apparatuses as that which opens toward unknown media, places, platforms, politics, and technologies.

All of these speculations have been performed live as collaborative endeavors, with amateur archival film projections or new media remixes on a screen, with live music and multiple readers/performers at conferences, festivals, and symposia. In many ways, these performances embodied the ideas that *Documentary across Platforms* attempts to open up. They moved ideas and images across platforms into different exhibition spaces, reverse engineering documentary theories in collaboration with communities.

PART I
PLATFORMS

Figure 1.1. *Sporting Life* (Philip Mallory Jones, US, 2016). Image courtesy of Philip Mallory Jones.

1

REVERSE ENGINEERING

Taking Things Apart for the New Global Media Ecology*

Reverse Engineering in Vietnam and Iraq

Engineers use reverse engineering to identify the components and interrelationships of a system, dismantling technologies in order to understand how their constituent parts articulate to create representations at another level of abstraction. Reverse engineering breaks codes and invents new forms, always building something better. It customizes tools for new uses in new interfaces, spaces, and technologies. Extended into a metaphorical model, reverse engineering becomes a way to conceptualize and analyze documentary media projects, combining machines, representation, and technologies in collage. In this sense, reverse engineering does not simply default to ideas such as pastiche or remixing, which center primarily on the presentational. Rather, reverse engineering can be a radical heuristic, functioning theoretically and practically to understand and intervene in the new media ecologies. It works in all levels of abstraction, taking things apart and rebuilding them in new ways.[1]

A theory and practice of reverse engineering in global media ecologies can only be considered within the transnational matrix of empires divided by race,

---

* This essay was initially delivered in 2005 as a keynote address for a conference at the University of Iowa, organized by faculty members Kembrew McLeod and Rudolph Kuenzli, called "Collage as Cultural Practice." The conference brought together a diverse group of artists, hackers, musicians, scholars, and writers for forums, panels, and workshops to discuss collage and appropriation as radical acts. My talk was titled "Reverse Engineering the New Global Media Ecology." Since I would be returning to Iowa as the Ida Beam Distinguished Visiting Professor at the university, I avoided formal academic presentational style and addressed media and politics with an organic structure evoking collage rather than linear argument. I projected a PowerPoint deck with images of the projects and live links to the websites in the paper, which served as one layer of the argument, showing a variety of approaches and styles of reverse engineering. Filmmaker Craig Baldwin remixed these images live as I spoke. The keynote was later revised into an essay published as "Reverse Engineering: Dismantling and Customizing for the New Global Media Ecology," *Afterimage* 34, no. 1–2 (2006): 66–72. To better situate the ideas historically, the essay from *Afterimage* was revised and retitled for this book.

class, gender, and sexualities. It serves in this context as a conceptual metaphor, a strategy, and a tactic. Most importantly, we must reverse engineer the amnesia and anesthesia that transnational capital and authoritarianism produces, replacing it with plural geographies, temporalities, and an incessant, insistent sense of community across differences. This must be based on a historiography of contiguities, pluralities, polyphony, and polyvocality, creating a new composition. For example, digital media artist Philip Mallory Jones creates paintings where each component represents a different moment of racialized history, connecting the disparate locations of the African diaspora, from Africa to the Caribbean to the United States. His work constructs contiguities from multiple geographic spaces to reverse engineer the separations that fragment African American diaspora histories, and thus creates a new imaginary zone of racialized historical reclamation.

Digital artist and engineer Natalie Jeremijenko's online open-source encyclopedia of labor conditions and manufacturing processes for consumer products provides another example of reverse engineering. By tracing a product back to its origins, her web project, *How Stuff Is Made*, combined economics, historical analysis, labor history, photography, science, and wikis to reveal the hidden transnational labor processes facilitating the manufacture of everyday products, moving them from the quotidian to the global.[2] For instance, the site revealed that nearly all US flags are manufactured in Chinese sweatshops.

A historical example of reverse engineering comes from the American war in Vietnam. North Vietnamese soldiers recycled metal from downed US warplanes, making booby traps to use against US ground troops. They refashioned US warplane tires into rubber-soled sandals that predated modern versions like Tevas and were ideal for tropical warfare.[3] They also recovered footage of napalm bombing from crashed US B-52s and used it as evidence of war atrocities. US footage was edited by the North Vietnamese, smuggled out of Vietnam, and then deployed to mobilize the international antiwar movement in films such as *US Techniques of Genocide in Vietnam* (1968).

Moving from historiography, at the core of video image processing and image/signal manipulation, reverse engineering of tools reveals the key components of experimental digital media, film, and video practices. For example, artists and toolmakers like Bill Etra, David Jones, and Woody and Steina Vasulka built new machines and tools, using schematics to create algorithmic mathematical art in collaborative processes that predate Photoshop and Combustion by twenty-five years. One early technologist manipulated the video image simply by inserting a screwdriver into the TV itself to short-circuit its stability, combining domestic objects as tools to dismantle old images and create something new.[4] Machinery was taken apart, recombined, layered, and collaged together to create new technologies and new imagescapes.

The use of collage in reverse engineering needs to be added to other interventionist tactics like copyleft, culture jamming, piracy, and pranks as strategies for resistance and intervention into transnational capital and empire.[5] Earlier, the Revolution in Military Affairs (RMA) forged complex linkages between the hardware and software industries and the government, connections that would help the military to develop modern digital warfare.[6] The USA PATRIOT Act, passed in 2001, broadly expanded surveillance and constituted "significant threats to civil liberties, privacy and democracy," according to the Electronic Frontier Foundation and many other individuals and institutions.[7] For instance, the Patriot Act authorized packet-sniffing technologies like Carnivore and eliminated basic constitutional protections like the need for a warrant.

For instance, in 2000, the US Department of Defense's vision statement, *Joint Vision 2020*, called for US forces to venture beyond conventional weaponry and strategy to "full-spectrum dominance" of the air, information, land, sea, and space. Alternative, independent, oppositional, and radical democratic media practices, therefore, need to expand and join forces in a countermeasure of full-spectrum resistance.[8]

A report published in 2004 by Andrew Blau and the National Association of Media Arts and Culture (NAMAC) entitled *Deep Focus: A Report on the Future of Independent Media* suggested the need for a conceptual shift: how might new technologies require rethinking the form and functions of media? The report suggested that the field might need to jettison 1970s thinking that positioned independent media as completely oppositional to commercial media. It argued that in these emerging public media ecologies, the borders between different domains of media practice have become blurred. The report explained that the relationship between commercial and other media has changed to such an extent that "the commercial/noncommercial distinction no longer serves the purpose it once might have."[9] In this restructured media ecology, inexpensive technologies have become accessible and ubiquitous, and forms, interfaces, platforms, and technologies have multiplied as a result. The popular *Bush in 30 Seconds* spots from Moveon.org in 2003 exemplified this, as did the marketing techniques of antiwar Flash animation circulated via email.

Deep Focus argued that computer games were "being embraced as a platform for critique and education," suggesting that public media needed a more multiplatformed environment. The report noted that gaming is a $7 billion-a-year industry, with Americans spending more on video games than movie tickets.[10] The need for expansion into multiple platforms is particularly critical because the military uses commercial war games to advance major strategic planning for innovation and training. The Department of Defense (DOD) leveraged their enormous investments in IBM, Microsoft, and Sony's gaming ventures by deploying the advanced technological capacities of the Xbox and Sony Playstation for military purposes.

A major strategic capability of the DOD resides in simulation technology, but the gaming industry's capabilities surpass the military's significantly. One article describing the military's interest in war games and gamers noted that "video games made better soldiers and sailors faster, safer, and cheaper."[11] In addition, the military developed its own gaming site to appeal to younger potential recruits.[12]

After the bombing of the World Trade Center on September 11, 2001, Osama Bin Laden was the most circulated picture on the internet. Gamers inserted his image into games so that it could be disseminated and shot at as a target. Many sites featured games where players could move the cursor to kill Osama Bin Laden and other Middle Eastern figures, militarizing the mouse and racializing the home computer screen with a national phantasm, generating youthful support for the war on terror.[13]

As a countermeasure, during the early to mid-2000s, several antiwar games inspired by reverse engineering tactics emerged on sites like newsgaming.com, watercoolergrames.com, seriousgames.org, and opensorcery.net. These projects combined interfaces and technologies—not just images or sounds—to create interactive antiwar collaborative environments. One of the most famous is *Velvet Strike*, an antiwar modification of the commercial multiplayer game called *Counter Strike*, where players join terrorists or counterterrorists. These examples suggest that the emerging new ecology for public media requires reverse engineering of not only technologies but also forms of oppositional media. This strategy requires us to consider collage not only on the visual and aural levels, but theorizing it as a new, more fluid, and shape-shifting system that layers networks, public spaces, and technologies together.[14]

Thus, a reverse engineering framework functions as both model and metaphor, where public media moves from images to interface, from fixity to fluidity, from object to iterative modularity, from disembodied to embodied. Covertly and without debate, the machinery of postcapitalism reorganizes empire and retreats into a dangerous invisibility. Life proceeds as usual, monolithic and somnambulant, without interruption, ignoring death and displacement.[15] These alarming, reconfigured, war-without-end authoritarian regimes operating in the new media ecology require us to think about images and discursive formations, oppositional public space and technology, as endlessly mobile circulations releasing multiple layers and voices. For example, after the Abu Ghraib incident, US Army and Central Intelligence Agency images of prisoner torture in Iraq were circulated to the public. Since nearly every soldier there had access to email and cellphones, unprecedented broad and largely uncensored real-time communications during war were inevitable. As a result, senior officers at bases in Iraq were given internet kill switches to enforce control over information flows in military networks.[16]

In these larger contexts, using reverse engineering to reconsider the form, function, and practices of public media requires action beyond manipulating images and sounds; it necessitates interrupting the networks in order to break into the machine and reorganize its parts. Independent and radical public media must operate inside the machine itself in order to function as a countermeasure to transnational global capitalism.

Malaysia and Geneva

According to the International Intellectual Property Alliance, copyright industries constitute the United States' largest export, exceeding even the export of military products.[17] However, boundaries between the two have become blurred. In the early to mid-2000s, the military's insistence on full-spectrum dominance (control over all dimensions and locations of battle) demonstrated the growing interdependence between communication industries and the military. According to Bruce Berkowitz in *The New Face of War*, 90 percent of military communications travel over commercial links.[18] He points out that decentralized digital communications have shifted war from the ground onto the networks. Because military fronts no longer exist as they once did, warfare relies on more dispersed tactics such as swarming and maneuvering to create disorder.[19] This new warfare also employs cyberattacks to disrupt digital communications and infrastructure and leverages digital support for ground operations. For example, a PalmPilot device was commercially produced specifically for special agents in Afghanistan and Iraq that provided GPS mapping, instant translation, scenario planning, tactics, and real-time communication. If captured or hit, agents were instructed to crush their PalmPilots with their boots and guns.

A salient example of this merger between new technologies and the military is the Institute for Creative Technologies at the University of Southern California (USC), bankrolled by the Department of Defense and the gaming company Electronic Arts. This alliance demonstrates the synergy between the entertainment industries, military applications, and simulation technologies.[20] Like the military, transnational media corporations seek their own full-spectrum dominance by owning or investing in as many distribution platforms as possible, a form of vertical and horizontal integration and market control. As Nitin Govil from the South Asian digital collective Sarai pointed out, Interpol asserted that intellectual property piracy finances global terrorism through DVD sales of Bollywood films, Disney children's movies, and Windows software. Interpol linked the global circulation of pirated information commodities with the rise of asymmetrical warfare between combatants using divergent and unpredictable tactics.[21]

Many political economists have commented on how post-Hollywood transnational media corporations have become intellectual property clearinghouses, commanding monopoly power over copyright, licensing, and trademarks. The Motion Picture Association (MPA), representing the seven major studios affiliated with transnational media corporations, uses their famous rating system as a front for their underlying goal: the worldwide policing of media industry copyright protections in order to solidify transnational corporations' monopoly.[22]

Piracy has existed for commercial purposes for some time, but in the mid-2000s, it was deployed politically as a counter to transnational copyright monopolies. In February 2005, Downhill Battle, a political group supporting participatory cultural practices and a fairer music industry, organized one hundred pirate screenings of *Eyes on the Prize* (1987 and 1990), the landmark public television documentary on the civil rights movement. Produced by Henry Hampton and a multiracial team of filmmakers, *Eyes on the Prize* was a fourteen-part project for PBS. The project secured rights to archival footage harvested from amateur films, television, and other collections for public television broadcast. *Eyes on the Prize* is now one of the most widely disseminated and screened documentaries in American history, in the collections of many university, public school, and public libraries.[23]

However, since the mid-1990s, rights clearance costs have escalated: it is more and more difficult to secure worldwide rights across different platforms. Some documentary filmmakers engaged with the *Eyes* controversy estimated that it would cost over half a million dollars to secure rights clearance, a small amount of money for a transnational media corporation but a sum beyond the reach of Blackside, the original nonprofit production company. The old VHS copies libraries originally purchased were deteriorating, and in 2004, it was no longer possible to buy a new copy of *Eyes on the Prize*.[24] At that time, Downhill Battle commemorated Black History Month by organizing screenings of *Eyes on the Prize* in public venues across the country, violating copyright law to bring public attention to this crisis. In this instance and others, copyright monopolies enable transnational media corporations to produce historical amnesia. Downhill Battle's intervention serves as an inspiring example of racialized reverse engineering film exhibition. After the screenings in 2005, Blackside, using grants from the Ford and Gilder Foundations, was finally able to renew rights to *Eyes*, and fourteen years later, in 2018, one can easily purchase copies on Amazon.

It is important to contextualize intellectual property and the control over image and branding within the restructuring of the communications and entertainment industries to monetize new technologies. Since 1989, large companies have focused on controlling the various media platforms with transnational, transindustrial, and transtechnological operations at every level.[25] In this scenario, products and images change, modularize, remix, and revise in order to move across many different forms, maximizing their penetration in markets across the globe.[26] The remediation of visuality expands beyond textuality and also represents global operations' asset management to maximize profit and ensure monopoly control.[27]

Transnational media corporations have shifted their focus from manufacturing to distribution, exhibition, and marketing, with the intent to control all the networks and spaces of media commodity circulation. Postproduction strategies reconfigure texts to suit diverse audiences and penetrate more markets. For instance, *The Matrix Revolution* (2003) was recut to delete a sex scene for exhibition in Singapore. Keanu Reeves, who is biracial, was transformed into an Asian kung fu star. The amateur, asymmetrical, collaborative, decentralized, interactive, and open-source modalities of digital culture present continuing threats to these media giants. They have responded by lobbying to extend copyright protections in the United States through the Digital Millennium Copyright Act (DMCA) and by instituting both vertical and horizontal integration to control technologies and means of distribution.

In December 2004, the MPA initiated Operation Eradicate in Malaysia and eleven other Asian countries in a move to not just crack down on copyright piracy of DVDs, CD ROMs, and CDs, but in a scorched-earth policy, to raid and then dismantle copying machinery and factories. Malaysia, one of the largest Muslim countries in the world, is among the biggest exporters of pirate entertainment software, enacting an estimated loss to the transnational media corporations of over $718 million per year.[28]

The MPA's action is best understood within the context of Malaysia's aggressive bid to enter the global information economy, the country's deep digital divide, and its continuing reliance on piracy. The Malaysian government launched the Multimedia Super Corridor in 1996 in an attempt to convert rubber and oil plantations south of Kuala Lumpur into a Southeast Asian Silicon Valley with the lure of a ten-year tax holiday, an elaborate digital infrastructure, and new cyberlaws covering intellectual property. As a result, 1,200 cybereconomy companies opened offices or manufacturing plants there, including Dell Computers, Intel, Lucent, Microsoft, Netscape, and Sun Microsystems. At the same time, the Malaysian digital divide in the early 2000s was extreme, with 90 percent of elementary schools lacking internet connections and at least 25 percent of East Malaysia without electricity.[29]

Piracy has been a pervasive above-ground activity throughout Malaysia. In Johor Bahru, a short cab ride across the Straits of Johor from copyright-compliant Singapore, three-story shopping malls feature small businesses specializing in American rap music, Bollywood films, computer games, Hong Kong action pictures, and software, all pirated. Piracy is the site of a contradiction between the Malaysian government's conspicuous efforts to ensure major players in the global economy that it obeys copyright and their covert promotion of underground piracy as a way to maintain political stability through full employment in a multiethnic Muslim area. Simultaneously, whether it is deliberate or not, piracy also functions as a way to resist globalization by earning money *from* Disney products, for example, rather than paying money *to* Disney.

In the context of a concentrated global media environment, reverse engineering means expanding access to tools that can circumvent the media monoculture and create space for a more diverse media ecology. In the United States, a small triumph related to media infrastructure occurred in June 2004 when the courts ruled against the massive deregulation of broadcasting in *Prometheus Radio Project v. the FCC*. The case was significant because it represented legal protection for what was formerly called pirate radio oriented to broadcasting within small geographic areas. Prometheus Radio promoted microradio, low-power FM stations that broadcast to a three- to seven-mile geographic area, and initiated community builds through radio barn raisings.[30]

Questions of democratic access to communications beyond the oligopolies of the media transnationals were also debated on the international level. The 2003 Geneva World Summit on the Information Society, a gathering of progressive international nongovernmental organizations (NGOs), created a Declaration of Principles. It supported interdependence and interrelationships among human rights, sustainable development, and affordable, equitable, and universal access to information and communication technology. Recognizing the needs of the least-developed nations, the declaration demanded respect for cultural and linguistic diversity and protection of the public domain by strengthening archives, libraries, museums, and collections. It shifted the language of the digital divide to the promotion of digital opportunity.[31]

India and Cambodia

Reverse engineering disassembles machines, programs, and tools, turning them to other uses. In countries like India and Cambodia, it employs 3-D computer-assisted design and manufacturing (CAD CAM) programs, making images of parts that translate the gaps between the physical and digital world. Reverse engineering functions as an interstitial practice in constant movement. Disassembly makes it possible to map the interrelationships among constituent parts and reassemble them in new ways. In the global information economy, global labor relations embody these processes. CAD CAM reverse engineering, software development, and the writing of code have been outsourced to India, where over one million people are employed in a $12.8 billion export industry that takes advantage of low wages in a country with a large educated population of English speakers.[32]

Moving from the digital and physical to the historical, interventionist collage also reverse engineers historical explanations and archives. Collage extends beyond aurality and visuality to reimagine machines, space, technologies of power, and tools.[33] Reverse engineering suggests moving off a single screen to many different interfaces, provisional exhibition zones, and multiple screens. It means combining machines with each other to reconfigure the interface and the spaces within which they operate.

At the Massachusetts Institute of Technology (MIT), Chris Csíkszentmihályi developed a mobile imaging system he dubbed the Afghan Explorer, an autonomous robot for remote cruising and imaging of geopolitical hotspots to procure news for the public as a workaround of Pentagon press restrictions in war zones. The machine was imaginary, like a child's remote-controlled automaton. The toy was reverse engineered, rebuilt as a faux remote-imaging device for Americans to secure blacked-out news and images. It purported to function as a translation machine between the physical and digital worlds of invisible war. However, rather than producing images, the toy functioned in the realm of imagination, calling attention to the wars we cannot see.

Subaltern historiography recalibrates historical method as a process of releasing the multiple stories that nationalism represses. This historiographic model has reverse engineered Indian nationalism by introducing the practices, struggles, and voices of the subaltern in South Asia into the narrative, dismantling national unities by exposing their inherent contradictions. Dipesh Chakrabarty contends that the historical is contradictory because it is by necessity plural, even as majoritarian ways of thinking attempt to neutralize heterogeneity.[34] He advocates translation across different registers and systems so that the radical potential of this repressed heterogeneity can be articulated and realized.[35] Subaltern historiographic methodologies provide ways to disassemble the constituent parts of the new media ecology and to relocate them within new contexts.

In this critical historiography, temporal disjunctures and plurality reconceptualize the archive and history to expose suppressed contradictions. In place of continuity and linear progression inhering in explanatory models of traditional historiography, these theorists advance a concept of contiguity—a spatial rather than temporal arrangement of artifacts and discourses. Focusing on contradictions, juxtapositions, and multiple layers, this historiography generates new meanings as well as new conceptualizations. The archive emerges as a constantly evolving recombinant space.

This reimagined archive combats the amnesia and anesthesia of authoritarian transnational capital with synesthesia and polyphony. Multiple and hybridized networked models insure the heterogeneity of public memories. Histories and stories are retold in new forms; interfaces and machines are taken apart and reconstituted in new formations. Historiographer Ranajit Guha contends that subaltern histories minimize the state in order to amplify the everyday. In the context of the new global media ecologies, reverse engineering shifts from the interface to the embodied, situating the everyday in specific places. Guha proposes that the ways in which multiple pasts interact comprise historical knowledge and explanatory models.[36] Reverse engineering utilizes a collaborative networked model that pays as much attention to collaging affinities, differences, machines, and tools as it does to deconstructing images.

A critically engaged public media must construct new imaginary zones through a multiplicity of perspectives and an amalgamation of differences. This enables us to reconfigure historical agencies and reenvision communities. For example, ethnographer and filmmaker David MacDougall suggests that cultural production necessitates a collaborative polyphonic process in order to dismantle power differentials and deconstruct domination. This collage of different voices creates a compound work that entails different cultural perspectives crossing and recrossing each other. It sustains a liminal zone through interconnections open to contingency and participatory performativity. As a result, these compound works activate new common knowledge across differences.[37] This collaborative reverse engineering of differences, histories, and tools redefines collage as mutable, performative, and spatialized. For example, the Not Channel Zero Video Collective founded in the early 1990s produced many works for the African American and Latino communities about racialized power in America such as *The Nation Erupts* (1992) and *X 1/2: The Legacy of Malcolm X* (1993). Founding member DJ/VJ Art Jones transitioned from oppositional documentary video to live remix performances in the late 1990s, and one of his collaborative works from the early 2000s was entitled *Dismantling Empire: Live!* (2003), performed as a VJ battle with digital artist Simon Tarr. Executed in real time with multiple computers, the piece was a live audio/visual performance and DJ/VJ battle incorporating multiple video streams, two screens, and prerecorded music. The performance remixed audio and visual elements from alternative media, commercial entertainment, and mainstream news to unpack the ways in which images work to validate the idea of a benign American empire. The performance reassembled embedded commercial media war journalism, remote-sensing technologies for combat, post 9/11 security and surveillance footage, and images of torture. Jones and Tarr reverse engineered the separations between different discourses, institutions, practices, sources, and technologies into a more embodied public knowledge. Through computers, music, and multiple screens, the performance took apart the networked nature of war and technology. It exposed the contradictions of each different network as they collided in the remix.

    S21: The Khmer Rouge Killing Machine (2002), a documentary by Cambodian filmmaker Rithy Panh, examines the genocide of over 1.7 million Cambodians by the Khmer Rouge. His film goes to the heart of how polyvocal historiography and collage of temporalities can break through collective amnesia, denial, and indifference. Through testimonies and reenactments with prisoners and guards of their experiences in Tuol Seng prison, he reverse engineers the strategy of the Khmer Rouge to reduce murder and genocide to the ordinary and exposes the horrors they perpetrated through that same quotidian detail and dispassion, allowing the surviving victims and the prison guards to confront each other through historical embodiment. A related project of reconstruction through reverse engineering is the Yale Cambodian Genocide Project. It functions as a portal of 22,000 biographic records, 6,000 artifacts and documents, and 5,000 images of victims killed in Tuol Seng, bringing to light material that has been dispersed, hidden, or lost in Cambodia.

Everywhere

A politics of collaborative reverse engineering generates imaginary spaces. It takes images, practices, and technologies apart to create provisional zones that mobilize imaginary geographies and reciprocal relations. Reverse engineering translates between the physical and the virtual and traverses between the embodied and the imagined.

Collaborative reverse engineering constitutes an act of refusal; it convenes forces against empire. It opposes any singular temporality or the imposition of any one story. Instead, it is polyvocal, opening up multiplicities. It argues that the political public media project must reconfigure and dismantle history in order to build new tools for historical transformation and transnational solidarities against empire and war. By customizing images, sounds, spaces, and tools, this way of thinking and acting demands that all of us together fearlessly and exuberantly enact ongoing reverse engineering across our differences. An anti-imperialist public media politics requires ongoing reverse engineering, rewiring and reconfiguring the global transnational media ecology.

Notes

1. For a more extensive and developed discussion of this concept of taking things apart as a key strategy of new media, see Dale Hudson and Patricia R. Zimmermann, *Thinking through Digital Media: Transnational Environments and Locative Places* (New York: Palgrave Macmillan, 2015), 21–56.

2. *How Stuff Is Made* originally ran on a website that is no longer live. It was a project that revealed the manufacturing process of common household items such as soap, cleaning supplies, brooms, food, and other items.

3. Karen Gottshang Turner and Phan Thanh Hao, *Even Women Must Fight: Memories of War from North Vietnam* (New York: John Wiley and Sons, 1998); Patricia Pelley, *Postcolonial Vietnam: New Histories of the National Past* (Durham: Duke University Press, 2002).

4. For discussion of these experiments and technological innovations, see Bill Etra, "Colorizers Come of Age," *Videography* 4, no. 4 (1979), 14–19.; and Sherry Miller Hocking, "The Evolution of Thinking Machines," *The Squealer* 15, no. 1 (2004), 5–8

5. For discussions of copyright, copyleft, and piracy, see Kembrew McLeod, *Freedom of Expression: Overzealous Copyright Bozos and Other Enemies of Creativity* (New York: Doubleday, 2005); Negativland, *Two Relationships to a Cultural Public Domain* (Sacramento: Seeland Media, 2005); and McKenzie Wark, *A Hacker Manifesto* (Cambridge: Harvard University Press, 2004).

6. Chris Hables Gray, "Perpetual Revolution in Military Affairs, International Security and Information," in *Bombs and Bandwidth: The Emerging Relationship between Information Technology and Security*, ed. Robert Latham (New York: New Press, 2003), 199–212; Michael Ignatieff, *Virtual War: Kosovo and Beyond* (New York: Henry Holt, 2000).

7. "PATRIOT Act," Electronic Frontier Foundation, accessed January 22, 2018, https://www.eff.org/issues/patriot-act.
8. Institute for Strategic Studies, *Joint Vision 2020: America's Military—Preparing for Tomorrow* (Washington, DC: National Defense University, 2000).
9. Andrew Blau, *Deep Focus: A Report on the Future of Independent Media* (San Francisco: National Association of Media Arts and Culture, 2005), 5.
10. Blau, *Deep Focus*, 5.
11. J. C. Herz and Michael R. Macedonia, "Computer Games and the Military: Two Views," *Defense Horizons*, no. 11–12 (April 2002), 1–8.
12. "America's Army Proving Grounds," US Army, accessed January 22, 2018, http://www.americasarmy.com.
13. Patricia R. Zimmermann, "Digital Deployments," in *Contemporary American Independent Cinema*, ed. Christine Holmlund and Justin Wyatt (New York: Routledge, 2005), 245–264.
14. Diane Waldman, *Collage, Assemblage and the Found Object* (New York: Harry N. Abrams, 1992).
15. Slavoj Žižek, *Iraq: The Borrowed Kettle* (London: Verso, 2004).
16. Irene Wiclawski, "For Troops, Home Can Be Too Close," *New York Times*, March 15, 2005, A16.
17. Stephen E. Siwek, *Copyright Industries in the U.S. Economy* (Washington, DC: International Intellectual Property Alliance, 2016).
18. Bruce Berkowitz, *The New Face of War: How War Will Be Fought in the 21st Century* (New York: Free Press, 2003), 138. Berkowitz's argument represents a promilitary position.
19. Berkowitz, *New Face*, 76–90.
20. "USC Institute for Creative Technologies Receives $135 Million Contract Extension from U.S. Army," Institute for Creative Technologies, press release, September 1, 2011, accessed January 22, 2018, http://ict.usc.edu/news/press-releases/usc-institute-for-creative-technologies-receives-135-million-contract-extension-from-u-s-army/.
21. Nitin Govil, "War in the Age of Pirate Reproductions," in *The Sarai Reader 04: Crisis/Media* (New Delhi: Sarai, 2004), 378–383.
22. See Toby Miller, Nitin Govil, John McMurria, and Richard Maxwell, *Global Hollywood* (London: British Film Institute, 2001).
23. "Fenwick & West Represents Downhill Battle in Fight to Make *Eyes on the Prize* Available for Public Viewing," Press Release from Fenwick and West, February 9, 2005, accessed January 22, 2018, https://www.fenwick.com/media/pages/fenwick-west-represents-downhill-battle-in-fight-to-make-eyes-on-the-prize-available-for-public-viewing.aspx; Katie Dean, "Cash Rescues *Eyes on the Prize*," *Wired*, August 30, 2005, accessed July 2, 2018, https://www.wired.com/2005/08/cash-rescues-eyes-on-the-prize/.
24. Katie Dean, "Bleary Days for *Eyes on the Prize*," February 9, 2005, *Wired*, accessed January 22, 2018, https://www.wired.com/2005/02/putting-eyeballs-on-copyright-law/.
25. For analysis of the politics of new technologies, see Aida Hozic, *Hollyworld: Space, Power and Fantasy in the American Economy* (Ithaca: Cornell University Press, 2001); and Dan Harries, ed., *The New Media Book* (London: British Film Institute, 2002).
26. For analysis of the reorganization of Hollywood in the transnational era, see Edward Jay Epstein, *The Big Picture: The New Logic of Money and Power in Hollywood* (New York: Random House, 2005).
27. For an explanation of the term "remediation," see Jay David Bolter and Richard Grusin, *Remediation: Understanding New Media* (Cambridge: MIT Press, 2000). They explain the term

as the process of new media technologies taking in, subsuming, and working with older legacy media technologies and their forms, rather than a total break from them.

28. Don Groves, "MPA Targets Asian Pirates: Aim Is to Protect Lucrative Holiday Season," *Variety*, December 6, 2004, accessed January 22, 2018, https://variety.com/2004/film/news/mpa-targets-asian-pirates-1117914447/.

29. Paramjit Singh Tyndall, "Multimedia Super Corridor: Introducing a New Economy in Malaysia," in *Information Technology in Asia: New Development Paradigms*, ed. Chia Siow Yue and Jamus Jerome Lim (Singapore: Institute of Southeast Asia Studies, 2002), 177–195.

30. Andrew Jay Schwartzman, Cheryl A. Leanza, and Harold Feld, "The Legal Case for Diversity in Broadcast Ownership," in *The Future of Media: Resistance and Reform in the 21st Century*, ed. Robert McChesney, Russell Newman, and Ben Scott (New York: Seven Stories, 2005), 156–171.

31. "Declaration of Principals: Building the Information Society—A Global Challenge in the New Millennium, Geneva 2003," World Summit on the Information Society, accessed January 22, 2018, http://www.itu.int/net/wsis/docs/geneva/official/dop.html.

32. Bhavesh Donga, "Why Outsourcing Software Development to India Still a Best Option," Addon Solutions, May 4, 2017, accessed January 22, 2018, https://www.addonsolutions.com/blog/outsourcing-software-development-india-still-best-option.html.

33. Waldman, *Collage*, 100–153, 284–322.

34. Dipesh Chakrabarty, *Provincializing Europe: Postcolonial Thought and Historical Difference* (Princeton, NJ: Princeton University Press, 2000), 42.

35. Chakrabarty, *Provincializing Europe*, 46.

36. Ranajit Guha, *History at the Limit of World-History* (New York: Columbia University Press, 2003), 22.

37. David MacDougall, *Transcultural Cinema* (Princeton, NJ: Princeton University Press, 1998), 135–147.

Figure 2.1. Still from *Buffalo Bone China* video, (Dana Claxton, Canada, 1997). Digital photo by Don Hall, courtesy of the MacKenzie Art Gallery.

2

ARDENT SPACES, FORMIDABLE ENVIRONMENTS*

Invocations

One long take: A broken bowl in the middle of the frame encircled by hands. One sound: the grind of broken pieces as they are fitted back together by fingers. The scraping sound both grates and reassures: you must listen closely to its jagged, insistent rhythms that intone the puzzle of shards of pottery. These sounds signify thinking through performing, figuring it out through piecing it together.

> No face.
> No body.
> No identity.
> No location.
> Only hands.
> Encircled.
> Enfolded.

The only place that matters is the bowl in front of the camera. A bowl, half shattered, half whole, its roundness real and implied, broken and whole, round

---

*In 2009 I received an email from a feminist scholar I had heard of but had never met. Janice Hladki, an Associate Professor in Theater and Film Studies in the School of the Arts at McMaster University in Hamilton, Ontario, has published feminist studies of disability, cinema, independent film, performance, and performance art. She was mounting a major exhibition of Canadian feminist experimental cinema entitled *Fierce: Women's Hot-Blooded Film/Video* for the McMaster Museum of Art, and invited me to contribute an essay on the works for the catalog. Hamilton is only three hours from Ithaca, and thus in our region of upstate New York and lower Canada. I felt it was important to be collegial. I also thought this project would be a way to learn more about experimental Canadian film. Janice sent me all the films in the exhibition, and encouraged me to write in a more lyrical way for an audience beyond specialists in screen studies. The works themselves with their vast range of approaches, styles, and tones, suggested the structure of this essay and propelled a more poetic strategy. The essay was published as "Ardent Spaces, Formidable Environments," in the catalog for *Fierce: Women's Hot-Blooded Film/Video,* McMaster University Museum of Art, Hamilton, Ontario, Canada, January 2010, 20–31.

and jagged. An endless cycle, assembled, taken apart, and fit together again, cradled in a woman's hands, holding together an object that can fall apart in the larger world beyond the screen.

This film, titled *Hope* (Dana Claxton, 2007) emblematizes what is at stake in the Canadian feminist experimental film and video work that appears in the *Fierce: Women's Hot-Blooded Film and Video* exhibition: hands around pieces to open up spaces for a relational location, an empathetic practice, an ardent public address, a newly landscaped ecosystem.

> Sharp edges.
> New sounds.
> Spaces between.
> Spaces inside.
> Space connected.
> Invocations.

The established media artists showcased in *Fierce*—Dana Claxton, b.h. yael, Maureen Bradley, and Allyson Mitchell—reveal the utter transformation of international feminist media practices. New vectors and new interrogations have sprouted out of the compost of identity politics and legacy forms.

For example, with its long continuous take in extreme close-up of a naked woman's back, *Birthday Suit Management* (Maureen Bradley, 2001) generates a new cartography of the body. It layers four gazes: the medical gaze of chiropractors, massage therapists, physiotherapists, acupuncturists and doctors; the probing gaze of the camera evoking aerial shots of landscapes; a desexualized body made voyeuristic object by long sensuous camera movements; a woman's autobiographical retelling of medical interventions after an accident.

These legacy genres mobilized disparate bodies of evidence—amateur film, animation, formal interventions, interviews, and voice-over to speak through silences—into hybridized forms that mixed genres together. Inserting images into absences, these legacy modes refuted a male-centered logocentrism with heterogeneity.

In contrast, the works in *Fierce* move beyond the text as an index for identity formation and identification: as invocations of a relational politics, they summon spectators into flexible environments. The mix of screenings, installations, loops, and viewing stations that make up this exhibition emblematize its conceptual movement into fluidities and sensualities.

The myriad genres traversed in this exhibition—documentary, experimental, found footage, hand processing, hybrid, installation, performative, popular culture—torque how to think through and enter into feminist aesthetics and politics. They unsettle an easily labeled, singular, feminist media practice. Their pluralities of address break open the liminal zones between the public and the private, between the personal and the political, between the nation and the region. Their transversals between the local, the regional, the national, and the global disconnect space from geography.

A visual Zen koan, *Melty Kitty* (Allyson Mitchell, 2007) condenses these pluralities and transversals: a candle in the shape of a cat burns and melts while lilting women's voices sing "Suicide is Painless," the *M*A*S*H* television show theme song. The image suggests candles lit in Catholic churches to remember the dead, but also invokes the pop, the public, the pun.

Polyphonies

In most narrative cinemas around the globe, music shores up a phallocentric narrative drive: an undercurrent, it expresses emotion beyond the verbal. It feels for us. It fills in the unknown spaces between action and character with excesses never spoken.

Music enters the body but is ultimately disembodied.

The works in this exhibition fiercely reverse the function of music, thwarting instrumental directionality. Alluding to music video, opera, and popular culture, the works align music with discourse, description, declarations, analytics.

Precious Little Tiny Love (Allyson Mitchell, 2003) suggests this polyphonic form with its one continuous take of the image broken into four quadrants, each with a statuette of a deer, a pig, a plastic lamb, or a rabbit in the billowing prairie. A woman's voice sings about what she eats: "I wish I didn't eat animals cause they don't eat me," and "I don't eat white flour. White sugar makes you rot." The plastic animal figurines contrast with the natural setting. The song adds another layer to the image, moving beyond this binary of natural/unnatural with a languishing indie rock aria about food consumption.

In these works, music invites the spectator into a participatory relation by offering a dialogic interaction, an opening, a passage. Layered with other images, these works generate polyphonic structures.

Electronic dance music pounds through *I Want to Know Why* (Dana Claxton, 1994) over iconic, clichéd images of First Nations people and landscapes made more abstract through their reduction to black and white pixels. The images function as motifs for new fugal structures, where two images flank another or are laid down in a strip alongside another image. The electronic dance music mixes with a voice describing racism and poverty: "My grandmother died of alcohol poisoning in a skid row hotel room . . . I want to know why," and "My mother OD'd at the age of thirty-seven, and I want to know why." This piece interrogates the idea that image is evidence; it proposes fugal recombinations to prompt new understandings.

The sound no longer serves the image, narrative temporal advancement, or emotion and refuses the postmodern strategy of creating ironies through disjuncture. Rather, the sound designs in these pieces build new structures out of layers with different melodic lines that intersect, cross, double.

This relational politics sustains the polyphonic epistemology of *Buffalo Bone China* (Dana Claxtom, 1997). It offers an empathic ritual to contemplate the First Nations' loss of the buffalo and the transformation of buffalo bones into china. With slow-motion shots of stampeding buffalo, a First Nations man screaming, a pink set of china edged with gold, long black hair dragged over the plates, and superimposed frames of buffalo skulls, this piece suggests the funeral rites. The nondirectional electronic soundscape inaugurates suspended temporalities of contemplation and participation.

The pieces in *Fierce* revamp image and sound relationships. They compose new feminist fugues in different keys.

> Minor.
> Major.
> Pianissimo
> Forte.
> Exercises.
> Exorcisms.

Microterritories

As the public and the private, the local and the global, the garden and the environment coil into each other, they sustain a sensual environmental politics that reconfigures feminist media practices. With its backward home movie images of a parade with floats of women, platform divers spiraling into a lake, and pulsating trance music, *Anwolek/Regatta City* (Dana Claxton, 2005) probes the colonization of first nation space by pageantry and public parades. Locations are imagined differently, with many intersecting and fluid layers in constant relational and interconnected movement.

At first, *My Life in 5 Minutes* (Allyson Mitchell, 2000) reads like a simple feminist queer autobiography: it jettisons the confines of the heterosexual nuclear family and weight watching for the liberations of lesbian collective identity and full bodied-ness. Punning the feminist autobiographical trope, *My Life* is composed almost entirely from family snapshots. However, in contrast to earlier feminist works, *My Life* constructs a microterritory for a more complexly queered identity with the addition of folk art–like drawings of a woman's face with words delineating traumas such as bulimia, cellulite, ill-wishers, and loss of control. Instead of a diary-like voice-over speaking that which is not spoken, the filmmaker sings a ballad about her life history that challenges the idea of pathos imbedded in the "voice" of documentary. The lyrics express interiority and subjectivity: "I traveled around a lot, and now I'm gay"

What I Remember (Maureen Bradley, 1998) and *Stranded* (Maureen Bradley, 2004) engage the environment even more explicitly. With shots of insects in bowls montaged with home movie–inflected imagery of young children, *What I Remember* graphs the parallels between childhood visual memories, the natural, and queer identities. The voice-over—or is it a performance or a parable or a put-on or a fantasy?—tells how a young woman met her first girlfriend.

In *Stranded*, a woman's voice describes Charlotte, a young woman repulsed by her dead hair cells. Underwater shots of various kinds of sea life in an aquarium and aboveground shots of grasses and trees sustain a microterritory of dead and living cells. While the voice-over suggests phobias and obsessions, the images engage a bigger world beyond the human, teeming with life emerging from wreckage or encasement.

Arab/Jewish partnerships, walls, and the blurred domains between public and private convergences in Palestine and Israel form another microterritory in *A Hot Sandfilled Wind* (b.h. yael, 2006). This winding together of separate domains is visualized by the layering of images of Israeli street scenes with images of destroyed homes, a public market, and traveling shots winding through city streets. Participants in a demonstration against the Israeli occupation by the antiwar group Women in Black hold up signs saying "This Wall Must Fall." A group of Israelis work with Palestinians to rebuild a bulldozed home. The film ends at a swimming hole, where people laugh and swim. Throughout, intertitles cascade through the frame in Hebrew and Arabic, doubling each other and the voice-over, imbedding a verbal microterritory of peace into the images themselves. "In this land, the ground is haunted, and each wind has a name," the voice-over, based on a poem by Nadia Habib, intones. "We have nothing else without the other," it commands.

These works figure the environment as an in-between zone engendering active manipulation, sensuous engagement, and incessant negotiation with autobiographies, borders, disabilities, genocide, health, histories, identities, land, sea, sexualities, and war. These works posit outposts from larger, more hierarchical and destructive constructs of nations and fixed identities. They also insist that the discarded, the handcrafted, and the quotidian are neglected feminist environments, microterritories of dialogic relation where the private and the political curl into each other.

Ardent Space

The feminist project in *Fierce* converts the linear, forward drive of the temporal into an open horizontal space. These works cluster together different ideas, image sources, and modes. They blend—but do not blur—aesthetics, discourses, elements, politics, position, and spaces into endless unfoldings and enfoldings.

The moving camera in *(of) Fences* (b.h. yael, 2001) visually refutes the spatial limitations of the metal fences erected to block demonstrators from the Montreal Free Trade of the Americas (FTAA) meetings. With slowed-down images of protesters with large x's over their mouths, helmeted police with shields, and complex electronic sound, *(of) Fences* winds together action and contemplation. An incantation and critique, text superimposes on the image: "Fences marshal forces, inequities . . . maintain elites . . . deny access." The piece ends with "fences preclude listening . . . fences enter my dreams."

Against the sensationalism, spectacle, and emotional excess of melodrama and action genres, these works insist on the tangible politics of everyday objects: bowls, rugs, plates, home movies, walls, fences, vegetables in markets, candles, grass, water, snapshots.

These works figure the hand, the handmade, and the handheld as tactile interfaces, a constant refusal to accept the world as it is. They remake the world through blending, folding, superimposing, and weaving. An antiwar homage to Canadian feminist filmmaker Joyce Wieland, *Afghanimation* (Allyson Mitchell, 2008) features a tableau shot of a rug woven by an anonymous Afghan woman in a refugee camp. Grenades and tanks in each corner surround a veiled woman. In stop action, a woman covers the rug by hand with colorful pieces of crochet, and then over that, tapes pages from the *Toronto Star*.

In *Fierce*, media work blends discourses, practices, and spectators, enfolding the polarizations, oppositions, and contradictions of earlier feminist works. A complex video essay on apocalyptic visions, disaster, environmental degradation, global warming, and secularism, *Trading the Future* (b.h. yael, 2008) enacts a liminal open space, a new ecosystem with mobile, multilayered relations ignoring national, epistemological, or material boundaries.

Throughout the works in *Fierce*, metaphors for fluidity and its generative engagements abound: dissolves, layered sound designs, meltings, moving cameras, scrolling words, slow-motion images, superimpositions, water.

These ardent spaces offer new cinematic ecosystems where what is fierce and necessary, visceral and conceptual, tactile and relational, layered and open, formidable and inviting, burst through.

Figure 3.1. *Petty's Island Libation*. Still from *Precious Places Project* (Scribe Video Center and Louis Massiah, US, 2005–ongoing). Image courtesy of Louis Massiah.

3

PRECIOUS PLACES

*Scribe Video Center, Philadelphia**

A VIGOROUS, CONTENTIOUS DEBATE UNDERLIES DOCUMENTARY THEORY, history, and practice: How do we understand the shifting power relations between filmmaker, subject, and audience? Corollary questions in this debate include: What are the ethics of representation? What, if any, is the effect of documentary images? What is the use value of documentary in the world? What is documentary's relationship to documents, archives, history? How do we understand the institutional parameters of documentary production, distribution, and exhibition?

To Badlands and Back Again (2005), a short community video produced by the Fair Hill Cemetery activist group as part of Scribe Video Center's *Precious Places* project, answers these questions effortlessly and poignantly. It shows how a working partnership between Philadelphia Quakers and concerned local African American and Latino residents transformed a historic cemetery from a dumping ground for garbage into a safe green space for the community.

In this short video, sustainability and environmental issues are not white, middle-class or corporate greenwashing, but multicultural, engaged political

---

*I first discovered the Precious Places Community Video Project at a meeting of the National Alliance for Media Arts and Culture in Philadelphia (NAMAC) in October of 2005. I had delivered a talk entitled "Media Histories and Media Archives" there. Now renamed The Alliance, NAMAC is a vital nexus for the independent media arts community, a place where distributors, exhibitors, funders, nonprofit organizations, producers, technologists, and a few academics converge to discuss unresolved challenges to the field. Unlike most academic conferences, NAMAC gatherings feature many activities and events that showcase the local independent media arts in the cities where the conference is held. At the Philadelphia NAMAC, I signed up for a bus tour of Philadelphia neighborhoods organized by Scribe Video. The tour featured stops at buildings, churches, and gardens where the community-produced *Precious Places* project had been shot in neighborhoods apart from the tourist areas, and where we watched the videos featuring their makers and community members in situ. Amazed at this form of imbedded collaborative documentary practice, I took many notes and decided to ask the Ithaca College librarians to order all the DVDs of this project. Later, I wrote a short, more journalistic-style piece about Scribe's *Precious Places* initiative entitled "Imbedded Public Histories," *Afterimage* 33 (2005): 5, 51–52. This version is slightly revised from the original.

activism that produces visible and usable changes in real places where people live and work. Although important early feminist and antislavery activists are buried in the cemetery, this knowledge was lost with the disintegration of Fair Hill into a haven for drug pushers and an eyesore in the community. The Quakers and community groups worked together to clean up the cemetery, disposing of the refuse and driving out the drugs and drug dealers. In the video, community members explain the landscape and drug-dealing clean-up process, and how they reclaimed the latent histories of the cemetery.

Scribe Video Center's community media and oral history project, *Precious Places* (2005), a video anthology of nineteen eight-minute short documentaries exploring the historical memories imbedded in public buildings, churches, monuments, parks, spaces, and street corners, constitutes an imaginative, empowering, and forward-thinking response to the philosophical conundrums plaguing documentary and to misrepresentations of development. The pieces employ a realist documentary style of interviews and cutaways to places, with precise editing and carefully considered, community-driven structure to advance storytelling as a collective and active historical enterprise. Taken as a whole, the DVD sizzles with polyvocal vitality that counters touristic propaganda promoting cities as places for high-end hotels, symphonies, theaters, and expensive restaurants.

The shorts on the DVD were produced by a wide, diverse range of organizations such as the African Cultural Art Forum, the Community Leadership Institute, the Germantown Historical Society, the Mt. Moriah Preservation Society, Odunde, and the West Girard Community Council. These pieces focus on specific places that have significant historical, cultural, religious or political meaning for the residents who live there, rather than for historians approaching the places as outsiders. Although aided by consultants, professional historians from Philadelphia colleges and universities, and experienced videomakers, *Precious Places* was conceived to document a particular place through the oral histories of residents as a response to a wide range of development initiatives that potentially destroy communities and their histories.

Precious Places moves documentary away from personal, individualistic, and idiosyncratic artisanal practices toward networked and collaborative interactions among filmmakers, neighborhoods, places, and scholars who create new histories. As a result, it constitutes more than an intervention into the conceptualization of documentary; the project shows how to embody polyvocalities and micrcohistories—large, sprawling, and difficult-to-materialize concepts imported from postcolonial studies—as a way to reclaim and revitalize ideas about the archive, history, and memory.

Started in 1982 and based in Philadelphia, Scribe Video Center is a nonprofit media arts center offering instruction in film, video, audio, and digital media to the residents of Philadelphia, Camden, and Chester. Scribe sees media production as a tool to help community groups and individuals explore personal, social, political, and cultural issues. It also engages in a variety of youth media projects, most notably its *Documentary History Project for Youth*, which provides young people with an opportunity to explore the history of Philadelphia.

Precious Places is not conceived along the lines of a traditional Oscar-nominated feature-length documentary project, where a director researches an idea and then searches for archival material, informants, and images to advance an argument, position, or point of view. Rather than this top-down, individualistic model of a single authorial vision, *Precious Places* advances a collaborative ethnographic and historical model, where community participants become the authors and not simply the subjects of community history.

In *Precious Places*, development and sustainability are reconceived from the perspective of communities, eminent domain, reclaiming parks, and restoring lost histories to particular buildings or blocks. This project operates as a microhistory that zeroes in on public places and individuals as part of the fabric of a community. It advocates for collective effort to revive communities through oral histories and actions that reclaim and rejuvenate these places and spaces. For example, in one of the short documentaries, *Putting the Nice Back in the Town*, the Neighborhood Advisory Committee works to restore the area. *Precious Places* counters the surface formalism that courses through the genre of the city film, typified in the works of Walter Ruttman (*Berlin: Symphony of a Metropolis*, 1927) in the 1920s or Godrey Reggio (*Koyaanisqatsi*, 1982) with the voices of participants and locations in specific community places such as buildings or parks.

Although much of documentary history and theory valorizes individual authorship, an equally long tradition of collaborative work exists, starting from Flaherty's *Nanook of the North* (1922). Subsequent examples appear in documentary history, including the Workers Film and Photo Leagues of the 1930s, George Stoney's *All My Babies* (1953), and his collaborative work on *You Are on Indian Land* (1969). Later, we see community media operations that started in the 1970s and early 1980s, such as Appalshop, Kartemquin, Third World Newsreel, Paper Tiger Television, and the entire cable access movement since the late 1970s. *Precious Places* extends this important legacy of collaborative community media by retelling the history of Philadelphia from very specific locations particular to people and neighborhoods, such as churches that were part of the Underground Railroad, the Friends Housing Cooperative, a community garden called Las Parcelas, the Mt. Zion Baptist Church, and the Uptown Theatre.

The *Precious Places* DVD anthology is significant in the history of media not only because it unpacks so many theoretical issues rippling through documentary, but because of the changes in communities and historical consciousness it galvanizes. Most films about development get trapped in a pastoral fantasy of technological civilization and malls devouring idyllic fields and forest landscapes, ignoring the history and potential of specific groups and neighborhoods in cities.

Precious Places advances a reminder that the environment is equally urgent for urban dwellers, people of color, and neighborhoods. It materializes a powerful, eye-opening, and collaborative response to diverse neighborhoods and the press of development that completely alters typical conceptualizations of cities, their inhabitants, and the links between sustainable development and history. In *Precious Places*, history is alive, and agency thrives.

Figure 4.1. Still from *boxing and collapse* from *Obsessive Becoming* (Daniel Reeves, US, 1995). Image courtesy of Daniel Reeves.

4

THE HAND THAT HOLDS UP ALL THIS FALLING

*The Works of Daniel Reeves**

D ANIEL REEVES, AN EXPATRIATE AMERICAN WHO HAS RESIDED in Scotland and France, is perhaps best known in the United States for his contributions over the last two decades to the evolution of the personal, poetic, experimental video documentary with signature pieces such as *Smothering Dreams* (1981),

---

* This essay emerged over the course of several years in the last half of the 1990s as I encountered video artists who worked with digital tools to process images. Through the legendary Experimental Television Center, upstate New York has a vital fifty-year history of video artists experimenting with inventing tools for image processing and manipulation. Daniel Reeves, an Ithaca College alumnus who attended the Cinema and Photography program in the late 1970s after returning from a tour of duty in Vietnam, is a key figure in that upstate video art scene that included Bill Viola, Philip Mallory Jones, Steina Vasulka, and Tony Conrad. When I moved to Ithaca in 1981, many people who learned of my interest in political documentary suggested I see Reeves's *Smothering Dreams* (1981), a recounting, using video processing and reenactment, of his harrowing Vietnam experience as a Marine. For many years, I taught that video in my documentary theory and history class. In 1995, I attended a Flaherty Seminar at Wells College entitled "The Camera Reframed," programmed by Marlina Gonzalez and Bruce Jenkins, both of whom worked at the Walker Art Museum in Minneapolis at the time. They screened Daniel Reeves's *Obsessive Becoming* (1995) at that seminar, although Reeves himself was not present. The piece seemed to combine many of my scholarly and political interests—amateur film, trauma, war, histories, new technologies, and lyrical writing. Two years later, the Flaherty Seminar was experiencing financial challenges and could not mount a full week-long seminar. They reached out looking for institutions to host what they called Flaherty on the Road, short three-day weekend seminars featuring screenings and discussions. I volunteered the Roy Park School of Communications to host a seminar I programmed with Michelle Materre, entitled "Explorations in Memory and Modernity." My dean at the time, Dr. Thomas Bohn, was excited about the prospect of hosting a Flaherty Seminar at the school and marshaled many resources to underwrite it. We invited Daniel Reeves to return because he was an alumnus of Ithaca College with a distinguished body of work. He not only showed *Obsessive Becoming* but mounted four installations in the campus art gallery. Six months later, I decided to pull together my thoughts to write an essay on his work for *Afterimage*. This essay is adapted from one that originally appeared in *Afterimage*, a journal published in upstate New York by the Visual Studies Workshop, called "Processing Trauma: The Media Art of Daniel Reeves," *Afterimage* 26, no. 22 (September/October 1998): 11–13.

Sabda (1984), *Ganapati: Spirit of the Bush* (1986), *Sombra a Sombra* (1988), and his epic masterwork, *Obsessive Becoming* (1995).[1] Historically, these works contributed to the legitimation of video as an art form and also helped to chart out the genre of the personal documentary that melded subjectivity with public histories and political agendas, carving out a space for documentary practice away from the objectivist and empiricist mass cultural locations that characterized much work inflected with identity politics during the 1980s and early 1990s.[2]

Since the production of *Smothering Dreams*—a visceral reenactment and psychic restaging of his brutal ambush experiences during the Vietnam War—Reeves has produced a stunning and evocative range of work in installation, multimedia, performance time-based art, photography, and video. Reeves's mystical, beautiful, and subjectively encoded single-channel work has somewhat eclipsed his equally dense and magisterial work in other media, such as installation and photography, that navigates more public territories in its disposition and reception.

Traversing multiple media formations and constructions, these various projects cover a complex terrain between the political nightmares of war, the necessity of spiritual renewal, and collective connection through appropriating technology for reimagined social rituals. All of the works suggest the urgency of constantly inventing new formal languages for visual and psychic exploration, deploying technology not as a fetish but as shamanistic medium to recover fractured memories, warped political sensibilities, and misplaced collectivities. Reeves's strategy merges art making as a spiritual practice with art reception as a historiographic methodology, an inscription of history upon both the body and the eye.

Both the single-channel and installation/multimedia works share an obsession with reworking trauma, ranging through child abuse, the environmental destruction of plants and animals, family violence, the Gulf War, nuclear war, the Spanish Civil War, and Vietnam. They reclaim the curative powers latent in the reprocessed and remade image. In trauma, the image emerges as the psychic pivot point, the place where precise repetition elides memory and prevents the moving forward inscribed in a narrativizing history.[3] The traumatic event, larger than life because it annihilates life and summons death, continually returns and cannot be controlled, extinguished, or tamed. It can only be integrated within a dialogic historical practice. In the content of the work of Daniel Reeves, trauma is engraved with death as well as figured in environmental destruction, psychic despair, and wars. As literary theorist Cathy Carruth has argued, "To be traumatized is precisely to be possessed by an image or event."[4]

Consequently, images, imagery, the imaginary, and imagined desires condense trauma and restage it. However, these traumas are always engraved by colonized, gendered, and racialized markings. As Stuart Hall has observed in his analysis of Frantz Fanon's theorization of the inscription of colonialism and race, it is necessary to get beyond facticity and fixity into "the practices of trans-coding and re-signing . . . to disturb, unsettle, and to re-inscribe."[5]

The anthropologist Michael Taussig has written about indigenous rituals that produce a "healing through images," a collective transformation of state terror into historical memory. For Taussig, the image holds possibilities beyond itself—it is a form of ritual, a site for performativity rather than fixed meaning or a stunted facticity. However, the image is not bound by solipsism and individualism but is instead collective and nomadic, creating networks that sustain resistance to the silencing produced by state terror.[6]

Daniel Reeves's body of work stages this healing through images, where processed and digitized video images revive the magic that technology and war suppress. This magic attempts to release pain and move toward a new collective reclamation of memory and history through imagery as a conduit to the psychic and political realms, rather than through a formulation of imagery as an identical index and referent for these realms. In other words, the images shed facticity and fixity, functioning more as associative links to larger, more layered narratives that generate meaning production through juxtaposition. Robert Jay Lifton has described how trauma requires that the repetition be disengaged; he writes, "The insight begins with the shattering of prior forms. Because forms have to be shattered for there to be new insight. In that sense, it is a shattering of form but it is also a new dimension of experience."[7]

This shattering of images and forms is exemplified perhaps most boldly in the design of *Obsessive Becoming*. This single-channel video moves from repression of shattered memories of family violence and sexual abuse; to witnessing larger political events like the Vietnam War, World War II, and genocide; to renewal and reconnection between family; and to larger collective politics as transformative and spiritually renewing. It doubles the sites of trauma, moving into psychic spaces and out toward more public war and genocide within the same visual zone through digital layering, superimpositions, and dissolves. In *Obsessive Becoming*, a variety of discordant images derived from archival footage of war, family snapshots, home movies, and science films are digitized and morphed into a continuous strip condensing fragmented images into water and fluidity. The layering of these disparate images and their image processing shatters them, releasing them from their repetitions and from indexicality. This layering strategy simultaneously problematizes signification as directly opaque referentiality and transcodes personal and historical imagery as impermanence and movement toward rather than repetition.

As a body of work, Reeves's videos push the possibilities of camera-vision to unlock authenticity and transcendence through seeing and revisioning, often in layering of images, slow-motion images, or associative montage connected through dissolves that function almost like metaphorical bandages to the traumas within. *Sombra a Sombra*, a poetic evocation of the Spanish Civil War through the poetry of Cesar Vallejo (read by video artist Juan Downey), consists of live-action imagery of various ruins and sites in Spain, where the emptiness of the compositions, devoid of humans, suggests death as an absence, as a void diagrammed by graphic compositional elements.

The act of shooting functions as an exorcism of personal trauma which resettles into spiritual resolution through transferring the Zen Buddhist notion of the present moment to the production process itself, a belief in the primacy of the image that counters postmodernism's severing of the sign from the referent to create new meaning. However, in Reeves's work, this insistence on some fractured referent in the real does not suggest a one-to-one correspondence between signifier and signified; his work functions as a foraging for signification itself, an archaeology of the visual as a space where trauma is scripted into memory. Slavoj Žižek refers to this process in *The Plague of Fantasies*: "In order to be operative, fantasy has to remain 'implicit,' it has to maintain a distance towards the explicit symbolic texture sustained by it, and to function as its inherent transgression. The constitutive gap between explicit symbolic texture and its phantasmic background is obvious in any work of art."[8]

For Reeves, the production of new referents as well as new signs drives the single-channel work and constitutes a refusal to accept imagery disconnected from the realms of the real; images and the imaginary function as processes rather than as memorialized and inert nostalgia. Shoshana Feldman has differentiated between the repetition of trauma and the forward dialogic movement of testimony. She writes, "The testimony in its commitment to truth is a passage through, and an exploration of, differences, rather than an exploration of identity."[9] Yet these images also insist on the fluidity and transformation of images. This strategy rejects veracity and verisimilitude as essentially a conservative practice that reflects a repetition: the images in Reeves's work operate as multilayered dialogic exchanges with other images, each enfolding a testimony of their visual traces into each other.

Reeves's single-channel video work exemplifies a virtuoso manipulation of a wide range of technologies—such as analog and digital, installation to photography, original footage to archival, single channel to multiple channel, and video, film, and computers—to shred, layer, and decompose images ranging from archival war images, to home movies, to images shot in France, India, Spain, and Scotland to excavate the psychic traumas entangled within their formal designs.[10] For example, nearly every one of Reeves's single-channel pieces discards the straight cut, a hallmark of discontinuous montage, opting for image processing, dissolves, digital layering, and superimpositions. This process suggests images as sedimentary layers, a geology of the self as composed with histories; public life; recovered, repressed imagery; subjectivities; and traumas.

This shredding and image composting is specified in Reeves's late 1970s image-processing techniques, his incessant use of digital morphing, digitized composite imaging, dissolves, and rotoscoping. In its deployment of technology to refashion vision as a way to repeal its mimetic, realist function, Reeves's work extends the epistemology of the radical political modernists of the early twentieth century such as Dziga Vertov. Vertov positioned technology as a facilitator of a new vision with his concepts of the kino-eye and montage that would dislodge the passivity of the fiction film, "the opiate of the people," through construction of new intervals and gaps between the image writing that summoned the spectator to labor on the signification of new revolutionary meanings. Vertov's position is counterposed to the more contemporary postmodernist movement of viewing images as surface texts to be deconstructed to reveal abstract political and ideological components not immediately visible.[11] The Vertovian project moves in two directions: deconstruction of old vision and reconstruction of new vision. With their haunting imagery and exquisitely complex, layered sound mixes by the sound-design artist Jon Hilton, the works offer a meditative spectatorship. They serve to create a public and psychic space that marks its difference from phenomenological experience through construction of a new kind of space in between the real and the fantastic, the present and history.

Additionally, Reeves's single-channel work often utilizes either poetry or poetic narration as another layer of memory piled into the video images themselves, locating the imaginary within the imagery. Combined, the layered imagery and the poetic writing invert the relationship between text and image: images detonate denotations, while spoken texts suggest textuality as infinitely associative and deferred. For example, *Ganapati*, a tape that situates the killing of elephants within a larger cultural death drive to destroy the earth, is composed of continuously scrolling script that dislodges the slowed-down images of elephants from their animality, linking them into a psychic symbolic structure about death, destruction, and land. In these works, Reeves arranges writing and images in order to create new ways of thinking and perceiving through a dense layering of imagery and language. These videos demonstrate that both text and image serve as discursive relations, infinitely sedimentary, sometimes mystical, always evocative.

Reeves's historically significant body of work is marked by a romanticism that threads the authentic seeing of Brakhage and the early 1960s underground film movement into concerns for the materiality of structural film of the 1970s.[12] This romanticism, which often anchors a totalized meaning finally within the self—the "I" position—rather than in a larger construct of a shared "we," constitutes a problematized movement in these works. This location within the subjectivity of the "I" can reduce readings to inner psychic excursions that hijack larger political iconographies as a way into the self rather than, per feminist aesthetic practice, as a continual transversal between private and public that completely reborders both.[13]

These works exhibit a tension between internalities and externalities. The production of the text reverts to the mysticism of individual vision. This nineteenth-century trope situates the artist as occupying a privileged outsider position often marked by a retreat from public accountability. On the other hand, the text's meaning production extends out toward a more spiritual collectivity and affinity through images and the imaginary. This dialectical strategy relies on an individual vision that produces the profilmic as a laboratory where trauma constantly infuses the real with death. It occupies a countermovement to film and video practices focused on more overtly political realms of identity politics or resistance to normalizing hegemonies. In Reeves's video work, resistance does not reject hegemony so reductively. Instead, through technological exorcisms, these works resist trauma that repeats and encircles itself. Reeves's video work continually pulls away from the real, positioning the text as a series of inscriptions, ciphers, repressions, displacements, and condensations, moving more toward Derrida than to realist cinematic documentary practices.[14]

As a body of work, Reeves's single-channel videos explore how the visual language of video and digital art migrates between the private and the public, a series of transversals, exchanges, and transformations. This negotiation between the personal and the political implicitly confounds the borders between them, evoking strategies of postcolonial conceptualizations about fluidity and hybridity. "Displacing is a way of surviving. It is an impossible, truthful story of living in-between regimes of truth," explains Trinh T. Minh-ha.[15] The nonlinear structure informing Reeves's works jettisons causality. Their layerings of image and sound exiles iconicity, anticipating digital multimedia architectures that rely less on linearity and more on multiple routes and paths on which to navigate many multiplicities.[16] Images, then, cannot be reduced to representations, but instead function as fluid parts of a visual ecosystem comprised of social, historical, political, environmental, and aesthetic layers that continually shift and mutate. The act of representation is transmogrified into multiple acts of juxtaposition. This layering functions as a translation of trauma into images, and images into architectures and geologies.[17]

Reeves's reenactment and consequent reenchantment—opening up mobilities between the private and the political, memory and history, the produced image and the archival one—precipitated pointed epistemological debate from audiences at the 1995 Flaherty Seminar and at a 1997 screening at Cornell Cinema, when *Obsessive Becoming*, a sweeping, poignant epic connecting Reeves's family dysfunction with representations of war and technology in twentieth-century modernity, was screened with the artist. The video invokes melodramatic tropes of conflicts between family and the larger world and the positioning of the spectator within pathos.

These audience debates interrogated the politics of reinscribing heavily encoded and overdetermined archival images from the Holocaust, the Warsaw ghetto during World War II, Vietnam, or the Gulf War with more solipsistic, personal issues such as abuse, war trauma, or the quest for spiritual enlightenment. Some argued that strategy reduces historical context into iconographic condensations standing in for and encapsulating individualized psychic trauma. Invoking cultural feminist Susan Griffin, Reeves contended that these images are interconnected: war manifests unbridled male power, and abuse suggests an invasion of war ideologies into familial psychic terrains.

The voice-over narration in *Obsessive Becoming* recounts Reeves's abuse as he ruminates on his family's psychic violence. The linear narrative of Reeves's family history invokes and reworks melodramatic codes, configuring contradictions between the family and public life as excess beyond language and rationality but located in mise-en-scène and the unconscious. This process is less overt than most political cinematic strategies. Melodrama collapses family life and economic life. In fiction, narrative structures displace and mask this contradiction between private and public. In documentary, this problematic is not displaced but instead mobilized as an associative dialectical structure that breaks open accountability, history, and responsibility. This application of a fictional structure to nonfictional material complicates and loosens up the subjective and the historical: the piece occupies an aesthetic space somewhere in between fact and fiction, melodrama and the unconscious. The visual practices of *Obsessive Becoming* materialize what theorist Paul Virilio describes as the "virtualization of real space," where cocooning, interface, and interactivity alter the experience of space and time.[18]

Materialized in layering and computer-generated effects, *Obsessive Becoming*'s image processing of trauma and war provokes debates about politics: virtualization dislocates politics and places it elsewhere, in a fabricated cyber/time/space. The political debates surrounding these raided iconographies erupt in the flattening affect and effect of the single-channel work, rather than the rhizome-like webs of new media projects that inscribe user driving as part of their design. New media projects reform the linear scopic drive of single-channel pieces into pluralities of readings, webs, and destinations. A central problematics of digital culture thus becomes how to locate these transitory, transitional, fluid dislocations with their ever-changing locations, meanings, readings, and spatialities. Raymond Bellour notes the new interfaces of sound/image/discourse: "We have gone beyond the image, to a nameless mixture, a discourse-image, if you like, or a sound image ('Son-Image,' as Godard calls it), whose first side is occupied by television and second side by the computer, in our all-purpose machine society. This is clearly where we can observe all the potentialities anticipated by the computer image, over and above the image itself, since it is produced by the same machine which, better than any other, can combine and relate interplays with images and with language to any conceivable extent."[19]

Reeves argues that his practice emanates from unresolved personal experiences that he works through during the image-making process, a therapeutic intervention into traumatic repetitions. At these two screenings, his interlocutors countered that these romanticized spiritual tropes drain historical context and power relations from the images. Thus, the computer processing depoliticizes images by anchoring them exclusively in personal registers rather than in what Trinh T. Minh-ha calls the feminist postcolonial dialectical "to and fro" that unsettles both the personal and the political into a plurality of differences.[20]

These debates about the political necessity of the archival images reside in melodramatic conventions, often considered radical because they mine contradictions between public and private, between family and larger social issues. This argument highlights ongoing debate in art and media discourse between artistic romanticized individuality identified with affective melodramatic narratives and auteurism versus the destabilizations of authorship and binary oppositions offered by postmodernism and postcolonial theory insisting on a meta-analytical dialectic. The latter unlocks texts to circulate within difference, frequently considered a more radical intervention. Reeves's work is neither one nor the other. Instead, these works morph between both positions, facilitating a series of destabilizations. Their artistic strategies circulate within and around genres rather than any fixed structure.

The Hand That Holds Up All This Falling was a Daniel Reeves exhibition that ran October 7–December 14, 1997, at the Handwerker Gallery at Ithaca College, Ithaca, New York. The exhibition featured four installations that reversed the individually encoded truth claims of the single-channel work: they exposed more collective global structures that, to invoke the title of the exhibition, held up the images. The installations jettisoned the analytically volatile and seductively beautiful personal romanticism of the single-channel piece. Instead, they exposed Reeves's preoccupations with the spatial and temporal architectures of images and with the elaboration of what Derrida has labeled "archive fever." For Derrida, the archive takes place "at the place of originary and structural breakdown of the said memory."[21] In the installations, this archive fever dismantles a repetition fetish to retain the past and incessantly recycle memory. The projects elaborate Derrida's arguments that the archive consists of substrata and layers superimposed on each other to produce a break with repetition.

The installations moved out from the individual artisanal mode of the videos into a more shamanistic collective model of production that enacted a ritual of community animation: during the week-long set-up at Ithaca College, over 150 students, faculty, staff, community members, and even deans contributed time and skills, placing rocks around *Eingang: The Way In* (an installation with video monitors inserted into large logs), painting gallery walls, or writing on glass windows. Embodying the title of the exhibition, many hands held up the falling of images, restoring community and handwork to virtualized prosthetic digital processes, the analog and the digital enfolded. These installations reclaimed public space as a fold between the archival and meditative, private and public, analog and digital, image and object, real and virtual. Thus, the enfolding process took priority over the restitution of referential signs.[22]

In the more public space of the gallery, spectators walk around and into the works, inserting their own physical presence and subjectivities into the pieces. The large scale of the installations foregrounded investigations into the healing powers of images through continuous and discontinuous montage between and on top of images, a simultaneously horizontal and vertical juxtaposition. These installations query how images can be retrieved to generate new archival relations and new substrata. In these installations, the personal explorations imbedded in the voice-overs, poetry, and image making endemic to the single-channel work dissolve into a plurality of voices, inscriptions, and encodings.

The exhibition was comprised of four separate pieces that together charted the one-hundred-year trajectory of image making, ranging from nineteenth-century lanternslides, family film, and commercial imagery to analog video images and digital compositing: *Eingang: The Way In* (1990), *Lines of Lamentation* (1997), *The White Television* (1977 and 1997), and a series of eight hand-painted digital composite images (1997).

The White Television reprised an installation that critiqued the Vietnam War: it projected slow-motion imagery of a performative, reenacted war produced for *Smothering Dreams* on a video monitor painted white. Reeves had crafted this piece while a cinema student at Ithaca College in the mid-1970s. This updated version of *The White Television* was mounted to engage undergraduates in the build during master classes offered as part of Reeves's residency as the inaugural Skip Landen Professional-in-Residence at the Roy H. Park School of Communications in October of 1997. It was closed to the public after the residency concluded.

Perhaps Reeves's most celebrated installation is *Eingang: The Way In*. It premiered at the High Museum of Art in Atlanta, Georgia, in 1990. It was subsequently remounted at Montage '93 in Rochester, New York; Harvard University in 1994; and sites in England, Scotland, and Ireland. The title derives from a Rilke poem suggesting the ineffability and urgency of vision. The installation recycled technology, images, and nature to create monumental public space for contemplation of the environment, broadly mapped as a constellation between nature, high technology, and the spectator's physical movement around the space. Most reviews described *Eingang* as a hauntingly spiritual work searching for inexpressible connections between nature and technology as well as the material and spiritual worlds.

Eingang consisted of seven large tree trunks three feet in diameter, reclaimed from a 350-year-old discarded New Mexico fir. The trunks' peeling bark suggested decomposition and erosion as an ecological art-making process. Each log was a different height ranging from twenty-five inches to forty-nine inches, creating a natural altar arising out of volcanic rocks and Scottish beach stones placed around the floor. Seven high-definition television monitors were inserted into the trunks, the screens flush with the surface. North Carolina egg rocks sat on top of each log, cascading over the video monitors mounted inside. The Handwerker Gallery was painted a burnt sienna that not only darkened the gallery space but invoked earth, soil, planting. A few key lights lit the trunks, suggesting moonlight entering a space of contemplation and participation. The high-definition television monitors within the tree trunks pointed to the contradiction between nature and technology.

Eingang oscillates between nature, ecology, and Zen principles of interconnectedness. However, the installation was more complex than an exercise in ecological spirituality. Repeating circular imagery in the shape of the trunks, the spherical bowls, and the arrangement of the logs, *Eingang* refutes a passive, immobile spectatorship. This circularity physically and psychically activates participatory spectatorship since the piece cannot be experienced without movement.

In *Eingang*, the darkened gallery space and the altar-like distribution of logs evoke the spatial configurations of a Catholic Church. In contrast, the movement of constantly changing images reflected in the spherical bowls, randomly accessed imagery, rocks deposited on beaches by the force of wave motion, and spectators' movements around the piece inscribe temporality. The installation combines a contemplative mode with a projection of what a transnational historiography of the senses might look like. The images depict every continent. The physical objects combine elements from Europe (the stones), America (the trees), and Asia (the monitors and high technology). Different historical periods form strata: the ancient lava rocks, the 350-year-old fir trunks, the water, images from the present, and Reeves's own personal archive of images unfolding within the trunks. *Eingang* suggests a post-1989, post–Cold War memorial to the end of arbitrary political and historical borders. It elaborates ideas about historical layers constantly moving within water flows, a strategy that suffuses *Obsessive Becoming*.

Another installation continues this exploration of linkages between nature, materiality, and spirituality. Shot over seven years in America, Europe, Africa, and Asia, Reeves's three-channel video installation, *Try to Live to See This* (1988) was a ninety-minute triptych organized around themes of water, earth, and fire, and fed into monitors. Bowls filled with distilled water were precipitously poised on top of the flat monitors. They reflected the monitor images in ghostly, distorted patterns that dislocated the images from their own materiality. A small glass plate filled with rice floated inside each bowl. Miniature three-inch-screen television monitors lay atop the rice. They picked up random signals from commercial television broadcasts that contrasted with the more formally complex images of landscapes, animals, and women workers from across the globe displayed on the larger monitors.

The exhibition also included eight large-scale digital paintings and prints that excavated relationships between trauma, historiography, the layering of substrates, and the iconography of water and flows. Reeves's two-dimensional work abandons digitality as hyperrealist verisimilitude, endemic to its commercial deployment in films such as *Titanic* (1997). In this work, Reeves deployed digital imaging techniques to question the photographic image and to materialize its multiple historical discourses: Reeves's work exposes the seams and folds between different registers of images. Four of the images were digitally processed from Reeves's own work, including a shot from his in-progress narrative feature film, *Perdu*. In this way, Reeves refuted the authenticity of his own image work by underscoring how all images eventually enter the archive.

Four other images, which Reeves entitled *Color Digital Paintings*, investigate the possibilities of digitality to pluralize the archive, repacking its discursive layers as sediments of power relations and political/psychic traumas. *Homage to the Lovers of Pompeii* (1997), a 24 1/2 by 24 1/2–inch Iris print comprised of over forty digital layers, is structured like a target with a flower in the bull's-eye. A rainbow, a man and a woman, words in German and French, mushrooms, a Chinese dancer, lips, a penis and a scrotum, a breast, and flamingos populate the frame. A target is layered over this collage, and elegant handwriting in French superimposed over the images sutures disparate imagery evoking sexuality, animality, and desire. While the digital processes expedite a new form of analytical montage within the image rather than sequentially across images, the analog handwriting illustrates how both the handmade and the discursive hold it all together.

Another digital painting entitled *Gas Masque* (1997), 34 3/4 by 24 inches large, interrogates this juxtaposition between the analog and the digital. An archival image of a mother and her two children wearing gas masks during what looks to be World War II is digitized, with colors and resolution decomposing. The full-frontal composition resembles news documentation that renders victims as icons for larger geopolitical issues. Through analog handicraft, Reeves restores historical context by surrounding the figures with gold hand lettering that describes the pervasiveness of illegal gas bombing in nearly every country. By layering the images with densely applied oil sticks in brilliant blue, green, orange, and red hues scratched in intricate patterns right on the image, he bears witness to trapped psychic traumas. Scribbling that figuratively inscribes inner turmoil disturbs the unities of the photograph, a kind of trauma writing.

Manos para la muerte (1997), a large 40 1/2 by 61–inch digital painting, similarly reworks the terror of war with imagery from the Spanish Civil War featuring crowds rushing around and leaders assuming power with their hands raised. Figures outlined in blue emerge from gray paint. Gray, red, and yellow oil sticks colored in intricately chaotic interconnected patterns viscerally illustrate how war traumas and fascism are etched onto bodies.

The exhibition also featured a site-specific installation on the glass walls of the Handwerker Gallery called *Lines of Lamentation* (1997), created especially for Ithaca College as part of the Reeves residency. Spanning 68½ feet in length across fourteen windows, 20 feet high by 24 inches wide, this work investigated how multiple languages write themselves as images. It revisited themes emerging in Reeves's single-channel work investigating writing and language as materiality. It also invoked layering as a strategy to question the referentiality of any image. *Lines of Lamentation* queried the act of translation and mediation, reimagining each as continual works in progress, always incomplete. It probed signification as a form of stratification, a sedimentary act requiring an archaeology of images, language, and *différance* suggesting Foucault morphed with Derrida. Each panel was composed of six layers, the centerpiece being a line of seven nineteenth-century lantern slides applied at eye level to the window and illuminated by daylight from the outside.

Across the top of all fourteen panels, Reeves composed a poetic text handwritten in gold ink. The text was filled with wordplay, political allusions to corporate downsizing and governmental inadequacies, and incomplete narratives about three angels, Aleph, Beth, and Gimel. To write, Reeves did a three-hour speed-writing session inspired by looking at the random distribution of lantern slides. Words denoting the content of the slides were written beneath. In contrast to the free-flowing poetic language of the top layer, three strips of 16mm sound magnetic film were taped to each window, evoking lost analog archives. The gallery provided a sound reader so that the viewer could run the sound head across to hear Reeves reciting the words written on the top layer. This process embodied the technological mediation in acts of representation and memory, activated by the physical movement of the body.

The bottom two layers of each panel consisted of handwritten translations of Reeves's narrative into over twenty different languages, including Arabic, Chinese, French, Farsi, Finnish, Hindi, Japanese, and Spanish. This multiplicity of languages deterritorialized and denationalized the images. It created a new social imaginary based on plurality, nonlinearity, and imaginative leaps. The first panel read: "Aleph, Beth and Gimel: We lived under lindens at the axle of this world. Our song was eaten by the great white father. Tearing pelvis from the phoenix, he made work and set us to it. The white birch buds headed in while alphabets and inventions ate the leaves from the trees." The lantern slides showed successive images of a birch tree, lettering, willow trees, washing, a skull, a tree, and buds. In *Lines of Lamentation*, Reeves explores how deterioration constitutes natural image processing and how history marks the text. The lantern slides were rusted, bent, dirty, and crackled. The images were burned and wiped out, with water, light, and air destroying their emulsions. Each slide edge was numbered and described, an atomizing, decontextualized classification system dependent on the referent. The act of writing on the window doubled this historical writing on the image.

Handwerker Gallery Director Thomas Somma, an art history professor at Ithaca College, observed that "*Lines of Lamentation* is conceptual art in the truest sense of the term. It is the idea of the artist, but the many hands that made it were not his hands, but the college community, the people who glued it to the glass, wrote the words."[23] The piece itself reveled in the different decorative handwriting styles of the scribes that materialized difference.

Somma contended: "The piece invokes the tradition of realism by breaking down the boundaries between the work of art and viewer—the college community is reflected in the piece as students walk by outside the gallery and their images are reflected into the piece, in much the same way as the Vietnam War Memorial in Washington. Yet [it] also creates a kind of postmodern dialogue between the high technology of *Eingang* and lantern slides. In this show, Reeves is creating a virtual dialogue with history in the confines of the gallery."[24]

The various pieces featured in *The Hand That Holds Up All This Falling* trace how fluidity in digital imagemaking is embodied in the physical form of water itself. The writing across separated panels attempted to heal fractured, fragmented traumatized imagery. These features remapped borders to restore a magical aura. Perhaps even more significantly, this show visually mapped archive fever by elaborating the substrata of history comprised of the handwork of the analog, imagery, the mutability of the real, the performative present, psychic imaginaries, rhizomes of the digital, shifting destabilizations of the past, and writing.

Derrida insists that "what is no longer archived in the same way is no longer lived in the same way."[25] *The Hand That Holds Up All This Falling* similarly intimates that the production of the future requires animating the past with hope, hand, heart, and life, rather than with the death drive. As Daniel Reeves writes in the last panel of *Lines of Lamentation*: "We gather at the shore, exchange greetings, clothes, gender, and launch homeward in the shadows of fallen temples, in the joy of resurrection at Arlington to the palm of the Diamond Cutter."

Notes

1. For penetrating discussions of these films as well as a particularly incisive interview with Daniel Reeves, see Marita Sturken, "What Is Grace in All This Madness: The Videotapes of Daniel Reeves," *Afterimage* (Summer 1985): 24–27.

2. For their provocative insights into the work of Daniel Reeves, I want to acknowledge the contribution of intensely heated discussions with Timothy Murray, Zillah Eisenstein, Ruth Bradley, Scott MacDonald, Erika Mohammed, and Michelle Materre. It is hard to know where

their ideas end and mine begin in this essay, so I thank them all for their generosity in allowing me to pirate their ideas and transform them into my own.

3. See Cathy Caruth, ed., *Trauma: Explorations in Memory* (Baltimore: Johns Hopkins University Press, 1995), 151–154.

4. Caruth, "Trauma and Experience: Introduction," in *Trauma*, 4–5.

5. Stuart Hall, "The After-life of Frantz Fanon: Why Fanon? Why Now? Why Black Skin, White Masks," in *The Fact of Blackness: Frantz Fanon and Visual Representation*, ed. Alan Reed (London: Institute of Contemporary Arts, 1996), 19.

6. Michael Taussig, *The Nervous System* (New York: Routledge, 1992), 6–30. For a trenchant discussion of trauma as it interweaves state terrors on the level of performance, see also Timothy Murray, *Drama/Trauma: Specters of Race and Sexuality in Performance, Video and Art* (London: Routledge, 1997).

7. Cathy Caruth, "An interview with Robert Jay Lifton," in *Trauma*, 134.

8. Slavoj Žižek, *The Plague of Fantasies* (New York: Verso, 1997), 18.

9. Shoshana Feldman and Dori Laub, MD, *Testimony: Crises of Witnessing in Literature, Psychoanalysis, and History* (New York: Routledge, 1992), 91.

10. Daniel Reeves, interview by Timothy Murray and Patricia R. Zimmermann, October 12, 1997, Ithaca, New York.

11. See for example, "Dziga Vertov on Kino-Eye: Excerpts from a Lecture Given in Paris in 1929," *FilmFront* 1, no. 2 (January 1935): 6–8. For a comprehensive overview of Vertov's writings, see Annette Michelson, ed. *The Kino-Eye: The Writings of Dziga Vertov* (Berkeley: University of California, 1985).

12. For an illuminating historical and theoretical discussion of the 1960s avant-garde, see David James, *Allegories of Cinema: American Film in the 1960s* (Princeton, NJ: Princeton University Press, 1989).

13. For a discussion of the feminist avant-garde's visual and political strategies to reconstitute private/public spaces, see Patricia Mellencamp, *A Fine Romance: Five Ages of Film Feminism* (Philadelphia: Temple University Press, 1995), 155–290.

14. Jacques Derrida, *Archive Fever* (Chicago: University of Chicago Press, 1997), 15. For a lucid elaboration of documentary's continual incorporation of realist codes, see Brian Winston, *Claiming the Real* (London: British Film Institute, 1995).

15. Trinh T. Minh-ha, *When the Moon Waxes Red* (London: Routledge, 1991), 21.

16. David Tomas, "From the Photograph to Postphotographic Practice: Toward a Postoptical Ecology of the Eye," in *Electronic Culture: Technology and Visual Representation*, ed. Timothy Druckrey (New York: Aperture, 1996), 145–153.

17. Gayatri Chakravorty Spivak, "Explanation and Culture: Marginalia," in *Out There: Marginalization and Contemporary Culture*, ed. Russell Ferguson, Martha Gever, Trinh T. Minh-ha, and Cornel West (Cambridge, MA: MIT Press, 1990), 377–393.

18. Paul Virilio, *Open Sky* (London: Verso, 1997), 70–80.

19. Raymond Bellour, "The Double Helix," in Druckrey, *Electronic Culture*, 199.

20. Trinh T. Minh-ha, *When the Moon Waxes Red* (New York: Routledge, 1991), 73–106.

21. Derrida, 11.

22. Gilles Deleuze, *The Fold* (New York: Bloomsbury Academic, 2006).

23. Thomas Somma, interview by Patricia R. Zimmermann, October 20, 1997.

24. Somma interview.

25. Derrida, *Archive Fever*, 18.

Figure 5.1. *Fall Roads Bus* (1981), photo by Michael Kientiz. Image courtesy of Michael Kientiz.

5

CARTOGRAPHIES OF IMPOSSIBLE AND POSSIBLE WORLDS

*The Photography of Michael Kienitz**

Elsewhere Is Here

A limp, unraveling shoelace cascades over worn, dusty sneakers. A little boy, maybe five years old, wears a fitted camouflage uniform with crumpled epaulets, a brimmed military-style hat covering his head. He grips the arms of a scratched wooden chair with his small hands. His feet do not touch the floor. He looks intently to the side, half of his face shaded by the hat, the other half lit by the sunlight.

This photograph by photojournalist Michael Kienitz is titled *The Little General* (Peshawar, Pakistan, 1984). It is one of thirty-six images from *Small Arms—Children of Conflict*, a moving retrospective chronicling three decades of Kienitz's photography. The exhibition maps how politically and economically driven conflict and violence envelop the bodies of children across the globe.

During the war in Vietnam, Kienitz sat in his political philosophy class at the University of Wisconsin in Madison. Outside, he could hear the screams and

---

* In 2007, photojournalist Michael Kienitz invited me to write an essay for a catalog to accompany an exhibition of his war photographs to be mounted at the Chazen Museum of Art at the University of Wisconsin, Madison. I had worked with Kienitz from 1977 to 1981, in the very political independent media scene in Madison, Wisconsin, doing print journalism, slide shows for various nongovernmental organizations, and documentaries. My journalistic work with Kienitz was a welcome, on-the-ground counterpoint to the abstract theories and dense histories that constituted my graduate program in communications at the University of Wisconsin. Reminiscent of that time when I was immersed in both theory and practice, this catalog essay presented a way to think about collaboration in documentary, the politics of image making, and direct address to the spectator. To prepare for writing this essay, I conducted two extensive interviews with Kienitz about his conceptualizations of photojournalism. He also sent me large eighteen- by twenty-four-inch prints of each photo so that I could work with them in analog form, spreading them out on the floor to look for conceptual and formal resonances. My essay was published in the catalog entitled *Small Arms—Children of Conflict: Photographs by Michael Kienitz* (Madison, WI: Chazen Museum of Art, 2007), 7–15.

chants of students involved in the antiwar movement. Later, he realized the local news media failed to accurately describe what he had witnessed—and heard—for himself. Television stations and newspapers emphasized raucous demonstrations and ignored the undisputed fact that police clubbed protesters with their nightsticks. These potent juxtapositions of philosophy and political action, disinformation and deliberate omissions, steered Kienitz to photojournalism. He never enrolled in a photography class. Photo reportage provided a compass to navigate the intersections between the theory of academia and the events unfolding in the material world.

Kienitz's photographs are radical, urgent, insistent, demanding, and clear. The images and their subjects address us directly, irrefutably, insistently. The people in these photographs look at Kienitz as he takes the picture. They collaborate with him in the process; they assent to be photographed. They look out, refusing to be objectified, pitied, or romanticized. Kienitz's careful compositions repudiate the adrenaline rushes of chaos. These images insist that elsewhere is here.

Small Arms—Children of Conflict rejects the drama of global struggle, political abstraction, and the horrific, violent spectacle of war. Instead, Kienitz's photographs laser in on individuals, their environs, and the everyday. These images insist we look at the specific and material daily lives of children who must live in political conflicts propelled and amplified by adults.

Risky Dislocations

The deliberate probing exemplified in *Small Arms* displaces the craving for action and the desire for frenzied, constant movement so entrenched in the practices of conventional photojournalism. This exhibition replaces the endless quest for narrative climaxes, the panic of the unexpected, linear time, the big story, the focus on the bloody, and false closure imbedded in these practices with its uncompromising opposite: a layered and often quiet denouement after the action has subsided, a pensive space focused on noncombatants in the environments and landscapes they inhabit.

These images do not ask us to turn inward. Rather, they invite us to consider the significance of the smallest actions, like a child sitting in a chair or young girls in angel costumes cupping pigeons in their hands. These images ask us to enter into the world and be part of it, to move beyond our own places of comfort into the risky territory of interaction, communication, and political engagement.

All of the potent, compelling images in *Small Arms* speak to a larger political and ethical world beyond representation, beyond their immediately discernible content. These photographs invite viewers to slow down, to pause, to locate themselves within a conflict zone, to think. They remind us to connect beyond difference, to gaze past the central subjects of the composition and move toward the edges of the frame. By looking *into* the images, we as spectators then can move *beyond* the images into the political and ethical questions of economic deprivation, political conflicts, violence, and war.

The Little General nudges the viewer into a relationship with the little boy, his chair, his costume. It refutes the distance that surveillance and voyeurism demand. It refutes the melodrama produced by spectacles of violence. *Small Arms—Children of Conflict* inserts the spectator into risky dislocations of the accepted, unexamined consciousness that all powerful and compassionate images command. These images do not capture the climax of the action as much as they recover the spaces of day-to-day life in landscapes and cityscapes ripped open and deconstructed by political conflict. Kienitz's photographs argue that poverty trumps war as an even more threatening and unacceptable form of violence.

Maps of Omission and Talking with Ghosts

Suspended between the horrors of the undeclared war in Vietnam and the endless morass of the war in Iraq, the photographs in *Small Arms* remind us that in this frightening era of worldwide aggressive economic reorganization, war, too, follows the contours of globalization. Violence has multiplied, mutated, spread virally, and dispersed to the places these images take us: El Salvador, Guatemala, Lebanon, Milwaukee, Mississippi, Nicaragua, Northern Ireland, Pakistan. The US government's efforts to destabilize democratic social struggles, economies, and politics lurk beneath all the conflicts registered in these images.

While on assignment in Central America and other regions in the 1980s, Kienitz observed that media corporations provided lavish budgets for meals, hotels, rental vehicles, drivers, and interpreters, a *cordon sanitaire* against political comprehension. Many international reporters enjoyed this economic privilege. Some holed up in their air-conditioned hotels and recycled information supplied by the US government. They often worked to meet deadlines rather than to understand and explain the complex situations engulfing them. They rarely discussed the conflicts with residents who endured the horrific disruptions and destruction. Photo editors wanted images of brutality. In the editing suites of the commercial broadcasters, Kienitz spotted broadcast technicians and reporters screening pornographic movies during breaks. News crews and photographers craved "bang bang," journalistic slang for action-packed spectacles of combat, blood, death, and emotion. This aesthetics of violent excess is war porn.

During his forty-year-plus career, Kienitz has alternated between commercial media assignments with their desire for spectacle and his own analytically questioning personal photography. When working for hire, Kienitz's editors paid him to produce American-centric and machine-fetishizing images. Yet as he shot his assignments for national publications, he decided to dig deeper to uncover a different story, a story that the US-based news magazines and newspapers ignored. He became fascinated by how people not directly engaged in combat coped and adapted to these extreme situations. His editors did not share his interest, asserting that images chronicling the plight of the everyday people would not hook national readers in the United States.

Rather than resolution, the images in *Small Arms—Children of Conflict* offer contradiction. They juxtapose disparate elements: the rubble of bombed cities and the physical exuberance of children, military uniforms beside babies and basketball, and the dead with the living. The dead who are buried in the fields and the cities do not haunt these photographs as memories. Rather, the subjects of these photographs are talking with the ghosts. The meaning of these images resides in that delicate interval between the living and the dead.

In this fleeting, ephemeral space created by an antiwar perspective, a position that recognizes that the horror of war is not only the moment of combat but also the effects on what and who remain after the tanks and soldiers depart, Kienitz's photographs marginalize war and its visual excesses. They do not document weaponry, machinery, combatants, military actions, or white male leaders landing on aircraft carriers proclaiming victory. Powerful antiwar art refocuses us on the human rather than the machine, on the particular rather than the heroic, on the contradictory rather than the unified, on absence rather than presence. These images visualize war as artifacts, aftermaths of combat in ruined cities and concealed landscapes. Neither foreground nor background, the drama of war relocates to an inert past. The children who dwell in the center of these images do not tritely suggest hope for the future—a popular-culture trope that reduces them to victims or icons. Rather, they encourage us to consider that those who live amid war also live and commune with ghosts.

The photographs in *Small Arms—Children of Conflict* convey symmetry and structure over disorder and the melodrama of conflict. The symmetry in Kienitz's work restores balance, suggesting that the act of making a photograph is a collaborative and egalitarian step toward imagining possible futures. The photographs center their subjects. At first, the photographs appear to function as portraits, but then our eyes disengage from the subject and drift to surroundings compositionally equal to or larger than the subject. These images bridge the impossible worlds of war and its dead and the possible world of the living, justice, and talking with ghosts.

Landscapes of Trauma

The children in *Small Arms* subsist in a liminal zone between two worlds: while their small bodies anchor them within the landscapes of trauma, their unemotional stares into the world outside the image express evacuation, refusal, exit. The images open an exchange between the two-dimensional image and the spectator. Here, trauma exceeds words and representation. It carves itself on the body, on the landscape, on the psychic imaginary. It speaks in fragments and exposes itself in breakage, holes, rips, and shards.

Makeshift Morgue (San Salvador, El Salvador, 1982) is an image split in half. The right side is weighted by two tables loaded with bloodied bodies, severed heads, and a dead woman whose painted toenails poke through her open-toed sandals. Boys and men crowd the left side of the image. They gaze at the dead. A young boy in a striped shirt places his hand over his mouth in either a gasp of horror or an attempt to stave off the stench of blood, body parts, and decomposition. On the far left, a slightly older boy in a soiled T-shirt looks out from the scene, the expression on his face neither sad nor happy. It is unclear what he understands about the death and conflict permeating the scene. One boy looks and the other boy looks away. Kienitz made this image at the height of the death squad activity in El Salvador.

The motif of children looking directly at the photographer and out from a landscape of trauma emerges in other images from El Salvador. In *Break Time* (San Salvador, El Salvador, 1981), a naked boy, his body coated in dust, perches on a rock in front of a makeshift wooden house with a gaping hole in the side. Discarded pieces of paper, plastic, rags, rope, and wood ring the house. The boy sips from a white mug. His eyes peer over the rim. The house and the barren ground engulf the boy.

On the other hand, *Natural Causes* (La Libertad, El Salvador, 1984) figures trauma as a triangle of gazes linking the dead with the living. A coffin, holding an elderly man with a piece of fruit for embalming propped in his mouth, angles across the bottom half of the image. At the top of the frame, two boys gaze into the window of the coffin. Between them, a boy peers out at us, his eyes directed off screen, his brow furrowed.

In these photographs, the starkness of the settings suggests that trauma is not individual and solitary, but social and contextual.

Here and There; Outside and Inside

Small Arms resolutely refuses to engage the plight of suffering children during war and destabilizing conflicts. This exhibition jettisons the fantasy of the photograph as an icon for passive distant mourning for victims. It discards the idea of children as delicate beings who must be contained, enclosed, pitied, protected, or rarefied. This exhibition documents children enmeshed in and surviving some of the most serious political conflicts of the last decades of the twentieth century. It not only looks at how they cope with political conflict, poverty, and war, but also how they escape all three through play or looking away. The photographs do not idealize children, nor do they invite nostalgia for lost innocence.

While these children may not be the agents of conflict, they cannot escape it. They possess agency in subtle yet complicated ways: they haul wood, stand, gesture, fly kites, look on, ramble atop bombed out buildings, and play in burnt-out vehicles. They are rarely photographed with parents or adults: they populate a parallel universe where war is distant, leaving its marks on the land but not on their diminutive bodies.

Yet the persistent specter of conflict, destruction, and poverty pervades these images. The children are inside these wars yet strangely outside of them, a persistent entanglement between here and there, within and without. Kienitz elected to photograph working class and impoverished children who survive on the fringes of cities, in community spaces, jungles, neighborhoods, streets, and wars. Children are the most visible and available subjects in these embattled treacherous zones. Adult men are off fighting and killing.

Kienitz journeyed to the interior of these conflicts to portray the plight of the mostly poor people subsisting in the aftermath. His project was underfunded and somewhat haphazard; he rode public transportation, rented cheap hotel rooms with no electricity, hitchhiked. As a freelance American journalist, he was able to abandon his economic privilege because he was independent of the large corporate news organizations. An outsider, Kienitz journeyed inside the countries to find his subjects. He did not subscribe to the policy of embedding: whenever possible, he would spend time with people from all sides of a conflict.

Small Arms contends that over there—beyond—is also here, where we live. The images from the United States, *Nazi Youth* (Milwaukee, Wisconsin, 1980) and *Flea Market Booth* (Tupelo, Mississippi, 1978) demonstrate an insidious violence: the brutality of racist white-power ideologies and the Ku Klux Klan that imbricates children into their webs of hate. These images remind us that hatred and violence also flourish inside the United States and not only outside its borders. These photographs ask us to recognize congruencies between the United States and the globe.

Incongruities and Contiguities

At first, the photographs in *Small Arms—Children of Conflict* appear incongruous. Their balanced, wide-angle compositions frame contradictions between broad political struggles and the daily lives of ordinary children. They seem to express a paradox between big events and small incidents. The children are always outside in public spaces. The interiors of private homes and public institutions like schools, churches, theaters, gyms, and union halls are absent. Parents, teachers, and authority figures rarely accompany these children who wander alone through empty streets and desolate, depopulated landscapes. They intermingle with other children. They confront the camera as an equal, refusing to present the clichés of hope and the future. Rather, they signify a present speaking with the past, emerging from it yet also liberated of its weight.

The mobility of these unsupervised children through landscapes of poverty and conflict alerts us to ideas beyond the simple shock of juxtaposition. It develops explanation through connection. Kienitz's photographs show the resilience, determination, and playfulness of children in the face of destruction. They also spur viewers to see the larger political and economic struggles in a new light. For example, the conflict in Northern Ireland is paired with a small toddler ambling down a street in *Belfast Street* (Belfast, Northern Ireland, 1981). The city street, row houses, and the empty space of a bombed-out vacant lot where an Irish Republican Army bomb factory once stood loom larger than the boy. A white cat prances on the remains of a doorjamb. The boy saunters in front of the rubble, his solitude larger than the environment.

Two other photographs shot in Northern Ireland also reinforce connections. In *Milltown Cemetery* (Belfast, Northern Ireland, 1981), a seven-year-old boy in a suit jacket covered with buttons naming dead hunger strikers leans one elbow on a tombstone inscribed with "Hopkirk, in loving memory of our darling son. Aged 7 years." The image insinuates that children die but also thrive. Age is doubled in this image: the boy who is buried is the same age as the boy leaning on the tombstone. In *Lads of the Murph* (Ballymurphy, Northern Ireland, 1981), five young ten-year-old boys smile exuberantly into the camera. Two of the boys position their fingers in peace signs, palms facing out. Another punches up his fist. A broken window and graffiti fill a rough stucco wall in the background of the photograph. Here, we are urged to consider how untapped pleasure erupts in the bodies and faces of five boys.

On the Ground, In the Landscape

Small Arms—Children of Conflict could be misinterpreted as a project that mourns lost innocence, a eulogy to children, those most vulnerable in times of crisis and war. However, to simply read these images as portraits of loss would be to ignore the compositional role of the landscape, which is as significant as the children and sometimes overshadows them.

Traditional portraiture honors the individual and his or her property. It operates on the assumption that personality, uniqueness, and essence can be captured and then elucidated through revealing precious gestures. Static and contrived, it monumentalizes the individual. It accentuates a solitary character and minimizes social and historical context. Kienitz's photography reverses the components of classical portraiture. He employs wide shots rather than close-ups. His images examine the relationships between landscape and people, rather than divining individuality. His images force the spectator to confront the materiality of decay, dirt, rust. For example, *Scavenger* (Esteli, Nicaragua, 1978) shows a young boy with ripped pants and a dirty T-shirt with a castle pictured on the front, hauling sheets of rusted scrap metal on his back. Two pairs of scissors dangle from his belt. The scrap metal spreads horizontally across the top of the frame, contrasting with the verticality of the boy hunched over a littered sidewalk.

In *The Search* (Bluefields Nicaragua, 1984), a young girl in a white sundress holds open the door to a dirt-floor shack. A hammock hangs above her. In the foreground, shadows of government soldiers on a house-to-house search for contras spread through the bottom quarter of the frame like tree branches or smudges on the image. The shack, the shadows, and the door dwarf the girl. In *Push Cart* (Nicaragua, 1984), one boy in sneakers without laces drives a wooden cart piled with firewood while the boy behind the cart pushes. The wheels are made of wood. A barren, depopulated landscape of dried bushes and distant mountains fills half of the background, the road and the boys the other half.

Kienitz's photography circumvents the visual tropes of power and the myth of the individual removed from social and political context. These images jettison essences of individuals and epic dramas of war. Instead, his images are carefully built from the traces that war and conflict leave behind: children, landscapes, and places. They concentrate on their human subjects and then allow us to drift into the deteriorating and degraded environments where these children play. As spectators, we are simultaneously in the landscape and on the ground with the subjects at their eye level.

Noncombatants at the Edges of War

Kienitz's photography probes and discloses the mechanisms children use to cope with trauma. Children and the elderly do not usually engage in fighting; they live on the edges of war, navigating its ragged borders and messy public domains. In the last decades, the number of noncombatants drawn into political conflict has accelerated at alarming rates, due in part to the increase in asymmetrical warfare and its various infiltrations. With its focus on noncombatants, *Small Arms—Children of Conflict* occupies a strong, insistent antiwar stance because it abandons, rather than glorifies, the epic and the destructive.

The condensed efficiencies of news deadlines dispense with in-depth reportorial work and the muckraking of investigative journalism. The time needed for intensive research translates into too high a price tag. In contrast, Kienitz's limited resources propelled him to capture images no one else had and no news organizations wanted. The daily life of noncombatants confused and blurred the reductionist message that good triumphs over evil and that US government–supported democratic troops fight corrupt insurgents. These so-called insurgents were usually indigenous people attempting to improve their economic and political existence.

In northern Lebanon, Kienitz hitchhiked or took taxis from one town to the next. Instead of fighting or incursions, he discovered only anticipation, rumor, speculation, and worry. He came upon a large hashish smuggling operation that exported drugs and imported guns. Children worked in the hashish factory and were paid with candy and colorful carbonated drinks. Traveling alone in the Bekaa Valley of Lebanon in the early 1980s, he was one of the first reporters to realize the existence of followers of the Ayatollah Khomeini (Hezbollah). Two images from Lebanon situate noncombatants at the edges of the action. In *Playground* (Beirut, Lebanon, 1982), four boys of around six years old climb on top of a disabled tank burrowed into a large hole in the ground. One boy balances on the cannon, while the others squat on the tank turret. The boys transform the tank from a killing machine into a play structure. In *Aftermath* (Beirut, Lebanon, 1982), a young boy in rubber flip-flops stands in the lower center of the frame, flanked by gutted overturned cars. Behind the cars, bombed-out apartment buildings sprout like abstract sculptures. The vast emptiness of the destroyed cityscape magnifies the boy's isolation.

Kienitz's own experiences in conflict zones parallel these images. In Nicaragua during the revolution, Kienitz slept in a hut in the jungle where large rats scurried across the rafters. He also walked all day through the jungle, trying to hook up with Sandinista rebels, whom he later discovered had been ambushed and killed. That evening after dark, he came upon a thatched roof hut over a tortilla oven. A *campesino* and his wife walked down the hill, illuminating the path with their lanterns. They served him a memorable delicious meal. They asked him what had been happening in the conflict. That morning, they had spotted government troops moving rapidly across their land to trail Sandinistas. The couple was unaware that a revolution had commenced. Kienitz was moved by the generosity of the impoverished people he photographed and their insistence to enter into conversation and exchange information. Often it was the poorest who offered him food.

Impossible and Possible

In most of these exhibition images, at least one subject looks directly out of the photograph; others gaze at something just outside the frame. These gazes do not permit voyeurism; they demand that we as spectators enter into a collaboration. They knit us into the image, insisting that we, too, are participants. In *Wood for the Oven* (La Pista, Guatemala, 1988), a young girl in an embroidered shirt carries firewood, the strap of the carrier over her head. She fills the center of the frame and looks directly out of the image. She seems to call out to us to join with her. This direct, unemotional gaze disciplines how we read these photographs. It also indicates the deeply collaborative relationship behind their production.

The fault line of ethics runs underneath virtually all documentary film and photography. What does it mean to produce images of those outside our own communities? What are the implications of the power differentials between those with cameras and comfort and their subjects who lack housing, food, or peace? How do image makers work through the economic differentials that allow them to leave while their subjects cannot? How do these images circulate, and how are they used?

Although impossible to answer, these questions dive to the very heart of documentary practice and representation. They present yet another contradiction for Kienitz to investigate. These dilemmas are nearly impossible to remedy; inequalities of power and money can ultimately only be balanced by radical social and political reorganization. Kienitz's photographs bring the philosophical complexity of these issues out into the open for examination. Taken together, they develop an architecture of gazes that support not only the subjectivities of the children photographed, but their refusal to be marginalized, pitied, or victimized. His photographic practice proposes joint inquiry that surpasses reportage.

Small Arms unequivocally dismantles the idea of a passive universalism and instead asks us to collaborate. The girl in *Wood for the Oven* and the boy with ripped pants in *Shoe Shiner* (Chichicastanago, Guatemala, 1988) do not ask for our pity. The direct address of their gazes insists on our participation and our collective action. Kienitz's photographs advance that we see what is possible, not what is impossible.

Moving Forward

Nevertheless, it is not sufficient to end this discussion in the unmapped territories of conjecture and abstraction. Let us instead move to the material and empirical terrain where we began—a photograph.

Falls Road Bus (Belfast, Northern Ireland, 1981) condenses and layers the concepts, issues, politics, and struggles infusing Kienitz's photographs. The skeleton of a bombed bus, cluttered with pieces of metal and wires, straddles the bottom half of the frame. The bus functions as a remnant of violence, an artifact from a previous altercation. The disorder of the random pieces of bumpers, engine, and handrails trace the intensity of the bomb, a cartography of trauma.

The bus looks empty, but ghosts waft through its debris. A five-year-old boy squats on the remains of the seat. He grips the metal wires, all that remains of the steering wheel. He drives the bus. He looks out of the frame at us, grinning, driving out of destruction, out of despair, out of chaos, and into some glorious territory he knows exists somewhere.

He is resilient: he has crafted something new out of the old; he has transformed the artifact into an imaginary machine that moves beyond the impossible. He is talking with the ghosts; they are his passengers, and with them he is willing the inert to move, the fragmented pieces to cohere, the real to transform into the imaginary. He smiles because he knows elsewhere is here. He smiles because he knows we will gaze at him and then look differently at the landscape he defies. He smiles because he knows in his bones that the photographer is with him, and we are with him—you are with him—driving somewhere else, together. Climbing over the ruins, we place our hands on the wheel, a circle that says all can be whole, a wheel of life, a wheel of the possible.

So now, let us look again at the photographs in *Small Arms*. Let us return changed. Let us return to a more engaged antiwar landscape where our own political stakes are challenged and disrupted. Let us travel to that place where we move with seriousness but also with joy, with intention but also with defiance. Let us journey to that place where the rubble of fear dissolves into dust and where we move forward, smiling.

Figure 6.1. Screenshot from *#Babylon '13 Cinema of A Civil Protest* (Babylon '13 Collective, Ukraine, 2014–ongoing).

6

BLACK SOIL

Chernozem *and* Tusit *in Ukraine**

BLACK SOIL WAS PACKED INTO A PLEXIGLASS SARCOPHAGUS two feet wide and six feet long. We stood in the basement of the Center for Urban History of East Central Europe in the UNESCO World Heritage–designated western Ukrainian city of Lviv, variously called Lemberg, Lvov, or Lwow depending on which country claimed or occupied it. I tried to take a picture, but the soil defied iPhone photography. Black soil. *Chernozem.*

RaeJean Stokes, assistant cultural affairs officer from the US embassy in Kyiv, pointed to the structure. "That's what Ukrainian black soil looks like," she said.

The second-largest country in Europe but not part of the European Union, Ukraine possesses 25 percent of the most nutrient-rich black soil on earth, part of a belt stretching from Croatia, across Bulgaria, Romania, Serbia, and Southern Russia. Once called "the bread basket of Europe," Ukraine wafts through the historical imaginaries of many countries that occupied, invaded, or border with it as a place where a bounty of grains grow. Ukrainian black soil—some of the most fertile on the planet—now lures international agricultural investors from Canada and large multinational corporations, including Cargill and Monsanto.

---

* Since 2011, I have served as an envoy for documentary for the American Film Showcase, a film diplomacy program of the US State Department's Bureau of Educational and Cultural Affairs produced by the University of Southern California (USC) School of Cinematic Arts. In this role, I have presented lectures and conducted workshops, master classes, and postscreening moderation on documentary across analog and new-media forms in China, Guinea, and Ukraine. Before I leave for a new place, I spend many months researching the country, reading books about its history and learning about its media landscape. My role as an envoy requires daily postings of my activities while on assignment back to the program producers at USC, a task that resonates with my early training as a print journalist. I always take spiral reporter notebooks with me, writing down my observations and documenting interviews I conduct with the various people I meet. These notes enter into my final report. Sometimes, as with this essay, my final reports evolve into creative nonfiction reflections of my experiences. This piece was originally published with photographs of my time in Ukraine in the online edition of *Afterimage: The Journal of Media Arts and Critics* in January 2017.

My reflection in the sarcophagus balancing my black mobile phone and black backpack obscured the black soil and impeded capturing the display in a photographic image. This structure spanned a large portion of wall, part of the permanent exhibition on World War I in Central Europe, 1914–1918.

Our guide, Volodymyr Beglov, explained that the installation had been designed to simulate a sensorium of what it felt like to be surrounded by soil during battle. World War I had inaugurated both trench warfare and chemical warfare. According to Volodymyr, World War I also marked the first time genocide and ethnic cleansing were mobilized as weapons of war. Nine million soldiers died from these battles. The exhibition featured many dazzling new media components such as four- by five-foot touchscreens, where one could tap on a photo of a poppy or a bandage or a woman's dress to decipher its deeper historical significance for the war.

The tour was marked by absences and gaps. Our guide Alyona brought us to empty lots, vegetable markets, and parks. Synagogues once stood on this soil in these places. The Nazis and then the Soviets razed the synagogues, rounded up Jews, and shot them point-blank in the back of the head just outside of Lviv. Alyona showed us small pictures of synagogues and Jewish street life on her mobile phone. She had culled these from the internet because the Jewish archives in Lviv are incomplete. She asked us to ponder the empty spaces in relation to the historical images, a low-tech augmented-reality interface of sorts. We walked through an excavation of a synagogue in the Lviv central district. It was transitioning into a historical commemorative site. There was no money to rebuild the synagogue, so construction workers replastered the one remaining wall that was crumbling into the churned-up, dust-spewing soil below.

On the long flight from Ithaca in upstate New York, I decided to memorize the map of Ukraine, a place I had never thought about much. I had watched the Vice News series short-form documentary war reporting from the Donbass for another project a year before. I admired the bilingualism of the reporter, his proximity to participants, and his full immersion in the action. But I needed the map to help make sense of the complex Ukrainian histories overwhelming my ability to unravel a through line or pattern. I was looking for a way of understanding since I was not a specialist in Eastern Europe, Russia, or the Soviet Union.

Black soil grounds Ukraine's shifting identities, languages, and borders. It was once part of the Habsburg Empire, then part of Poland in the western Ukraine. It was a sovereign state between 1918 and 1921, and then became part of the USSR in 1922. The Nazis declared Ukraine to be part of Germany and occupied it from 1941 to 1944. The Soviet Union's dominion over Ukraine resumed in the post-1945 period. Then in 1991, it became a post-Soviet republic. Demonstrations, student protests, and hunger strikes against corrupt centralized governments erupted in 1991, 2004, 2013, and 2014, the people organizing to reclaim their black soil, fighting for sometimes abstract but always urgent demands for transparency, for freedom to travel without a visa to the European Union, and against corruption. These demonstrations summoned a nationalism that seemed different from other nationalisms of unified identity and protected borders, a nationalism reclaiming histories dismembered, buried, and ghostly. I met people who spoke Russian under the Soviets as children, and then, as adults, painstakingly learned Ukrainian phrase by phrase.

Growing up Irish Catholic in Chicago, I would often hear about Ukrainians, but mostly because their Eastern Orthodox churches sported domes rather than spires with crosses. They were referred to as "DPs" (displaced people), shadowy immigrants fleeing something big and political never discussed openly.

Memorizing the map, I wanted to know which cities were in the East where an undeclared civil war (or global face-off between Russia and the West, depending on one's news sources) continued to erupt. I wanted to know where the Crimea—which the Russians occupied in February 2014 after the Maidan Revolution—was located. I wanted to know specifically where Chernobyl was situated, as it loomed large and placeless in my mind as a nuclear disaster, a transnational radioactive cloud, and a monumental and continuing environmental catastrophe. I needed to decode the fluid cartographies of Belarus, Moldova, Poland, Romania, Russia, and Ukraine. I wanted to imprint in my mind the names of cities I could not properly pronounce, pinning them and my confusions on the map. That way, I thought, I would dig my mind into the geography that grounded people and references—a small way to specify place and people beyond the large, vague, revolution- and war-obsessed Western media representations of Ukraine.

Black soil infused the complex histories I fought to understand that unsettled my preconceptions about Ukraine. Black soil of the borderlands, the bloodlands, the blood-soaked and contaminated lands, the lands straddling the imaginary hallucinations of both East and West. As historian Timothy Snyder soberly reminds us in *Bloodlands: Europe between Hitler and Stalin* (2012), in the borderland regions of the Baltics, Belarus, Poland, Russia, and Ukraine, more than fourteen million people died at the hands of Hitler and Stalin between 1933 and 1945. In a land with the richest soil on earth, a central-government-induced famine from 1932 to 1933 was promulgated to install Stalin's farm collectivization across the Soviet Union; 3.3 million perished from starvation in Ukraine alone.

The April 26, 1986, explosion at the Chernobyl nuclear power plant, the largest nuclear disaster in history, contaminated the soil with radioactivity. This year marked the thirtieth anniversary of Chernobyl, now no longer the name of a place but a word equated with disaster. In *Borderland: A Journey through the History of Ukraine* (2015), Anna Reid contends that the Soviets' faulty machinery and improper protocols prompted the accident. Their cover-up provoked citizen political outrage. For some writers, the catastrophic Chernobyl accident not only disgorged radioactive fallout across Europe, but was the first salvo to undo the USSR. One young man I met at Indie Lab at America House Kyiv, who uses the pseudonym M. Vadimskiy, had produced a rough cut of his slow-moving, careful portrait film entitled *The Farm: Zone 2* (2017). The film follows a middle-aged man displaced from Donetsk in 2015 due to the ongoing conflict there who moved to Chernobyl to farm, a quiet story with chilling implications. In seeking safety, the character had moved from a war zone to a contaminated zone.

Before I left, many friends in Ithaca asked me why I was traveling to a war zone. They worried for my safety. While in Ukraine, I received some emails from other colleagues asking me to describe how it felt to be in a country at war. I appreciated these queries. They catapulted me into a discomfiting, fragmented, transitory interstitial zone between Western media representations (or fantasy projections) of Ukraine and my embodied experiences there walking the streets of Kyiv and Lviv and talking to filmmakers and programmers in theaters and in smaller, more intimate workshops.

Before I arrived, almost every book I read about Ukraine invoked the word "crisis" as a catchall for a country in "transition": *Ukraine Crisis: What It Means for the West* by Andrew Wilson (2014); *Frontline Ukraine: Crisis in the Borderlands* by Richard Sakwa (2015); *Crisis in Ukraine* by Gideon Rose (2014). These narratives posited Ukraine as a country of citizen uprisings, Communists, deaths, the European Union, famines, independence, many occupations, revolutions, Soviets, Vladimir Putin, and continual war. Few of these books mentioned the crushing poverty of Ukraine: I heard a story that elderly people diagnosed with cancer refused medical treatment in order to avoid bankrupting their children.

Sitting in my hotel room in Kyiv watching CNN International analyze the 2016 US presidential contest as an election in which voters were aligned against rather than for candidates, a strange realization percolated through this haunting space. From my third-story fancy hotel window, I observed the shining domes of St. Michael's Monastery, frequently called St. Michael's Golden-Domed Monastery, which had served as a makeshift hospital for the wounded from the Maidan protests. This beautiful monastery was in a dialectical montage with the large-screen TV blaring CNN. This trip was the first time I had lectured in public about documentary film and new media in a place with an ongoing war and a Russian occupation, two years out from a massive people's revolution.

With very little reporting from Ukraine beyond what many I met referred to as "Putin's Russian narrative," and sporadic armed fighting in the East, the queries I received reflected the impact of what I now assess as an almost total news blackout. These friends' questions suggested the reductionist condensations of Ukraine into one destabilized, overblown image of men with guns occupying decaying public buildings. The projections of Putin-approved news cover over a much more variegated territory composed of vital sedimentary layers of different histories, media practices, people, roads, soils, and spaces. In contrast, nearly every other day, a filmmaker or a guide or a State Department escort would casually insert a story about "the crowd-sourced war in the East," where Kyivans leave plastic buckets in front of food markets to raise money for weapons and bulletproof vests for the army. I heard stories about women making *varenyky* (Ukrainian dumplings stuffed with meat or fruit) to deliver to soldiers on the front.

Jesse Moss and I delivered our separate talks on "Film as a Type of New Media" to a group of sixteen people not involved in media at all. We were at the First Lviv MediaTeka, a space in a library dubbed a "third space" where people could gather without paying. Light bursting in through the windows from the sunset nearly erased our PowerPoint images projected on a newly painted white wall. Afterward, Shari Bistransky, the US embassy cultural affairs officer, mentioned that no international news organizations operated any bureaus in Ukraine, so there was no ongoing coverage of the region. Instead, international journalists arrived for the Maidan Revolution, with hundreds of thousands in the streets singing the national anthem and battling police and security forces. These journalists covered the subsequent war in the East, tagging along after bands of men hauling Kalashnikov rifles. After the ceasefire, they left.

Before I left the United States, the *Economist* ran two stories about Ukraine. One described a government minister who resigned his post.[1] The other detailed the information technology boom in Ukraine, now reconceived as a European business outsourcing haven comparable to India for its low prices.[2] According to Ukrainian filmmakers I met, if you could speak and type in English, you could earn significantly more than the average salary of $300USD a month.

Flying back from Munich, I realized that Ukraine in wartime resonated more with the quiet, everyday images of people attending classical music concerts in military uniforms and going to work with helmets in the short film *Listen to Britain* (UK, 1942, directed by Humphrey Jennings and Stewart McAllister) than with the overblown spectacle of guns, soldiers, and napalm in Vietnam pictured in *Apocalypse Now* (United States, 1979, directed by Francis Ford Coppola). Rather than news images of bands of men with guns in Donestk occupying buildings or tracking stories of female sex slavery favored by the young male freelance newshounds prowling around Ukraine, I observed quieter gestures, hints, inflections, intonations, reflections, and traces. A young man in a screening at the American Independence Film Festival in Lviv revealed he was from Donetsk. He was one of the over one million internally displaced people in Ukraine from the war in the East.

A young journalism student from the National University of Kyiv-Mohyla Academy told me she wanted to create a new media project about returning soldiers. This week, back in Ithaca, I realized that hers was the journalism program that developed the stopfake.org site, a bold online initiative whose website states its mission is to "check facts, verify information, and refute verifiable disinformation about events in Ukraine covered in the media." I have intermittently followed this muckraking site post-Maidan, usually prompted by enthusiastic Facebook posts from colleagues who know more than I do about Eastern Europe and Russia. Many journalism colleagues admire stopfake for its determined insistence on a strategy of rigorous refutation of media fabrications based on fact-checking.

It was not until after my talk on collaborative new media practices to journalism graduate students at Mohyla that I realized that Mohyla was the university where this groundbreaking online journalism project—also a collaborative endeavor like the new media documentary projects I had shared in my lecture—had been developed.

In March 2014, just after the Maidan uprising—also known as the Revolution of Dignity—faculty members, alumni, and other journalists contributed to stopfake to counter Russia's propaganda and disinformation war with facts. The site debunked the story that Sweden intended to export Ukraine's black soil, a narrative repetition and remix of old legends that the Nazis had shipped sacks of Ukrainian black soil to Germany. I learned from Anna Sumar, a Ukrainian staffer at the US embassy in Kyiv, that National University of Kyiv-Mohyla Academy was more "Western" than the other universities. I asked her what that meant. She said they had instituted transparent systems to prevent students from bribing faculty for grades.

I met filmmaker Andril Lytvynenko at a small workshop on indie documentary. He had produced a quietly surreal film entitled *In the Fields* (2014) about the largest biodiversity region in Europe, called Askania-Nova, a place of virgin steppe. Askania-Nova held layers of different histories composted together; a German established it in in 1898, the Red Army claimed it in 1919 and declared it a sanctuary park, the Soviets remade it into a research center, and independent Ukraine affirmed its importance. At the screening, lost in references and places and headset translations, I pulled up a map of Ukraine on my iPhone to find it. I discovered it was adjacent to Crimea, the region that the Russians occupied in 2014.

The filmmakers, guides, professors, programmers, students, and US State Department representatives I met denounced the ascendancy of the "Russian narrative"—propaganda discounting the Maidan Revolution and claiming that "fascists" populated Kyiv. Although I had read articles online dubbing what was happening in Ukraine "the new Cold War" (in fact, there is a website by this name that tracks events in Ukraine, newcoldwar.org), I did not hear one person—American or Ukrainian—invoke this term, with its residual evocations of a bilateral, pre-1989 world. I heard the term "frozen war" to describe the continuing military skirmishes in the East between pro-Russian partisans, pro-Ukrainian volunteers, Russian-supplied mercenaries, separatists, Ukrainian army members, and unemployed workers after the brokered ceasefire on September 2014. At the Dovzhenko Film Archive, the young, intellectually driven archivists explained a current curatorial and research project to find films about the Donbass region, the "frozen war" zone in the East.

Decorating the visual landscapes of restaurants, screenings, streets, and workshops were the colors of the Ukrainian flag—yellow and light blue. Faded flags were draped from apartment balconies. A young man with a tattoo of the flag on the top of his right hand smoked a hand-rolled cigarette, gazing out over the trees in an urban Kyiv park hidden behind nineteenth-century apartment buildings. A young woman furiously scribbled notes in a small black notebook in the Indie Lab workshop, her long dreadlocks rippling down to her waist, each one tinted yellow or blue. At the outdoor craft market in Lviv, down the street from the Leopolis Hotel, a woman vendor stood behind a crudely assembled wooden table displaying wristbands and hairpieces tightly braided from yellow and blue ribbon, spread out in a carefully designed pattern, like a museum art installation.

Black soil cascades through my reflections on the time in Ukraine. Black soil under my feet held contested lands, horrific geographies, and wars over territories and languages. Black soil was tilled in order to make a stand and reclaim the land, a history unraveled by many other overlapping Eastern European and global diaspora histories almost unknown in the United States. Black soil returned me to a place to ponder deaths across decades that fertilize the soil in blood and bone and the memories deep below the surface. Black soil evoked for me what grows up from the land rather than what descends down from authorities or fantasies or ideologies or state-manufactured narratives.

As I ambled around Kyiv armed with an umbrella and a bilingual map, my first stop centered on the Maidan Nezaleshnosti. I wanted to feel the space and pay homage to the "Heavenly Hundred" killed by the Ukrainian security forces. By some accounts, as many as eight hundred thousand Ukrainians marched in demonstrations during the months of the Maidan Revolution in 2013–14.

This journey might have been the only time I visited sites I had first seen in documentaries. I had viewed this legendary square in the Academy Award–nominated feature *Winter on Fire: Ukraine's Fight for Freedom* (2015, directed by Evgeny Afineevsky) and in *Maidan* (2014, directed by Sergey Loznitza), two very different documentaries in style, argument, and approach. I met Ukrainian filmmakers who sharply criticized both films because the directors, one of Ukrainian heritage currently working in Israel, and the other a Ukrainian national producing films in Europe, did not actually live in Ukraine as regular residents. They had privilege. They had visas or different passports. They lived elsewhere.

Both films repeat images of the winged woman on top of the tall pillar monument in the middle of Maidan Nezalezhnosti, which means "independence square." I went there but could not quite see the winged figure with the sun backlighting her. Back at the InterContinental Hotel, I spied other women bursting out of the key-coded elevators each morning in skin-tight short lycra dresses, four-inch heels, hair to their waists, and heavy dark eye makeup. I wondered if they were prostitutes, part of Ukraine's sex trade and internet bride business, propelled more by poverty than sexuality. At the Maidan, my eyes drifted down to the pictures of the dead taped to the concrete foundation, a makeshift memorial of the "Heavenly Hundred" who were killed during the Maidan uprising.

Black soil helped me get my head around the range of media I encountered in Ukraine. The ten books I read before my trip—by historians, journalists, and think-tankers prepping transnational business ventures—referenced the black soil of Ukraine as a way to transnational economic success through agriculture. As a place with potential where plants can grow and soil can be plowed, black soil loomed as a metaphor for the explosive media practices I encountered.

This term anchored my conclusion that many different media ecologies have emerged from the fertile soils of the Maidan people's revolution, the legacy of the Soviet state, the occupation of Crimea, and the "frozen" civil war in the Donbass region that would keep Ukraine destabilized and out of the European Union. As I posted on Facebook and in emails to colleagues back in the United States, it felt as if a Ukrainian Documentary New Wave was ascendant, like grain emerging out of the earth in the steppes.

Film Quarterly (full disclosure: I am on the editorial board) contacted me about launching a campaign to post shorts emerging from this Ukrainian Documentary New Wave, post-Maidan cinematic practices about everyday people, local battles, small places. Shorts rather than features, designed for sharing rather than festivals, these films chiseled out space for voices from the ground. Ella Shtyka and Dmytro Tiazhlov, coprogrammers of the American Independence Film Festival and Indie Lab, supplied a careful selection of Ukrainian independent shorts drafting a different map of Ukraine from the ground up. The films crafted stories about bold journalists, Orthodox priests fighting for LGBTQ rights, corrupt police, citizen fights against unauthorized construction, a pro-Russian teenager, and romance at the Maidan barricades.

This rich humus of black soil emerged at the American Independence Film Festival in Kyiv and Lviv. The American films offered a way to enter into issues laced through the unresolved and unfolding Ukrainian imaginary: civil society, energy concerns, internally displaced people, people-centered initiatives, and the reclamation of lost histories destroyed by state ideologies.

In addition to shorts, the black soil of Ukrainian cinema birthed large-budget feature films about the Maidan protests in 2014. *Winter on Fire* operated with a more popular-culture narrative arc and characters to chart the revolution. *Maidan,* a film that I deeply admire, elaborated this historic event with formal rigor, long-take tableaus, and insistence on the collective. After I met the director, Chad Garcia, after a screening, Jesse Moss suggested I download Garcia's *The Russian Woodpecker* (United States, 2015) to gain another view of the conspiracy tales encircling the Soviets and Chernobyl. The film charted a different, more individual psychogeography of Chernobyl through performative documentary style. In my hotel room after a long day of watching, lecturing, and listening, I watched it on my tablet with headphones via a streaming service from the United States.

At a dinner party with Ukrainian filmmakers, I met twenty-one-year-old Alexandra Chuprina. So excited that she kept apologizing for her English, she told me about urgent, street-smart, anonymous short-form documentations of events in Ukraine. The #Babylon '13 Collective designed and produced these films for Facebook reposting, a platform used more than email in Ukraine. The one hundred filmmakers of #Babylon '13 ranged from professionals to amateurs, from established to young. They filmed Crimea, Donbass, the Maidan, and soldiers.

From my experiences and observations, I developed the category of the Ukrainian Documentary New Wave. Each day, I encountered a staggering range of different and urgent documentary practices. At Indie Lab at America House, a short, direct cinema-style film chronicled a teenage Russian nationalist in Donbass and a collaborative new media archival project followed Kyivans criticizing the decommunization laws to remove statuary traces of communist ideology. The same day, Tiazholov, a documentary filmmaker as well as codirector of the Indie Lab initiative, told me that his hometown had been renamed, the Russian name removed and new Ukrainian name installed. Oleksandra Mykolyshn, the head of promotion at the Dovzhenko Film Archive, gave me a catalog of Ukrainian films published by the Ukrainian State Film Agency. Sixty-two feature-length Ukrainian documentaries spanned topics including Crimea, the Donbass, the environment, gypsies, identity, the Maidan, and soldiers.

Black soil, chernozem: histories grown fallow are bursting out, fertile, hoed, rooted, turned over, and tilled.

On a warm Saturday night after a sold-out screening at the American Independence Film Festival, Jesse and I sauntered back to the hotel with Stokes, ambling down a large boulevard called Vul. Khreshchatyk. The street was closed to traffic that night, and karaoke, jazz groups, rock bands, and young singers with guitars peppered the sidewalks. Large groups circled around them.

People in groups, arms entwined, rambled slowly through the street, down the sidewalks, through the Maidan Nezalezhnosti (Independence Square). Some cuddled on benches. Some carried beers, forbidden but tolerated. Stokes shared that there was a word in Russian and Ukrainian for these leisurely walks with others in public places. I could not pronounce the word. In an email to me after I returned to the United States, Stokes wrote that the word was *hulyaty*, which translates roughly as "to stroll." It made sense that this collaborative activity in public demanded its own word. The contrast with US cities and even my own small college town where everyone walks fast and never saunters together, could not be more pronounced.

Later, back in Ithaca, I asked for linguistic help on Facebook to snare this elusive word I could neither say correctly nor remember accurately. Marina Orekhova, the Ukrainian line producer for *The Babushkas of Chernobyl* (United States, 2015, directed by Holly Morris and Anne Bogart), about intrepid women who farmed in the Chernobyl Exclusion Zone, responded. I liked her feisty, fiercely intellectual, and artistic denunciations of various films made by outsiders about Ukraine's transition. She suggested the word was *tusit*. I realized that the concept of strolling together in public engendered many words and forms, from leisure to demonstrations to just being with others in streets blocked off. Tusit. Hulyaty.

Ten days before, I had sat in coach on the Lufthansa plane to Newark, trying to make sense of jumbled layers of experiences, conversations, readings, and thoughts from Ukraine in my gray notebook to write my report. I started to think about how nothing is ever unified or stable, that everywhere we go—not just Ukraine—is always in transition, a word often levied as camouflage for political instabilities. I want to revise the word "transition" more positively, as an unsettling that connects the earth with the sky, histories with what is yet to come.

I considered that the notions of black soil and walking with others in public space needed to be embroidered together like the *vyshyvka*, the acclaimed Ukrainian decorative embroidery hanging from clotheslines strung in the outdoor markets, colorful threads grounded in white linen and moving in impossibly intricate patterns.

Tusit and vyshyvka suggested different registers of the same movement, strolling with others as a needle with saturated red thread, exploring space, listening, watching films, discussing, embroidering a life. Talking with others about documentaries large and small in publics with sold-out audiences or with only sixteen people activated an intellectual tusit: a sauntering together through ideas without an agenda, a meandering to reclaim a conceptual street and to shut it down from traffic. An intellectual, cinematic, artistic tusit. Chernozem and tusit. Black soil and wandering, together.

Notes

1. "Corruption in Ukraine: Dear Friends," *Economist*, February 13, 2016, www.economist.com/news/europe/21692917-ukraines-grace-period-tackling-cronyism-may-have-run-out-dear-friends.

2. "Ukraine's Restless East: The City Beta-Testing Ukraine's Revolution," *Economist*, May 27, 2016, www.economist.com/news/europe/21699545-russian-speaking-kharkiv-it-industry-one-few-things-thriving-city.

PART II
REVERSALS

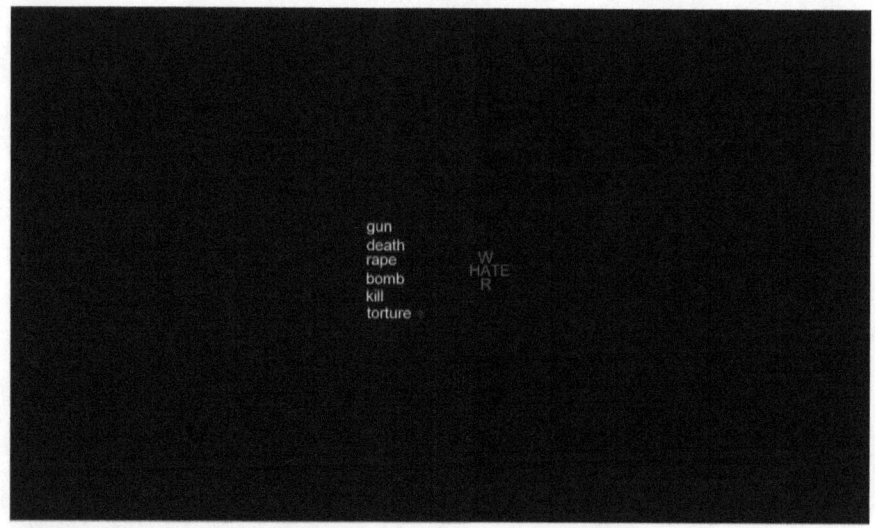

Figure 7.1. Screenshot from *Wordswar* (Matt Eberhart, Germany, 1999).

7

MATRICES OF WAR*

Sorties

The seventy-eight-day United States–led NATO bombing campaign in Kosovo in the Spring of 1999 produced over three thousand bombing sorties and 650,000 refugees. The Old World moral order envisioned the bombing as destructive of life and its environs, a necessity to restore coherency and order through technological mastery over catastrophe.

---

* A Serbian ethnically based nationalist war unfurled in the former Yugoslavia between 1991 and 2001, producing atrocities, ruins, and deaths. In 1991, Croatia and Slovenia declared their independence. During the 1992–1995 Bosnia war, horrific atrocities were committed against Muslims, which were widely considered to be ethnic cleansing and genocide. In 1995, 8,000 people were killed at Srebenica. This ten-year war broke up the Yugoslav state and claimed between 140,000 and 200,000 lives. The war in Kosovo ran from 1998 to 1999, with the army of the Free Republic of Yugoslavia (FRY), comprised at this time of Serbia and Montenegro, fighting the Kosovo Liberation Army. In 1999, to end the massacre and atrocities against Kosovo's Albanian population and to stabilize the region, NATO enacted a bombing campaign against Serbia.
  During this period, central New York colleges and universities held many public teach-ins about the civil wars in Yugoslavia, ethnic cleansing, genocide, rape, and anti-Muslim aggressions. I heard my close friends Asma Barlas, Zillah Eisenstein, and Aida Hozic, colleagues from the Ithaca College politics department, speak at these events and sometimes joined them as a speaker discussing the visual representations of these deadly conflicts. I began to parse out the complex political, structural, and psychic relationships between these racialized and ethnically framed wars on the ground and the cyberwars in the networks. For instance, media coming out of Belgrade accused the Albanian Kosovars of trafficking in human organs, a charge that was unsupportable given the lack of medical facilities in Kosovo that could support sterile organ harvesting and had the means to get harvested organs to transplant recipients. Nevertheless, many in the Western European media found the accusation credible and disseminated it online. I discussed the role of cyberwars in getting NATO on board with the US military's policy of intervention at invited talks at Oregon State University, Cornell University, Hobart and William Smith Colleges, and MIT during this period of the Yugoslav wars. My longtime friend Laura Marks, the Canadian/American film and new-media theorist, was curating a section of the International Short Film Festival in Oberhausen, Germany, in May of 2001. She had invited me to present a talk and select a short program of work engaging the war in Kosovo for the festival. Among film festival devotees, it is known simply as the Oberhausen Film Festival, but its official name is actually Internationale Kurzfilmtage Oberhausen. Founded in 1954, it is one of the oldest festivals in the world promoting

Human Rights Watch reported that the bombing campaign deployed a "higher percentage of precision-guided munitions than in any other major conflict in history." Nevertheless, Yugoslav civilian deaths still occurred during Operation Allied Force, during all kinds of weather, with all kinds of bombs, in almost every kind of attack, and on every type of target.[1] In *Virtual War: Kosovo and Beyond*, Michael Ignatieff observes that the war in Kosovo only felt like a war for the Kosovar Albanians who were under attack on the ground and for the Serbian civilians killed in air strikes. It mobilized civilians as well as spectators; once the bombing started, the war was calculative rather than visceral. The actual number of Allied combatants was small: 1,500 members of a NATO air crew and 30,000 technicians and staff.[2] The 1999 NATO bombings marked a huge shift from weaponry to computers that military analysts called "the revolution in military affairs" or RMA.

General Wesley K. Clark, Supreme Allied Commander, Europe, relied on American-supplied intelligence, aircraft, and precision ordinance. Ignatieff points out that the bombings were "fought and won by technicians and Clark's team produced a virtuoso display of technical improvisation."[3] Sortie planners at European and stateside airbases used SIPERNET, a US military network, to calculate targets through the analysis of aerial reconnaissance, military significance, collateral damage, moral assessment, and legal evaluation.[4] Arthur and Marilouise Kroker identify this virtual war as "all about beta-testing: systematic program testing of virtual warriors in their virtual flying machines."[5] The bombings functioned as laboratories for conversion from analog wars of bodies to virtual wars of imaging and calculation that concealed the racialized phantoms that propelled them.[6] In a perverse inversion, the regime of cyber-civil wars engaged the psychic production of a digitized catastrophe. The NATO campaign targeted the networks and circuitry of the digital: in late April 1999, planes bombed a Serbian television station and electrical grids with special graphite ordnances.[7]

Amid this perversity where life is robbed of its own death, images of war are no longer stable, fixed, or singular. The images and their imaginaries are multiple, sedimentary, mobile, and linked. No longer significations, these war images functioned as vectors of movements and interfaces between images and social imaginaries. No longer images, they mapped nodal points in invisible digital networks.

Pierre Lévy argues that the art of cyberspace constantly resamples, remixes, and remakes images. These processes obliterate the borders between author and

---

and investigating short-form film ranging across experimental works, video art, advertising, music videos, and many hybrid forms. Since my fellow historian Jan-Christopher Horak (now the director of the UCLA Film and Television Archive) was also going to be there, I felt compelled to think through the issues of war imagery within some theorizations of archives and historiography. I later combined these thoughts and arguments into an essay entitled "Matrices of War," *Afterimage* 29, no 1 (January/February 2001): 18–23.

reader, creator and interpreter.[8] These mutations in the art and information domains create open works that function more as environments and landscapes than as a particular message or image. They blur "distinctions between emission and reception, creation and interpretation."[9]

As mediations through images, the seventy-eight-day Operation Allied Force fixated in nostalgic historical formations, where phantasmatics of World War II, Vietnam, and the Gulf War were imbedded within the images and imaginaries so profusely that they deleted history with a dangerous transparent narrative impulse. Explanation exceeded words. Incomprehensible phantoms etherized history. Psychoanalyzing this trauma, Robert Jay Lifton has shown that "the insight begins with the shattering of prior forms. Because forms have to be shattered for there to be new insight."[10] In the images produced by the transnational media corporations, the historical fantasy became a modality of transparency rather than a modality of agency. The 1999 Kosovo crisis required that forms be shattered in order to break open the multiplicities of historical temporalities.

The digital surround also inscribed the bombings of Serbia and the destabilization of Kosovo. Digital militarization promoted warfare without bodies.[11] Ubiquitous cyber-networks reduced war to screens. War multiplied across various screens such as computer, cinema, gaming, television, radar, and satellite. The digitalization of the crisis in Kosovo formulated war as a flat image to be manipulated and calculated by anyone and everyone.

The Archive of Contiguities

This migration of bombings across multiple screens announced the death of signification. The image no longer functioned as a fetish object. These screens formed networks through which images circulated, were reprocessed, rerouted, and repressed. In this world, historical engagement, meaning, and location recedes. The networks must separate and refuse the social and political meanings latent in the contiguities among images. While continuity underpins a historiography organized around temporal progression, contiguity suggests a series of discourses, practices, and temporalities that, although discontinuous, are adjacent to each other. As an organizing structure, continuity extends beyond a concept of historical context. Critical historiography postulates that the past is created rather than found. Various networks digitize meaning as an unconnected series of bits and bytes whose endless reorganization lacks agency and can never be productive.[12] Without productive relations and dialogic engagements that create new contiguities and spaces for provisional collectivities, all that remains is psychic disorder, a hystericized individualism, and social isolation, propagating a depoliticized virus.

The archive and memory, then, function with a quite opposite strategy, foregoing recombination for superimpositions to generate new substrata. Jacques Derrida writes how the archive presses toward layers rather than separations: "The semantics of the archive, of memory and of the memorial ... accumulate, capitalize, stock a quasi-infinity of layers, of archival strata that are at once superimposed, overprinted, and enveloped in each other."[13]

The NATO bombing campaign produces and displays phantasms where digitality evaporates the body in traumas not so much as representations but as reverberations between archival layers. NATO member nations were divided over the introduction of a ground war. The British wanted to send in the troops, while the Germans were opposed.[14] These land war debates indicated the shift of war from the ground to the dematerialized beyond of deterritorialized digital networks.

Symptoms

When Slobodan Milosevic removed the opposition Radio B92 website from its server in Belgrade, NATO/Bill Clinton bombed Serbian television stations, the very same stations used by reporters to beam out Milosevic's propaganda. The Pentagon spammed the internet in Serbia with QuickTime movies of Clinton's exhortations. While Milosevic programmed Hollywood films *Wag the Dog* (1997) and *Apocalypse Now* (1975) as the bombs cascaded down, the United States programmed its own film festival with the cyber-war male fantasies like the Hollywood blockbuster *The Matrix* (1999) and the horror of the high school shootings in Littleton, Colorado. Milosevic also interrupted television programming in Kosovo during the bombing to screen various films from the World War II period depicting Serb heroism against the Nazis.[15]

In World War II, Hollywood collaborated with the US military, creating a mise-en-scène for patriotism, nationalism, and militarism to unite the nation through narrative. As Hollywood movie studios retooled for the war effort, films' visual design was militarized and then mobilized for national unity.[16] However, in the globalized era where the nation-state has evolved into an international police force monitoring destabilizations, eruptions, and civil wars, these fantasies of national unity have lost their utility.

By 1999, the NATO bombing campaign's visual imaginaries manifested this decline in the utility of the image itself as an agent of war, inspiration, and national unity. Mise-en-scène was no longer militarized but virtualized, an immersive experience where the real and the virtual cast off distinction and meaning. An article in the *New York Times* observed that despite virtually continuous coverage and live reports from the refugee camps, the NATO bombings failed to stimulate military recruitment. While one could connect with Serbians via email, the digitized bombing strategy kept the war remote. One scholar commented, "War has become a movie that other people do, and something we watch rather than something we engage in."[17]

In August 1999, the US Army gave $45 million to the University of Southern California to fund a research center to "develop advanced military simulations" to attract designers to translate these digital military modalities into video games and game park rides. Historically, the military has innovated technology that eventually diffused to consumers, such as the standardization of 16mm film, transistor radios, and computers.[18] In the post–Cold War era, however, games and special effects are more sophisticated than military imaging systems. The National Research Council encouraged collaboration between the defense and entertainment industries to develop more emotionally captivating simulation technology.[19]

Aida Hozic has observed that as the Southern California military and aerospace industry contracted in the post–Cold War period, the film industry expanded. The migration of the high-technology military sector into Hollywood backlots fueled the digitalization of Hollywood in the 1990s.[20] Department of Defense–funded firms moved aggressively into special effects, computer design, and interactive entertainment, three areas aligned with military simulation technologies.

Phantoms

Beyond Serbia, the bombings produced ideological phantoms[21] circulating around the war and NATO's intervention, specters haunting the image landscapes. Digital networks became burial grounds where the bodiless move through new techno-landscapes. Phantoms haunted the image networks: death infiltrated these cyber-networks equating the digital with the eternal. Photojournalism psychically displaced the physical and the material with an image; although cyber-pundits prophesized the end of the body, it persisted in etherealized forms. The bombings of Serbia permeated other forms, like images of Littleton, natural disasters like tornadoes, and what people saw on their computer screens. Phantoms resist virtualization and infiltrate many networks. While the corporeality of death recedes, the digital penetrates the body as a wound. Films such as *The Matrix* (1999) narrativize these wounds with images of holes in the head through which data streams. Analyzing the NATO bombings, Arthur and Marilouise Kroker contend that the "virtual war is one perspectival remove from experiencing the actual consequences of violence."[22] *The Matrix* refracts its murders, shootings, and beatings, producing a phantom border between the analog and the digital.

In July 2000, a group of US-based film producers called FilmAid International proposed to screen blockbuster Hollywood films for Kosovar refugees. One organizer proclaimed, "Refugee camps are really appalling places, but films can make them better. It's like relief for the soul, relief from the boredom, trauma and anxiety of those places... two hours of fantasy can go a long way."[23] Although these phantoms assumed many shapes, they always denied death.

White

The Matrix interfaces with Littleton, Colorado, and Littleton interfaces with Kosovo. If Kosovar Albanians are racialized as Muslim, then the Littleton shootings are racialized as white. While Littleton staged the repressed phantom of the digital, video games were blamed as the engine of death drives, and the Kosovo refugees occupied an orientalized "other" bombed into primitiveness.[24] The Littleton victims inverted Kosovo, mourning the death of "whiteness."

In his book *White*, Richard Dyer argues that white image culture reduces black people to their bodies, while white people are distinguished by that which cannot be seen such as spirit, transcendence, intelligence, and mastery over space and time. For Dyer, whiteness hinges on disinterest in the corporeal and alliance with abstraction, distance, separation, objectivity, the disembodied, and otherworldliness. All genres of imagery move toward whitening: halos and extra lighting create skin tones suggesting transcendence from the material world.[25] While Littleton whitens, the bombings in Kosovo blacken.[26]

This repressed violent underside of the racialized digital erupted in the shootings in Colorado where two white male teenagers made an armed assault against students at Columbine High School. The *New York Times* called the rash of shootings in schools across the country "a new kind of domestic terror." As Orlando Patterson speculated in an op-ed piece in the *New York Times*, "What if the high school shooters were black?"[27] Turning his attention from the bombing in Serbia, in a speech at the same time as the bombing sorties, President Clinton contended that Columbine "pierced the soul of a nation."[28]

Many articles subsequent to the shootings posited a causal relationship between excessive internet and computer game usage by teenagers and the escalation of school shootings. This displacement of the bombings in Serbia by out-of-control teenage violence suggests that the revolution in military affairs generates a hysterical phantasmatic discourse about violence, bodies, racialized fantasies, and digitality.

The psychic landscape narrated in images revealed the blurred borders between the bombings (viewed from without) and Littleton (a threat from within). In the middle of the bombing campaign, a photograph in the *New York Times* on April 29, 1999, showed students gazing at makeshift crosses for murdered classmates dug into a hill overlooking the Columbine school.[29] This image doubled countless representations from the war in the Balkans featuring equally makeshift grave markers, but with real bodies. In Littleton, these handmade, unofficial markers memorialized the dead while its compositional structure of the image balanced the crosses with the living.

In another op-ed piece in the *New York Times*, Maureen Dowd observed the irony of Vice President Al Gore's admiration for *The Matrix* in the wake of the Littleton shootings. She pointed out that the film's "balletic and epic ode to violence" attracted an "obsessively devoted audience of young computer savvy males." Dowd claimed that "the violence has a terrible beauty and the death seems merely virtual."[30]

Shattering Smooth Flows

According to Slavoj Žižek, cyberspace can be characterized by "the frictionless flow of images."[31] These digital networks and flows of images incarnate realism in new ways. Upgrading seamless Hollywood narrative structures, they replace psychoanalytic identification with physical immersion. Through a repetitive constancy of image, their technological surround locks out all other sensations beyond the visual and banishes metacommunicative cognitive apparatuses.

This new configuration of digital realism no longer depends on concealing the means of production. Instead, it creates an infinite flow and production of images, collapsing time and space by means of the instantaneous, the immediate, and the immersive. For Paul Virilio, the digital accelerates real time as an "escape velocity," dispelling history, the geophysical, and sensation.[32] Strapped into these digital accelerations, critical analysis must then deaccelerate to slow down the flow and to expose and open up the gaps.

By downshifting from the swift, linear, smooth narratives of the Serbian bombings, the image flows that constitute new formations of continuity can be shattered to produce clashes, leaps, and associative montages. Žižek has observed that the West requires Bosnia and the Balkans to be fixed and victimized so that it can project its phantasmatic content onto this timeless space.[33] Consequently, it is necessary to break apart the timelessness, the smooth flows, the chimeras, and the fantasized historical that evacuates history. This strategy necessitates moving beyond the images to occupy the interstitial, the constantly shifting provisional grounds between contiguous history, digital antiwar art, films, photographs, and underground video tapes. Trinh T. Minh-ha refers to this production of gaps as the "cinema interval," the space between the images where contradiction and juxtaposition generate meaning.[34]

The 1999 NATO bombings repressed the interval. The incessant destruction of bridges in Serbia materialized this psychic movement. By devising a reformulated radicalized theorization of interface, these imaginaries can decelerate, their montages and breakages exposing dangerous digital flows and invisible imbedded networks. Rather than multiple mediations, interface suggests a way these various screens ricochet off each other. For example, Peter Weibel has argued that "in the age of electronics, the world is becoming increasingly manipulatable as an interface between observer and objects."[35]

Through different associative routings, the interstitial and the interval can be recovered to restore social collectivities and generate a historiography that creates the past through continual recovery of abandoned objects and displaced temporalities. Associative repatterning combines with deductive argumentation. As the interstitial widens, a landscape for agency emerges that rejects morbid individualism and a hierarchical control that incarcerates.

Digital Pathologies

The bombings in Kosovo and Serbia unmasked the pathologies of the digital and opened up possibilities for reconfiguration within an interface. With these bombings, digital memory downloaded on both radar and psychic screens. In this way, visualities of many registers disturb and infect each other. The posthuman digital suspension of history and its replacement with immediacy, speed, and immersion are so pervasive in digital discourse that its practice is to produce phantasms that become naturalized.

The traumas implied by the digital reside not in how it eliminates the analog, but in how it amputates history and historiography. For example, writers as different as Francis Fukuyama, a political scientist, and Jean Baudrillard, a critical theorist, have argued that history ended after the revolutions of 1989 in Eastern Europe.[36] Yet their arguments locate history within events, rather than within networks and interfaces. As the NATO bombings illustrated, history did not end, but was suspended and restaged as smooth digital flows.

The war stripped images from CNN and the *New York Times* of their histories, their meaning, their politics, their stories.[37] These images are spectacles of empathy, virtual and meaningless. Aida Hozic argues that the NATO bombs did not bomb Belgrade, they bombed politics.[38] Around the world, public spheres for debate and community diminished. Disconnected images of refugees and fighting machines assumed the shapes of these absent public spheres. They cannibalized each other, refueling binary oppositions. They operated like mirages, promising that somewhere amid the amorphous cyber-networks, ubiquitous computing, and surveillance, referents and living human beings persist. Within these destructive fixities that function only as deadly projectiles and phantasms, it is important for analysis to move beyond the fantasies *of* the image to the interfaces *for* images. The postphotographic, postcinematic era constantly mutates. Because it continually morphs referents and signs, recovering the interface and the interstitial is critical.[39]

If the fixed, stable celluloid image is dead, reduced to a ghost inhabiting visuality but no longer defining it, what interfaces articulate the phantom desires latent in the bombings? The opposition between the digital and the analog as well as the virtual and the real requires unsettling and diffusion. To restore the political, these deadly separations need to be rerouted. The historiographic emerges in these interstitial spaces.[40] Borders between the digital and the analog as well as the historical and the future manufacture a fantasy of an inside and an outside. Analyzing the Bosnian conflict, Žižek argues "the gaze of the innocent observer is also in a way nonexistent, since this gaze is the impossible neutral gaze of someone who falsely exempts himself from his concrete historical existence, that is, from his actual involvement in the Bosnian conflict."[41] Neutrality is thus a fantasy. We are all bombed. We are all refugees. We live with the phantoms of death.

In *Remnants of Auschwitz: The Witness and the Archive*, Giorgio Agamben discusses how the Holocaust has been framed within a discursive veil of "incomprehensibility," which confers the "prestige of the mystical" on the Nazi's systematic extermination. Agamben writes: "To say that Auschwitz is 'unsayable' or 'incomprehensible' is equivalent to *euphemein*, to adoring in silence, as one does with a god. Regardless of one's intention, this contributes to its glory."[42] Incomprehensibility shrouds the Kosovo crisis as spiritual redemption through digital technologies. Matrixes of war, then, need to replace images of war.

The bombings displaced both Serbs and Albanian Kosovars. They killed history. These bombings produced refugees as a timeless, incomprehensible chaos within causal narratives. They materialized the circuits in the new transnational digital economy where money and information move across borders yet productive relations are imbedded, invisible, encrypted.[43] The post–Cold War era produces and thrives in a culture of encryption; secrets and crypts become pervasive.

Narrative Calibrations

With the 1999 bombings, narrative forms were not so much emplotted, Hayden White's well-known term for the structures of modernist historical practice, as they were calibrated.[44] Calibration entails several meanings that help position Kosovo's psychic stagings. First, it refers to inspecting quantitative measurements, exemplified in the *New York Times*' daily counts of bombs, the military, and the refugees. The second meaning is akin to gradations of quantity on thermometers or measuring cups. In Kosovo, this strategy was perhaps best exemplified in discussions in the US Congress about causal linkages between expenditures and bombs. A third definition of calibration refers to the correct calculation for weapons by observing where projectiles hit. Thus, all calibrations hold the capacity for destruction and death. In an essay called "Digital Apparitions," Vilém Flusser suggests that calibrations form the genetic tissues of the digital: "People discovered that although the world may be unimaginable and indescribable, it is calculable."[45] In calibration, analog images materialize calculations and algorithms, distilling the multiple sedimentary layers of relationships between the digital and the analog. The analog transforms into a metaphor for the digital. While calibration performs translation, it also disposes of discourse and dialogic engagement. Calibrations create connections based on separations.

CNN and the *New York Times* narrated a simple, unified story with characters, rising action, and an apparition of a chasm between East and West. This epic adhered to nineteenth-century realist narrative structures of transparency and referentiality: primitive, deep-seated ethnic hatreds versus NATO's digitally enhanced precision aerial bombing. This narrative invoked nineteenth-century tropes of coherency that twentieth-century modernism dismantled.[46] For Žižek, narrative's primordial form is fantasy: "Narrative as such emerges in order to resolve some fundamental antagonism by rearranging its terms into a temporal succession.... [It] bears witness to some repressed antagonism."[47] The deification of Kosovar suffering and destruction and the heroicization of patriarchal nationalism mobilized a realist transparent narrative humanism. The narrative of the Kosovo war, with its demons and heroes, perpetrators and victims, moves the NATO intervention from the virtual back to the corporeal. Žižek demonstrates that this humanitarianism demands that victims depoliticize through (re)narrativization.[48] Hayden White argues along similar lines in his discussion of the *Challenger* explosion: "Insofar as the story is identifiable as a story, it can provide no lasting 'psychic mastery' of such events."[49]

A repetition fetish emerged in the structure of the *New York Times'* images during the bombing. Three visual elements staged the *New York Times'* narration of the war: bombing patterns and changing borders; maps of the former Yugoslavia marking troop buildup; masses of refugees near destroyed houses, and world leaders and NATO military commanders. These images functioned as hieroglyphs of traumatic repressions. Across several months of bombing, these three sectors did not shift, but repeated. These images dramatized calibrations. They transferred NATO high-tech, digital bombing apparatuses into analog forms. They were not camouflage, but screens. They transposed the calculations, computers, and measurements of radar screens into the physical forms of airplanes and nation-state officials. The bodies and blood from the sanitized Gulf War returned in the bombings, recalibrated as narrativized projections of digitality.

NATO members, the United States, France, Austria, and beyond were imaged in medium shots. Diplomats in suits signified rationality against the irrationality of the dirty and ragged refugees. The chaotic compositional mass of refugees was calibrated against the patriarchal calm of world leaders. The refugees stood and moved while world leaders sat, their suits repressing the trauma of abandoned clothes and homes. Clinton, Jacques Chirac, General Wesley Clark, and Viktor Chernomyrdin signified a named white masculinity against the anonymity of the racialized refugees framed as beyond time and historical content. The NATO leaders represented their nation-states while the refugees remained stateless.

NATO leaders were positioned within discourse: they talked and huddled, their utterances propelling narrative. They moved policy forward despite the demise of history and nation states. In an image accompanying an April 29, 1999, *New York Times* article, Clinton held a press conference on the air strikes. He read from a podium on the left of the image. On the right, filling two thirds of the frame, aides huddled in different groups. Rational discourse motoring plots across national borders mattered more than presidents, even as Clinton conflated the economic sanctions and military campaign with the "humanitarian challenge."[50]

A May 6, 1999, *New York Times* image replayed these tropes. Clinton ate a hot dog with military personnel at Ramstein Air Base in Germany. His luminous image filled the center of the frame, while the nameless, indistinctly pictured soldiers crowded around him. He gesticulated, talking about "the war, the military's recruitment problems and military pay."[51] Psychoanalytically, one could say that Clinton did not eat a hot dog, but devoured Milosevic as an act of symbolic castration. When he bit into the hot dog, the nature of this war reframed this "bite" as a "byte." This analog image metastasized the digital through calibration.

Yet despite the narratives that situated him as other, Milosevic was simultaneously visualized as parallel to Clinton, a named man in a suit suspended in speech that no longer had any meaning. Each image deferred to the digital and the technological. NATO images linked the masculine to digitality and the deployment of high-technology weapons and planes. Milosevic's masculinity was refantasized as predigital, the direct inverse of NATO. Although NATO possessed explosive capabilities, it was Milosevic who was, in fact, explosive: his revivalist nationalism, invoking a "Greater Serbia," did not convert to digital algorithms.

These photographs operated as national imaginaries: NATO's transnational capital was digital, while Milosevic's nationalism was analog. This very separation demanded penetration. Kosovo, then, staged the digital divide in a new way: the digital was invisible while the analog was visible. These male figures reverse Vladimir Propp's schematas that realist narratives require a hero.[52] Instrumentality, rationality, and technocracy supplant the heroic, stripping away bodies, history, place, and time. Milosevic, then, becomes the bad Fordist manager oblivious to the post-Fordist virtual economy. The charred remains of masculinity propelled the war narrative: NATO was male. Marked by a feminized psychic lack, absent nation, food, safety, or warmth, these photos constructed the refugees as infantilized, female, and vulnerable.

A world away, another image inscribed the digital onto the natural. A color photograph of a neighborhood in Moore, Oklahoma, leveled by a tornado appeared on the front page of the May 5, 1999, *New York Times*.[53] Its composition mirrored the imprint of the bombings in the Balkans, domesticating and naturalizing aerial reconnaissance. As a formal design, the flattened landscape resembled a computer circuit board.

Monuments and Victims

The NATO bombing produced imagery that performed a phantasmatic imaginary, an epic Hollywood film where mighty men and high-tech bombing machines saved Kosovar women wearing headscarves and elderly Albanians sitting in wheelbarrows. A contradiction between history and the future motored these narratives: the Albanian Kosovars reduced to a pretechnological state propelled the false humanitarianism of high-tech bombing.

NATO staged a neat binary opposition that effaced these brutal, bloody operations. It installed a simplistic causality in place of explanation: refugees massed together around fires fueled by foraged twigs can only secure redemption through high-tech planes and bombs.[54] Nameless masses in dirt, rain, and snow on one screen, shiny multimillion-dollar planes deploying the latest computer technology on the other. One set of images on the ground, the other in the air. Sky and earth, digital and corporeal: the one cannibalizing the other.

In *Trespassing through Shadows: Memory, Photography and the Holocaust*, Andrea Liss contends that images of the Nazi exterminations during World War II always run an ethical risk if they depend too much on false realisms, the mimetic, and the monumental. She cautions that empathy assumes that an act of horror can be fully understood. In contrast, Liss draws attention to various Holocaust memorials that perform the work of antimonumentality, such as the decision to name the people in the images displayed in the Holocaust Museum or installation artist Christian Boltanski's commemorative shrines to the ambiguities of memory during Nazi occupations and exterminations. Liss argues that Boltanski rejects the capacity of the photograph to function as a document and a "rhetoric of victimology."[55] He circles around memory to interrogate how the viewer gets caught within the sentimental, the inauthentic, the universal, and the nostalgic.[56] Rather than artifacts or evidence, Liss advances images as questions and enigmas, fulcrums to activate questions into the shifting configurations of image, history, memory, and mourning.[57] She advocates an epistemological connection between mourning the referent and producing active analytic signification.[58]

The post–Cold War era and its digital economy have rehabilitated monumentality and victims both psychically and physically. The discourse around Kosovo condensed all twentieth-century wars. The war in Kosovo was likened to a "Holocaust," a narrative repetition of World War II and fascism.[59] The war in Kosovo was figured as another Vietnam. The war in Kosovo replicated the bloodless, postmodern Gulf War. These metaphors and analogies ambush the new politics of the digital networks with simplistic nostalgia.

A full-page ad in the April 30, 1999, *New York Times* suggested the political complexities imbedded in deploying history as metaphor.[60] Sponsored by the American Jewish Joint Distribution Committee Coalition for Kosovo Relief, the advertisement deployed a realist image of a Kosovar woman in a large crowd of refugees gazing into the distance, disengaged. She holds a sleeping child. A headline over her chest exclaimed "One month after Passover, we are witnessing an exodus of biblical proportions. But it's not about freedom." Near the bottom, a quote from Elie Wiesel: "We as Jews are responsible, morally and humanly responsible, for helping victims everywhere. In Kosovo, they need our help and deserve our solidarity." This image folded in another image of suffering: Dorothea Lange's famous *Migrant Mother* from 1936. Both images collapsed universality and individuality into a monument to maternity. The victim and the monumental are conflated into the woman's body; she is a stand-in for the feminized nation of Kosovo. Masses of refugees swarmed behind the mother, an out-of-focus tapestry of suffering. Newspaper photojournalism images of Kosovars and Serbs rephrased the visual iconography of World War II and Nazi concentration camps. These image structures imbricated prior historical formations to displace the digital warfare irradiating the cyber-militarized economy. By replacing mourning and history with phantoms, they elided death.

A May 20, 1999, *New York Times* photograph reprocessed the digital through condensation. The section heading above it read, "Crisis in the Balkans: Evidence of Atrocities, Talk of Desertions."[61] A frame grab from a Kosovar journalist's videotape, the image chronicled the dead lined up on the ground, documenting the massacre of 127 Albanian Kosovars. The cutlines asserted that CNN had televised the original video. The image was also calibrated with NATO's aerial images of mass graves, but its digitalization diminished the atrocities.[62]

Jay David Bolter and Richard Grusin contend that the digital does not constitute a paradigmatic break but is rather a series of contiguities with other media. They use the term "remediation" to describe how the digital cannibalizes previous media formations. Rather than a new form, the digital is recombinant.[63] Just as the imagery of Kosovo conjured the extermination of Jews, this photograph remediated amateur video, the archival, and surveillance. Its CNN broadcast sustained an analog form for global satellite communication. The digital verified the analog while the fantasized historical verified the image. This image, then, did not in fact evidence slaughter, but instead demonstrated the racialized residue of how the new digital networks undergird war.

The interfaces between images loom more significant than the images alone. After the bombings concluded, Žižek argued that the language of "universal human rights" depoliticized the NATO intervention by creating victims.[64] Yet when images enter the circulatory systems of the digital networks and reconnect with discourse, their function changes. They transform into historical agents and mobile interfaces.

The Human Rights Watch website section entitled "Kosovo: Focus on Human Rights" and its special section on "Tragedy in Pictures" exemplified this movement away from images ossified in residual historical formations to a strategy of images mobilized to create what Derrida has identified as an archive that always opens to the future.[65] The site contains a series of photo essays to complement the Human Rights Watch written work "uncovering abuses by all parties to the conflict in Kosovo."[66] The 105 images on this site suggested that the multiple replaces the unique image of evidentiary truth, contextualized as one layer of the horrors the Kosovar refugees endured rather than as historicized fantasy projections. Unlike photojournalism's narrativity, these photographs mobilized agency in tandem with the written documentation and testimonies gathered by Human Rights Watch, yet this documentation eschewed a false coherency and realism. Its exposure of incoherence deployed images with the assumption that they are always incomplete archival traces constantly in search of new contiguities. These photographs retained a humanistic, traditional realist documentary aesthetic that privileged the Kosovars as subjects. Nevertheless, their context of the Human Rights Watch website suggested antimonumentalism: they were grouped in historical patterns rather than as illustrations, a crucial difference from more commercial photojournalism. Categories include "A Village Destroyed October 1999," "Return to Kosovo June 1999," "Peace Deferred June 1999" and "Refugees April 1999." These images served as nodal points for inquiries into a constantly expanding archive. Thus, the Human Rights Watch site's architecture was built upon mobile vectors and changing interfaces rather than static, essentializing images.

Pivoting Delirium

Discussing the documentary film *Who Killed Vincent Chin?* (Christine Choy and Renee Tajima, 1989), Bill Nichols emphasizes the primacy of argumentation, political trauma, and death, arguing that the development of epistemological genealogies requires new analytical architectures. For instance, *Who Killed Vincent Chin?* embraces a discourse of delirium rather than sobriety. Mixing multiple editing and analytical strategies, the film restores "feeling and bodily sensation" to conceptual abstractions.[67] These juxtapositions activate a "web of relationalities" that alters epistemological structures. This web demonstrates "the logical impossibility of explaining the whole by means of any part and accounts for the reluctance to name the framework in which apparent disorder can assume pattern and meaning."[68] Nichols analyzes how the film's radical and visceral intervention opens previously blocked pathways to knowledge and action. He employs the word "pivot" to describe how the film activates historiography: it "pivots dialectically between past and present, present and future. . . . This pivoting upholds a tension between the particular and the general, the local and the historical."[69]

Digital art produced about the Kosovo crisis echoed these tactics Nichols identifies to disembowel narrative unity. These works did not manufacture new imagery to counter ideologically contaminated dominant commercial imagery. Rather, they produced pivots of delirium fraying coherencies. In their essay "Digital Delirium," Arthur and Marilouise Kroker observe that in the digital image speed economy "the real can no longer keep up to the speed of the image. Reality shudders and collapses and fragments into the vortex of many different alternative realities."[70] Rather than smoothing over phantasms, these works radically recalibrated war through digitality. Some digital art doubled these two concepts: the web of relationalities and the pivot to produce not images, but dialectical interfaces between traumatic gaps and elisions. The interstitial extracted the image out of the regimes of coherency, narrative, and ossified temporality.

During the Kosovo crisis, the website www.jodi.org worked with a default mode and rerouting. Jodi interrogated the search engine as the materialization of knowledge.[71] Through various random strategies to search and access sites, jodi .org proposed that the web interface maps relations between sites and codes rather than generating new images. These cartographic strategies presented delirium as the repressed image of the cyber-networks. They changed the fantasied control of search engines into an immersion into and an interrogation of the search engine itself. Jodi maneuvered the user from outside the machine to inside the machine of the digital networks.

Jodi.org inverted the modality of associative strings typical of commercial search engines by performing a psychic reversal through system crashing and parodying how people access information.[72] During the Kosovo crisis, when a user signed on to jodi.org, she/he was instantly routed to the B92 website, which delivered news of the bombings from a Serbian dissident point of view. No matter how many times the user would try to type in jodi.org to attempt to locate other search engines or net art, the B92 site loaded up. During this period, Milosevic attacked B92 and forced it to move to another server in The Netherlands.

In jodi.org, the pivot intervenes into transparency with a historiography of replacement: it forfeits its URL to Radio B92, generating more public space for it to occupy. Jodi.org deconstructed the vast amorphous discontinuities of the digital networks with directionality and contiguity, and thus inserted the user into the repressed delirium of the war. The inability of the user to experience anything other than the B92 view of the bombings wrote new codes of delirium through the pivot.

Interstitial Operations

During the bombing campaign in 1999, the International Action Center (IAC), a US-based foreign policy political action group, produced a twenty-minute videotape entitled *NATO Targets* (1999). IAC sold the tape for twenty-five dollars through its listserv and direct mail. The tape exemplified how circulatory transactions were adapted for the new matrices of war that migrate between analog and digital forms. It did not function as a fixed media object but as a node within a network of shifting relations and political necessities. *NATO Targets* intervened into interstitial relations: it maneuvered between the digital and the analog, between the real and the virtual. It refused the imbedded digital grids of the bombings by demonstrating their impact on real bodies. *NATO Targets* rejected the repurposing of historical tropes like "the Holocaust" and the phantasms of chaos and incomprehensibility. It disarmed the fissures between Serbia and the United States, between the inside and the outside.

Directed by Gloria La Riva, the short documentary featured former Attorney General Ramsey Clark touring Serbia to assess the bombing. Clark travels to bombed hospitals, workplaces, apartment buildings, and factories. The film's documentation of bombings and the victims in the hospitals awaiting medical care invoked the realist documentary representations of the Workers' Film and Photo League newsreels from the 1930s, remediating their strategies with the new technologies of camcorders.

NATO Targets remapped contiguities, visible evidence, and the morality of bombing. The tape pirated news footage from CNN and NBC that described the bombings as a "high-tech war." It intercut news footage of the city of Pristina after the bombings with camcorder shots recorded during the destruction. Rerouting the high-tech air war through on-the-ground bodies and places, *NATO Targets* invented a new matrix that restored context and consequence to historical actions.

In *NATO Targets*, Daniel Bernstein, a reporter from Pacifica radio, explains that during the bombing, journalists became "stenographers for the Pentagon." He decries the attacks on civilians in churches, libraries, schools, bridges. He analyzes the Rambouillet peace agreement as a NATO declaration of war on Serbia. *NATO Targets* produced a dialectic between militarized imaginaries and camcorder images. It disarmed the cyber-networks with bodies on the ground: a boy in a coma, a paraplegic young woman with metal cluster bomb fragments imbedded in her legs, a maternity hospital with rows of babies and limited medicine.[73] Serbian doctors explained the difficulties of medical care during wartime. The tape's function extended beyond muckraking the bombings' effects on civilians. Instead, it pivoted between a plurality of formations: it replaced the phantasmatic with historical explanation and contiguities.

Polyphony

If the archive depends on superimpositions, layers, and substrata, what new forms engage the historical? Cyber-wars require fragmentations that refuse layering, repressing violence with velocity and obliterating contiguities. How can both the dialectic and dialogic be restored?[74] Developed during Operation Allied Force, the Weakblood website, developed by Reiner Strasser, was a gallery of hyperlinks to a diverse array of antiwar Internet art.[75] It sustained a new interstitial historical structure between the analog and the digital, based on creating an endlessly open text where sites link to other sites, a digital *mise-en-abyme* into violence, technology, and genocide. Many pieces exposed digital networks: various vertical and horizontal scrolling functions on the computer screen revealed the image structure.

Nearly all pieces linked to Weakblood morphed historiographic analysis with digitalization. The user created montages to generate new antiwar argumentation. For example, Elson Froes's piece *Autopsia das Utopias* (Autopsy the Utopias, 1999) graphically embodied the contradictions between peacekeeping and bombing: a blue screen with the white letters UTOPIA alternated with a red screen with the black letters AUTOPSIA, looping the interstitial zone between the future and death. Matt Eberhart's piece *Wordwar* (1999) created a linguistic montage of collisions.[76] Scrolling down the left revealed the words "gun," "death," "rape," "bomb," "kill," and "torture." Headlines on the right proclaimed, "Words of war, words of hate." *Wordwar* transformed the dictionary of violence into performance.

Weakblood disarmed the matrices of war by composing a layered fugal structure utilizing counterpoint. Many pieces reprocessed commercial images, dislodging their false coherencies. For instance, Veronik Menanteau constructed a loop animation from three previously disconnected news images: a baby, a bomb, and a star nebula. A title scrolled underneath which read, "Shame politics . . . if only one political leader would stand up and have courage to say frankly: let's stop this running for power for money." The piece mobilized a polyphonic structure between images, words, and movement.

Rather than offering evidence, the Weakblood site rerouted the vectors of cyber-wars into historiographic meditations. Weakblood proposed the endless mutability and mobility of images as historical artifacts and mixed temporalities. Weakblood functioned contrapuntally. Archival layers responded to each other as Weakblood detonated incomprehensible phantasms through historiographic explanation, connection, and fluidity.

Fugues

The matrices of cyberwar demand new architectures. To revitalize and reanimate political agency, the historiographic must be rewritten as a fugue in many voices in order to combat the vaporization of history. The radical possibilities of the digital do not reside in how it refashions temporality and spatiality. Rather, digital affordances hold the possibility to reimagine the archive as mobile. They can articulate reconstructed layers in order to substitute a plurality of images and temporalities for one static image and one historical event.

These networks circulate and collide, shattering linearity and dismantling calibration. Restoration of the historical archive requires a fugue-like structure constructed out of contiguities rather than one single image. With their variations, embellishments, and polyphony, digital fugues hold the latent possibility to rewire history and the future. Their emerging and continually changing circuitry holds the untapped and yet-to-be-realized possibility of crashing the networks booted up by the military and the transnational media corporations.

Notes

1. Human Rights Watch Report, "Civilian Deaths in the NATO Air Campaign," February 7, 2000, http://www.nyu.edu/globalbeat/balkan/HRW020700.html.

2. Michael Ignatieff, *Virtual War: Kosovo and Beyond* (New York: Metropolitan Books, 2000), 4.

3. Ignatieff, *Virtual War*, 111.

4. Ignatieff, *Virtual War*, 100–101

5. Arthur and Marilouis Kroker, "Fast War/Slow Motion," accessed January 22, 2000, http://www.ctheory.com/e76.html.

6. See "Aerial Images," at http://www.sping-2.com; Michael Evans, "NATO Dropped Thousands of Bombs on Dummy Road, Bridges and Soldiers . . . and Hit Only 13 Real Serb Tanks," *London Times*, June 24, 1999, voti-agent <agent@blast.org; Florian Schneider, "Border Camp '99" June 25, 1999, voti-agent<agent@blast.org; Robert Fisk, "Yugoslavia: Is NATO Killing People Because It Doesn't Like What They Say?" April 24, 1999, at www.igc.org/trac.coerner/worldnews/other/372.html; Tim Smart, "USA: Count Corporate America Among NATO's Staunchest Allies," April 13, 1999, www.igc.org.trac.corner/worldnews/other/373.html.

7. On April 23, 1999, NATO bombed the main building of Serbian television and two weeks later began attacking the Serbian electrical system. See Tim Judah, *Kosovo: War and Revenge* (New Haven: Yale University Press), 222–264; Carlotta Gall, "No Water, Power, Phone: A Serbian City's Trials," *New York Times*, May 4, 1999, 14; and Michael R. Gordon, "NATO Air Attacks on Power Plants Cross a Threshold," *New York Times*, May 4, 1999, 1.

8. Pierre Levy, "The Art of Cyberspace," in *Electronic Culture: Technology and Visual Representation*, ed. Timothy Druckery (New York: Aperture Foundation, 1996), 266–267.

9. Levy, "The Art of Cyberspace," 270.

10. Cathy Caruth, "An Interview with Robert Jay Lifton," in *Trauma: Explorations in Memory*, ed. Cathy Caruth (Baltimore: Johns Hopkins University Press, 1995), 134.

11. For a historical overview of the relationship between the US military and digital innovation, see Richard Wise, *Multimedia: A Critical Introduction* (New York: Routledge, 2000), 9–41.

12. For a definitive discussion of digital coherency as mark and index of the corporate, see Sean Cubitt, *Digital Aesthetics* (London: Sage Publications, 1998), 123–151. For an explanation of the historiographic differences between continuous structures and contiguous formations, see Alan Munslow, *Deconstructing History* (London: Routledge, 1997), 128–133.

13. Jacques Derrida, *Archive Fever* (Chicago: University of Chicago Press, 1996), 22.

14. Eric Schmitt and Michael R. Gordon, "British Pressing Partners to Deploy Ground Troops," *New York Times*, May 18, 1999, 10; Michael R. Gordon, "NATO Says Serbs, Fearing Land War, Dig In on Border," *New York Times*, May 19, 1999, 1, 8; Eric Schmitt, "Germany's Leader Pledges to Block Combat on the Ground," *New York Times* May 20, 1999, 1 and 12; Daniel Ellsberg, "Contemplating a Fatal Mistake," *New York Times*, May 21, 1999, 27; Jane Perlez, "3 Options for Washington, All with Major Risks," *New York Times*, May 21,1999, 12.

15. Tim Judah, *Kosovo: War and Revenge* (New Haven: Yale University Press, 2000), 228–242.

16. Thomas Doherty, *Projections of War: Hollywood, American Culture, and World War II* (New York: Columbia University Press, 1993), 4.

17. Diana Jean Schemo, "Kosovo War Doesn't Do Much for US Recruitment," Week in Review, *New York Times*, May 16, 1999, 6.

18. For a discussion of how the military innovated media technology and impelled its diffusion, see Patricia R. Zimmermann, *Reel Families: A Social History of American Film* (Bloomington: Indiana University Press, 1995).

19. Andrew Pollack, "Trying to Improve Training, Army Turns to Hollywood," *New York Times*, August 19, 1999, A14.

20. Aida Hozic, "Uncle Sam Goes to Siliwood: Of Landscapes, Spielberg and Hegemony," unpublished manuscript, 14–20.

21. See Jacques Derrida, *Spectres of Marx: The State of Debt, the Work of Mourning, and the New International* (New York: Routledge, 1994), 95–158.

22. Arthur and Marilouise Kroker, "Fast War, Slow Motion" July 14, 1999, www.ctheory.com/e76.html.

23. Jesse McKinley, "Film Fantasy as a Tonic for Refugee Children," *New York Times*, July 4, 2000, 1, 3.

24. Asma Barlas, "Kosovo: U.S. Foreign Policy and the Media," speech at the Teach-In on Kosovo, Ithaca College, Ithaca, NY, April 15, 1999.

25. Richard Dyer, *White* (London: Routledge, 1997), 1–68.

26. The web site www.pocho.com played on this repressed racialization of the bombings by pointing out that the GIs who had been held captive by the Serbs were Latinos whose release was negotiated by Rev. Jesse Jackson. In addition, the bombing of the Chinese Embassy in Belgrade also signified the eruption of this repressed racialization. See Susan Sachs, "3 G.I. Prisoners Reach Freedom in Good Health," *New York Times*, May 3, 1999, A1, A12; Susan Sachs, "3 Captive Soldiers Tell of Isolation in Yugoslav Cells," *New York Times*, May 1, 1999, A1, A10; Seth Faison, "Embassy Blast Churns Political Tea Leaves," *New York Times*, May 16, 1999, A11; Jane Perlez, "White House Is Bracing for a Chinese Backlash," *New York Times*, May 16, 1999, A11. For analysis of more globalized racialized violence in Colombia and Rwanda, respectively, occurring simultaneously to the Balkan crises of the 1990s, see Gabriel Garcia Marquez, *News of a Kidnapping* (New York: Penguin, 1996) and Philip Gourevitch, *We Wish to Inform You That Tomorrow We Will Be Killed with Our Families: Stories from Rwanda* (New York: Farrar, Strauss and Giroux, 1998).

27. Katherine Q. Seelye, "New Reign of Domestic Terror," *New York Times*, May 28, 1999, 12; Orlando Patterson, "When 'They' Are 'US," op-ed, *New York Times*, April 30, 1999, 34.

28. Katherine Q. Seelye, "Killings in Littleton Pierced the Soul of the Nation, Clinton Says," *New York Times*, May 21, 1999, 13.

29. Photograph by Monica Almeida, *New York Times*, April 29, 1999, 15.

30. Maureen Dowd, "In the D.C. Matrix," op-ed, *New York Times*, April 28, 1999, A29.

31. Slavoj Žižek, *The Plague of Fantasies* (London: Verso, 1997), 156.

32. See Paul Virilio, *Open Sky* (London: Verso, 1997), 119–145.

33. Žižek, *Plague of Fantasies*, 61–62.

34. Trinh T. Minh-ha, *Cinema Interval* (New York: Routledge, 1999), 33–50.

35. Peter Weibel, "The World as Interface: Towards the Construction of Context-Controlled Event-Worlds," in Druckery, *Electronic Culture*, 343.

36. Stuart Sim, *Derrida and the End of History* (London: Icon Books, 1999), 3–29.

37. For a discussion of how images negotiated the Balkans as a zone of incoherence, see International Action Center, *NATO in the Balkans: Voices of Opposition* (New York: International Action Center, 1998).

38. Aida Hozic, "The War in Kosovo," speech at Hobart and William Smith Colleges, Geneva, NY, April 6, 1999.

39. David Tomas, "From Photograph to Postphotographic Practice: Toward Postoptical Ecology of the Eye," in Druckery, *Electronic Culture*, 145–153.

40. Hayden White, for example, has argued that "the past is a place of fantasy," and that the historian's task is to transform these fantasies through writing. See interview with Hayden White, in *Encounters: Philosophy of History after Postmodernism*, ed. Ewa Domanska, (Charlottesville: University Press of Virginia, 1998), 16–21.

41. Žižek, *Plague of Fantasies*, 18.

42. Giorgio Agamben, *Remnants of Auschwitz: The Witness and the Archive* (New York: Zone Books, 1999), 32–33.

43. For explanations of how transnational corporate capital is built upon digital networks across borders, see Dan Schiller, *Digital Capitalism: Networking the Global Market System* (Cambridge, MA: MIT Press, 1999) and Robert W. McChesney, Ellen Meiksins Wood, and John Bellamy Foster, eds. *Capitalism and the Information Age* (New York: Monthly Review, 1999).

44. See Hayden White, *Metahistory* (Baltimore: Johns Hopkins University Press, 1973).

45. Vilém Flusser, "Digital Apparition," in Druckery, *Electronic Culture*, 243.

46. Robert F. Berkhofer, Jr., *Beyond the Great Story: History as Text and Discourse* (Cambridge: Harvard University Press, 1995), 26–44.

47. Žižek, *Plague of Fantasies*, 10–11.

48. Žižek, *Plague of Fantasies*, 17.

49. Hayden White, "The Modernist Event," in *The Persistence of History: Cinema, Television and the Modern Event*, ed. Vivian Sobchack (New York: Routledge, 1996), 32.

50. "In Clinton's Words: 'Speak with a Single Voice,'" *New York Times*, April 29, 1999, A14.

51. Agence France-Presse photograph in *New York Times*, May 6, 1999, A22.

52. See Vladimir Propp, *Morphology of the Folktale* (Austin: University of Texas Press, 1990).

53. Photograph by Jeff Mitchell of Reuters, *New York Times*, May 5, 1999, 1.

54. It is essential to note the contiguity between the US Department of Justice's antitrust case against Microsoft's bundling and Operation Allied Force. For a concise exposition of the Microsoft case, see John Heilemann, "The Truth, The Whole Truth, and Nothing but the Truth: The Untold Story of the Microsoft Antitrust Case," *Wired*, November 2000, 260–311.

55. Andrea Liss, *Trespassing through Shadows: Memory, Photography and the Holocaust* (Minneapolis: University of Minnesota Press, 1998), 43.

56. Liss, *Trespassing through Shadows*, 49.

57. Liss, *Trespassing through Shadows*, 77.

58. Liss, *Trespassing through Shadows*, 48.

59. This invocation of the Holocaust is a repetitive trope in Balkan War iconography, typified in the well-known and controversial image of Fikret Alic, a Bosnian Muslim, who looked to be imprisoned behind barbed wire. As subsequent reporting has demonstrated, he was not in a concentration camp, but at a collection center for refugees. For an analysis of this image and its circulation see Thomas Deichmann, "The Picture that Fooled the World," *NATO in the Balkans*, 165–178.

60. Coalition for Kosovo Relief advertisement, *New York Times*, April 30, 1999, A25.

61. Photograph, *New York Times*, May 20, 1999, A15.

62. Paul Virilio, *The Information Bomb* (London: Verso, 2000), 58–68

63. Jay David Bolter and Richard Grusin, *Remediation: Understanding New Media* (Cambridge, MA: MIT Press, 2000), 53–84.

64. Slavoj Žižek, "NATO, the Left Hand of God? On the Self Deception of the West, or Why the Conflict in the Balkans Will Not Come to an End Anytime Soon," July 1, 1999, voti-agent, agent@blast.org.

65. Derrida, *Archive Fever*, 36.

66. "Kosovo: Focus on Human Rights," Human Rights Watch, accessed July 1, 2018. https://www.hrw.org.legacy/campaigns/kosovo98/reports/shtml.

67. Bill Nichols, "Historical Consciousness and the Viewer: *Who Killed Vincent Chin?*" in *Persistence of History: Cinema, Television, and the Modern Event*, ed. Vivian Sobchack (New York: Routledge, 1996), 65.

68. Nichols, "Historical Consciousness," 59.

69. Nichols, "Historical Consciousness," 62.

70. Arthur and Marilouise Kroker, "Digital Delirium," in *Digital Delirium*, ed. Arthur and Marilouise Kroker (New York: St. Martin's, 1997), ix.

71. For a discussion of jodi.org as a live performance of reshuffled code and HTML, see Peter Lunenfeld, *Snap to Grid: A User's Guide to Digital Arts, Media and Cultures* (Cambridge: MIT Press, 2000), 80–84.

72. The creators of the website www.jodi.org assert "we serve no content." It is a collaboration between Dirk Paesmans (Belgium) and Joan Heemskerk (The Netherlands) to create collages of materials found on the net and to deliberately create confusion through producing system crashes and dead-end navigations through the internet.

73. For a discussion of the political significance of refiguring ground wars in an era of aerial reconnaissance, see Patricia R. Zimmermann, *States of Emergency: Documentaries, Wars, Democracies* (Minneapolis: University of Minnesota Press, 2000), 87–115.

74. For a discussion of how digitality can engage a dialectical history, see Vivian Sobchack's discussion of the morph as dialectic and dialogical in her essay "At the Still Point of the Turning World: Meta-Morphing and Meta-Stasis," in *Metamorphing: Visual Transformation and the Culture of Quick-Change,* ed. Vivian Sobchack (Minneapolis: University of Minnesota Press, 2000), 131–158.

75. See http://netartefact.de/weakblood. I thank Timothy Murray for introducing me to this site.

76. This idea of collisions between images originated with Sergei Eisenstein. For a discussion of the montage of collisions, see David Bordwell, *The Cinema of Eisenstein* (Cambridge: Harvard University Press, 1993), 111–138.

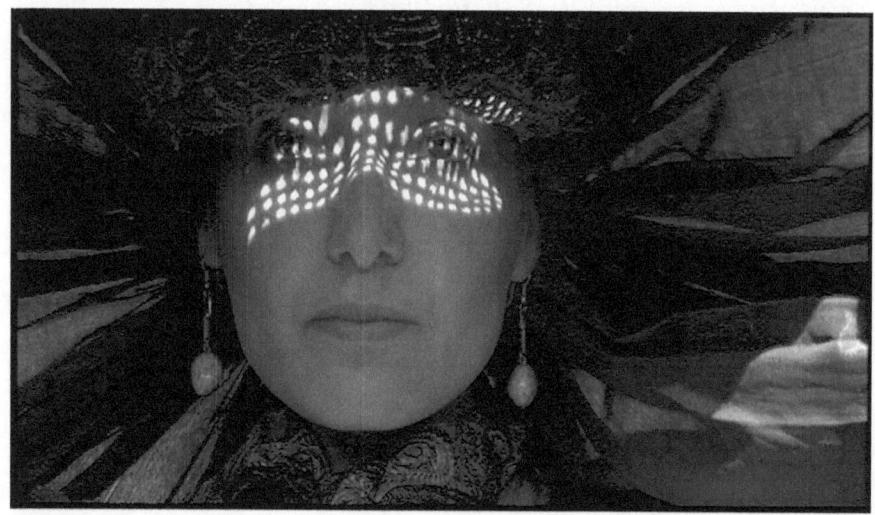

Figure 8.1. Screenshot from *Kandahar* (Mohsen Makhmalbaf, Iran, 2001).

8

BLASTING WAR*

Mohsen Mahkmalbaf, the Iranian New Wave film director, published a powerful essay in 2001 in *Monthly Review* titled "Limbs of No Body." He described the destruction of Afghanistan over the last twenty years.[1] The body was the world that amputated its limbs, among them, Afghanistan.

During this period of digital terror, the USA PATRIOT Act mobilized various email investigation and commercial digital data-mining technologies against people both within and outside the United States. These invasive and authoritarian regulatory acts created an atmosphere of paranoia. They employed the digital to disembody and to disempower.

I want to turn this system inside out in order to reembody and reempower analysis, critical art, digitality, people, and politics. We must resist any and all architectures of disembodiment; they remove dissent from justice; gender from race; privacy from security; labor from manufacturing in the global economy; and war from geography. These ideas—as well as all of us gathered here today—are limbs of one body.

Our choice in this endlessly morphing swirl of phantasmatic nationalist discourse is quite simple: we are dead, or we are alive. We must issue a call to humanity not as some universalized abstraction, but as a specific dialogic action *across*

---

* In September 2002, Timothy Murray, a professor of comparative literature, English, and film and a longtime friend, invited me to speak at Cornell University at his Digital Terror Workshop and Conference, sponsored by CTheory Multimedia and the Rose Goldsen Lecture Series. A year after the bombing of the World Trade Centers on September 11, 2001, I gave myself an intellectual goal to avoid writing a traditional conference paper on digital terror, as I thought it would dissipate the complexities of the political climate and ensuing resistance of the time. Instead, I opted for an approach that could accommodate a mosaic of ideas, countries, and media practices. A month later, Tara MacPherson invited me to be one of the plenary speakers at the Race in Digital Space Symposium at the Museum of Contemporary Art in Los Angeles, organized by the University of Southern California and MIT in October 2002. There, I presented a paper that expanded on my ideas first introduced at Cornell, in a talk entitled "Blasting, Streaming, and Flashing War." I developed these ideas with more research into the military and the entertainment industry, eventually publishing these talks as an essay titled "Blasting War," *Afterimage* 30, nos. 3 & 4 (Winter 2003): 4–5.

and *with* difference. And we must look to the dead, everywhere they exist, and insist on forging connections among them. It is important to remember that the people who perish each day from AIDS in sub-Saharan Africa equal the dead of two September 11ths.

We need to see, and then to see more, through a digital ultrasound of all of the complicated, messy, invisible politics that evade us. We can choose: we are limbs of no body, or we are limbs of one body.

In response to the war resolution vote in Congress in 2002, my aim in this essay is to think through the notion of blasting war. Blasting enfolds many meanings from different historical epochs and disciplines, and here, it is the thing we need to connect the limbs to the body. Blasto, in biology, means embryonic cell formation.

To blast is to open up, to make, to form.

To blast is to proclaim.

To blast is to criticize vigorously.

Blasting is not a thing or a statement; it describes a process.

Mohsen Mahkmalbaf's film *Kandahar* (2001) blasts away our imaginary projections of Afghanistan as a place of death, drugs, amputation, bombed buildings, death, drugs, murder, rubble—a place of absence. Instead, with an expansive compositional strategy of color, form, and line it creates a place of presence. The real and the imaginary twist together: sand, *burqas*, poverty, *madrassas*, and people trying to live their lives with the help of prosthetic legs cascading from the sky.

In *Kandahar,* a Canadian/Afghani woman journalist travels into Afghanistan to search for her sister. Despite the *mujahadeen* and the Taliban, the film genders the nation through the vision of a diasporic woman. Its narrative folds many stories into one. In the final shot, the journalist looks through the screen of her burqa at a distant city; not only are we inside Afghanistan, we are inside the burqa. We are not reaching our destination. We are not ending the story. We are looking out through a screen, beyond ourselves.

To blast is an expression of reprobation.

USA Today, CNN, and President George W. Bush's speeches describe the tragedies of September 11 as a seismic historical shift, where nothing is the same after and where history is blasted away like rock in a mountain needing removal for a new tunnel. Books on Islam proliferate, but Islam is seen as separate from the West, however we might characterize it in this post–Cold War world. Books on 9/11 crowd bookstores, but history continues to be reduced to therapeutic, repetitive narratives.

In this view, a new epoch in history begins with the horrific assault on the United States. But as Robert Fisk has pointed out, Palestinians in Lebanon might assume that a reference to the September massacre refers to the Christian militia's slaughter (thought to be masterminded by the Israelis) of 1,700 Palestinians in

Beirut, on September 14, 1982.² Arundhati Roy, Ariel Dorfman, and Zillah Eisenstein have reminded us that September 11 is also the anniversary of the Chilean coup, where 10,000 died, and other anniversaries of horrific and wrongful death and genocide, each different, each requiring our mourning.³ Around the world, many September 11ths occupy history, not only one. Iranians killed by Iraqis. Guatemalans killed by their government. African Americans, Cambodians, East Timorese, Rwandans, and Yugoslavians murdered across many Septembers. The deaths surround us with a virtual archive—never spoken, invisible, not connected to the others. These dead are the limbs of one body.

When George W. Bush proclaimed in his speech to Congress on September 21, 2001, that "either you are with us, or you are with the terrorists," he blasted away history. He insisted on this binary despite the fact that our globalized, flexible, borderless economy riddled with asymmetrical warfare without nation states, and invisible terrorists who blend in as suburbanites and family men render it utterly inoperative. As Philip Rosen has argued, a radical historiography must replace the pursuit of authentic, immobilized pastness with a dynamic sense of multiple temporalities.⁴ These multiple temporalities must collide and produce bursts of energy if we are to see anything at all.

The mediated, immobilized pastness of September 11 throws out an anchor to stabilize our anxieties. But on September 12, Bush replaced Afghanistan with Iraq, coalitions with global domination, corporate criminals with war resolutions, Osama Bin Laden with Saddam Hussein, and a plummeting economy with war.

More than a decade earlier, in the era just after the Gulf War and the end of the Cold War, Dick Cheney, Colin Powell, and Paul Wolfowitz outlined exactly the same plan in their Defense Planning Guidance Report. They directed the military to retool for cyber, laser, and electronic warfare capabilities in order to dominate outer space, inner space, digital space, private space, domestic space, entertainment space, international space, and national space, a system identified as full-spectrum dominance.⁵

In the digital age, war is no longer debated. It has been shorn from death. It is branded. Bush advisor Andrew Card declared that the war plans against Iraq were delayed until September because you don't want to introduce a new product in August.⁶ Yet, on August 6, 1990—the same date as the bombing of Hiroshima—the US imposed sanctions on Iraq, and over one million Iraqis died, half of whom were children, as a result.

Iraq poses a question for our politics: to borrow Edward Hallet Carr's title from his 1961 book, *What Is History*? In 2002 alone, the US military executed thirty bombing missions into Iraq. Would we have declared war on Iraq when the image marketeers identified a good launch date? Or did the war continue on for over a decade anyway with all of George W. Bush's speeches functioning as performance art to camouflage the realignment of the US military with transnational capital? By 1992, capital spending on information systems exceeded capital spending on industrial age items such as mining, construction, and manufacturing equipment. At that time, the Department of Defense shifted to an explicit policy of strategic information warfare because of the threat of open networks, no borders, and easily available software.

To blast is to blow air through the mouth to spray away decay.

Slavoj Žižek asked what we should make of the greatest power in the world bombarding Afghanistan, one of the poorest countries in the world, as retaliation? He observed that Kabul already looked like downtown Manhattan after September 11.[7] The most high-tech country in the world bombed a nation with barely any electricity and no paved roads. The Department of Defense briefings explained that Afghanistan was not "target rich." The geography of war was reorganized: within minutes of the first bombing of Afghanistan, the United States repositioned forty communications satellites over the country and bought all satellite time to prevent independent imaging from outer space.

Yet, as US ground forces and CIA agents penetrated, they captured not only what they thought were Taliban operatives, but hard drives from almost any computer they could find. Yet, as Pakistani investigative reporter Ahmed Rashid points out, US military and oil companies have been involved in Afghanistan for twenty years.[8] US popular culture depicted the end of the Taliban in images of urban Afghani women disposing of their burqas, the importation of Indian musicals on video, and satellite dishes hammered from soup cans.

Variety boasted a headline "Post-Taliban Production Rebounds."[9] The article explained that the West—however now defined—was no longer limited to Mahkmalbaf's *Kandahar* for a point of reference. The Locarno Film Festival hosted an Afghan Film Day. But the Taliban destroyed 2,700 films in the Afghan film archives, another note in the history of analog images incinerated. And in a move of which the Taliban would likely have approved, the US consulate denied Abbas Kiarostami, the Iranian film director, a visa to attend the New York Film Festival.[10]

Afghanistan's history speaks dismemberment even before the US bombings. Over the last twenty years, 2.5 million Afghans died from war, militarization, famine, and lack of medicine. Ten percent of the population perished, and another 30 percent migrated to other countries in search of food and water. Over 6.3 million Afghanis are refugees—three times the number of Balkan refugees.

But Afghanistan's was not the only history to be rendered invisible. In this period, it is as though Harry Potter's invisibility cloak covered the globe like a digital effect in a Hollywood film. Take an example from Africa, where US interests obliterated the visibility of the people on the ground. Angola is an oil-rich country that US Secretary of State Colin Powell visited. According to Medecins Sans Frontieres, after twenty-seven years of war, 30 percent of the Angolan people were malnourished from famine, with mortality and malnutrition rates five to ten times emergency threshold levels for international relief agencies.[11]

These histories articulated with the contemporaneous actions of Attorney General John Ashcroft. He responded to the terrorist attacks by arresting six thousand people in two months with little or no evidence. But let us not amputate Ashcroft's actions from other acts of aggression against otherness in US history: the Palmer Raids against Eastern European immigrants and communists in 1917 and 1918, the incarceration of Japanese Americans during World War II, and the Red Scare. The USA PATRIOT Act, "rammed through Congress" as the American Civil Liberties Union (ACLU) describes it, with very little debate, expanded government power to invade privacy, imprison people, and punish dissent.[12] Under the Terrorism, Information and Prevention System (TIPS), the government militarized citizens and service workers to spy on people in their homes.

Law enforcement agents then garnered a sneak-and-peek provision to enter a house or office with a search warrant when the occupants were away, photograph whatever they deem necessary to fight the war on terror, and confiscate any communications equipment.

To blast is to bomb, explode.

In an opinion piece in the *New York Times*, Susan Sontag wrote that the war on terror is a vague, ill-defined misnomer designed to keep us engaged in endless war. She pointed out "this is a phantom war and therefore in need of an anniversary." She argued we are fighting Al Qaeda, not terror.[13] Perhaps war was simply a vacuous invocation and cover for the complete reorganization, realignment, and mobilization of the state, the military, information infrastructures, and transnational capital. Tom Ridge, head of Homeland Security from 2003 to 2005, not only requested exemptions from Congressional oversight, but also demanded that corporate records and infrastructures be exempted from the Freedom of Information Act. Perhaps an authoritarian coup d'état occurred within our own borders in the United States. Perhaps Bush himself was virtual.

This endless phantom war that is really not war lacks images and news: an invisible war. The Department of Defense initiated the strictest press protocols in US history. Reporters had no independent access to military personnel anywhere. They covered the story from destroyers 2,500 miles away in the Indian Ocean. All images had to be approved or were supplied by the Department of Defense. 3D virtuality replaced muckraking. CNN transformed into our collective burqa.

We must rewire for cyberwar. Bush's new war and the wars that will follow will no longer be total wars like World War II, Vietnam, or the Gulf. They will be nodal wars, practiced and perfected in the war on drugs in the United States and Latin America and the civil wars against the cultures of difference and public arts practices. Nodal wars are no longer wars of images and propaganda. Instead they institute the policing and circulation of virtuality in asymmetrical warfare.

Since the end of the Cold War in 1989, the military converted to a plan called the Revolution in Military Affairs (RMA). The twentieth century moved wars into the air and off the ground. In the twenty-first century, war is etherized by digitizing it. The 1999 bombings of Serbia signaled a decisive shift in the military from weaponry to cyber-infrastructure. One thousand five hundred bombing sorties required 30,000 computer technicians, engineers, and analysts. The largest military contract in US history—200 billion—was awarded to Lockheed Martin, an aircraft manufacturer, erasing differences between planes, weapons, and computers. The CIA targeted financial networks and organizations that might have harbored Al Qaeda money, employing the hackers they once pursued for copyright piracy. The Predator, an unmanned spy plane, could also engage in reconnaissance. Commando Solo, a special operations communications plane, dropped anti-Osama reward leaflets and blasted world beat hip-hop music over Afghanistan like a mobile rave machine.[14]

Digital technologies developed for the Cold War migrated into and merged with the entertainment industry. The information sector represents more than 15 percent of the US economy. Copyright products such as film, video, games, and software constitute the largest US export. Firms that depended on military financing from the Department of Defense moved into special effects, computer design, and interactive entertainment.

These digital conversions do not so simply mark a technological shift. They signal a political economy reorganization from a military-industrial complex to the military information media entertainment complex. BBC News announced that the military had convened a group of screenwriters of action and cult films like *Die Hard* (1998), *Fight Club* (1999), and *Being John Malkovich* (1999) to brainstorm terrorist scenarios.[15] Computer games outsell Hollywood films. Collusion persists: Michael Powell, son of Colin, was installed as head of the Federal Communications Commission in 2001, serving until 2005. He peeled back rulings on media concentration. He endangered the diversity of voices and opinions on broadband internet, which the ACLU and many US and Canadian media rights organizations considered one of the most important free speech issues of the twenty-first century. Unregulated media transnationals work to control all portals and filter content.

Network news executives bemoaned how to cover a war with no clear enemy; no single location; no beginning, middle or end; no images; no news bureaus in Central Asia; and no advertisers. Executives worried about a war without clear coordinates and a sense of place.[16]

To blast is to infect injuriously.

Ethnic anxieties escalated: Muslim, South Asian, and Arab men were tracked, interrogated, and rounded up on two hundred college campuses. A Muslim woman was subjected to a humiliating body search at O'Hare Airport in Chicago when she refused to remove her head scarf. Visitors from specific countries were put on watch lists to be fingerprinted. In the United States, pro-Palestinian college faculty were targeted.

The Department of Homeland Security, the second-largest federal agency, institutionalized ethnic anxieties. It had more armed federal agents than any other agency. It limited openness and accountability, threatened the Freedom of Information Act, and advanced racial profiling. It had the potential to turn whistleblowers into enemies of the state. The budget allocations for Homeland Security demonstrated that racialization of anxiety can be translated into dollars: the largest budget area, more than fifty times that allocated for twenty-first-century technology, was designated for securing America's border.

On the internet, anti-Osama, anti-Arab gaming sights multiplied into the hundreds. The image of Osama Bin Laden was the most circulated digital skin on the internet for gamers, with George Bush second. These games expressed that which George Bush, whose endless claims that we have no quarrel with the peoples of Afghanistan and Iraq, repress: they were the fantasmatic projection of power over the unknowable, the invisible, and the unfindable. They had titles such as *Bye Bye Bin Laden, The Kill Osama Game, Bend Over Bin Laden, Slap Osama, Capture Bin Laden, Where's Osama Bin Laden Hiding?*, and *Special Ops*. These games displaced the Revolution in Military Affairs. They elaborated the digitalization of warfare with the psychic manifestation of racialized, gendered, and sexualized hatred. These revenge fantasies operated as the psychotic underside of the national phantasmatic that pledged restraint and precision bombing. The user's mouse and keyboard exploded and deleted Arab men, a pathological, racist compulsion.

These interfaces racialized computer keyboards as white, American, male killers for whom linear narrative eroticizes death. Our psychic imaginaries merge with the machineries of war. Touch merges with the fantasy of the screen now figured as Arab, male, silent. The blasts of explosions emanating through audio speakers flood aural space.

To blast is to produce a shockwave.

To blast is hot air on steel to smelt something new.

In the end, I am not sure what shapes our politics and critical art will assume in this slippery, chaotic, authoritarian world. I only know we need both. Echoing the narrative of *Kandahar*, indymedia journalists Jeremy Scahill and Jacquie Soohen traveled to Baghdad to report the invisible story of Iraq through daily webcasts on iraqjournal.org.

Perhaps, through digital art as a prosthesis of hope and a shockwave of peace, we can relearn that if we are alive and not dead, we are all, in fact, limbs of one body.

Notes

1. Mohsen Makhmalbaf, "Limbs of No Body: The World's Indifference to the Afghan Tragedy," *Monthly Review*, accessed February 25, 2018, https://monthlyreview.org/2001/11/01/limbs-of-no-body/.
2. Robert Fisk, "Terror in America," *The Nation*, October 1, 2001, accessed November 12, 2017, https://www.thenation.com/article/terror-america/.
3. Ariel Dorfman, "An Open Letter to America," *Guardian*, September 7, 2002, accessed September 5, 2017, https://www.theguardian.com/world/2002/sep/08/september11.terrorism4; Arundhati Roy, "The Algebra of Infinite Justice," *Guardian*, September 29, 2001, accessed September 5, 2017, https://www.theguardian.com/world/2001/sep/29/september11.afghanistan; Zillah Eisenstein, *Against Empire: Feminisms, Racism and the West* (London: Zed Books, 2004).
4. See Philip Rosen, *Change Mummified: Cinema, Historicity, Theory* (Minneapolis: University of Minnesota Press, 2001).
5. "Excerpts from Pentagon's Plan: 'Prevent the Re-Emergence of a New Rival,'" *New York Times*, March 8, 1992, accessed October 4, 2017, http://www.nytimes.com/1992/03/08/world/excerpts-from-pentagon-s-plan-prevent-the-re-emergence-of-a-new-rival.html?pagewanted=all.
6. For a discussion of George W. Bush's war plans in Iraq, see Ken Auletta, "Fortress Bush," *New Yorker*, January 19, 2004, accessed September 13, 2017, https://www.newyorker.com/magazine/2004/01/19/fortress-bush.
7. Slavoj Žižek, "The Desert of the Real II: Is This the End of Fantasy?" *In These Times*, October 29, 2001, accessed September 13, 2017, http://www.lacan.com/zizekdesertwo.htm.
8. See Ahmed Rashid, *Taliban: Militant Islam, Oil, and Fundamentalism in Central Asia* (New Haven: Yale University Press, 2000).
9. Melanie Goodfellow, "Post-Taliban Production Rebounds," *Variety*, September 16, 2000, 20.
10. Celestine Bohlen, "One Visa Problem Costs a Festival Two Filmmakers," *New York Times*, October 1, 2002, accessed September 13, 2017, http://www.nytimes.com/2002/10/01/movies/one-visa-problem-costs-a-festival-two-filmmakers.html.
11. "Angola: A people trapped in civil war," Medicins San Frontieres, November 1, 2000, accessed September 13, 2017, http://www.msf.org/en/article/angola-people-trapped-civil-war
12. "Surveillance under the Patriot Act," American Civil Liberties Union, accessed September 13, 2017, https://www.aclu.org/issues/national-security/privacy-and-surveillance/surveillance-under-patriot-act
13. Susan Sontag, "Real Battles and Empty Metaphors," *New York Times*, September 10, 2000, accessed September 13, 2017, http://www.nytimes.com/2002/09/10/opinion/real-battles-and-empty-metaphors.html
14. Jim Garamone, "U.S. Commando Solo Takes over Afghan Airwaves," *DOD News*, October 29, 2001, accessed September 13, 2017, http://archive.defense.gov/news/newsarticle.aspx?id=44603
15. "Army Turns to Hollywood for Advice," BBC news, October 8, 2001, accessed September 13, 2017, http://news.bbc.co.uk/2/hi/entertainment/1586468.stm
16. See Douglas Kellner, *From 9/11 to Terror War: The Dangers of the Bush Legacy* (New York: Rowman and Littlefield, 2003).

Figure 9.1. Screenshot from *"Roots of Islam" 9/11 Moments* (Louis Massiah, US, 2001–2002).

9

DIGITAL DEPLOYMENTS*

Deployments

In the twenty-first century, the term independent film requires a serious overhaul and updating. Digital interfaces, platforms, programs, and technologies continue older entertainment industry economic models with their focus on distribution and exhibition, but also open up new formations such as online festivals, Flash, and streaming that reconfigure the relationship between shorts and the feature film industry. In a multiplatformed media landscape that spans broadcasting, film, games, the internet, satellite, video, and video on demand, the divisions between technologies blur as works migrate between different platforms with different interfaces. This migration of media works across technologies, where the

---

* After the attacks on the World Trade Center and the Pentagon in September of 2001, the independent media sphere expanded to digital interfaces, unleashing virulent anti-Arab and anti-Muslim racist shorts in Flash software and streaming as well as oppositional work. Around this time, I noticed independent media was shifting to short forms utilizing new technologies that circulated in email forwards. At the time, I was teaching a large lecture course on Hollywood and American film at Ithaca College, so I was spending significant time thinking about the industry. The course ended with a week about independent film. Nevertheless, as I watched these new short pieces (including very racist pieces) circulate on email, I started to think about how older ideas about independent film could not address these new terrains focused on infiltrating media flows.

Between 2001 and 2006 as the war and racism escalated, I gave several talks that theorized these developments at the Declarations Symposium on Design and the Public Sphere at Concordia University in Montreal, Canada, in October of 2001, and more locally in upstate New York at the Cornell Institute for Public Affairs at Cornell University in February 2002, the University of Rochester in March 2002, and Hobart and William Smith Colleges in April 2002. I also further unpacked these ideas as the invited plenary speaker at the Race in Digital Space Symposium at the Museum of Contemporary Art in Los Angeles, organized by the University of Southern California and MIT (thanks to Tara MacPherson for the invitation). Later, my longtime colleagues Christine Holmlund and Justin Wyatt invited me to write about independent documentary for an edited volume. My essay about this new independent media ecology reworked these talks to create a more systematic argument about how these newly emerging forms both connected to and also suggested change in both Hollywood and independent film histories. The essay was published in *Contemporary American Independent Film*, eds. Christine Holmlund and Justin Wyatt (New York: Routledge, 2006), 245–264.

transnational media corporations function as distributors and exhibitors rather than producers, has also complicated the definitions of the term independent film operating since the 1970s; it is not so easy to draw a line between analog and digital, dominant and oppositional, film and video, profit and nonprofit, as it might have been in 1974. Decades ago, independent media could be identified through its aesthetic, ideological, and structural differences from corporate media: different formal strategies, narrative structures, and voices; nonprofit, oppositional, and political.

Independent film forms a vital part of the entertainment industry, functioning as a way to outsource risk, innovation, and project development. As a result of concentration, conglomeration, and risk aversion, the transnational media corporate economy has instituted a more horizontal business model based on exploiting a transindustrial and transtechnological environment where flexibility is achieved through outsourcing production and where production costs are reduced through endless repurposing of archives into different platforms. Whether corporate, independent, or oppositional, media across all forms function in circulatory networks typified by constant movement between platforms, users, and different economies of scale (big budget tentpole films, independent features, and digital shorts). The independent film sector has transformed into a vital wing of the transnational entertainment industry, integral to propelling innovation, a place to outsource risk to achieve higher profit margins.

This essay is a provisional redefinition of independent film by triangulating four intersecting salient formations of exhibition within the transindustrial economy. It attempts to map how this economy interacts with and relies on independent narrative modes within its complex, multilayered digital environment. It explores the dependencies between the media transnationals and the independent film sector; Flash animation as a pervasive software program unique to the web; the reinstitution of exhibition as a major feature of the transnational media sector's retailing of media products; and streaming technologies as a site to track the conflation between production and distribution in the digital realm, which may provide more access for independents in point-to-point exhibition. These four sectors provide different altitudes from which to assess the changes in distribution and exhibition as the analog and digital combine and intertwine. Each one demonstrates that independent narrative film needs to be redefined as a form of cinema that moves across different platforms and through different audiences and economies, rather than the more static model of a feature-length film on celluloid that plays in theaters and film festivals. These four sectors elaborate the impact and realignments that new digital technologies precipitate in the indie landscape; they offer a contradictory environment of increased concentration mixed simultaneously with increased access. As two modalities unique to digital networked media of the web, Flash and streaming are important because they suggest the imagined broadening of the indie scene from features to shorts. These two technologies also evidence how the retail aspect of film exhibition is not only multiplatformed across analog and digital, but also multiple in terms of how it addresses spectators as either groups assembled in a theater or individuals sitting at their computer terminals.

This horizontally networked universe that extends from the analog world of theaters and the digital domains of online festivals, Flash, and streaming presents a vast landscape that is simultaneously global, regional, local, and individual. One way to examine its operations and practices is to focus on how independent filmmakers have represented the events of September 11 and the subsequent war on terror. Digital interfaces offer affordances of a rapid response to world events. Media artists can enlist digital platforms as a way to insert their point of view into the horizontal circulatory networks of transnational media practices, a major difference from previous political events like the Gulf War, the civil wars in Central America, or the Vietnam War, where independent media networks worked in opposition to the absences of dominant media by creating different networks of production and distribution that often operated like parallel universes to the entertainment industry.

Media artists produced a variety of documentary and experimental shorts to memorialize the trauma of the attack and the ensuing war on terror, such as curator Jay Rosenblatt's *Underground Zero* (2002) project, a four-hour compilation of short narrative, documentary, and experimental media artists' responses to the World Trade Center and Pentagon bombings. The enlistment of these digital interfaces—by both antiwar and prowar movements—demonstrates how digital technologies together with networked communications offered rapid responses to world events within circulatory networks via Flash animation, streaming, and websites. However, these new technologies and emerging interfaces are not just new ways for progressive voices and cultural difference to be heard. As this essay will argue, these technologies have also functioned as a kind of a return of the repressed, expressing racism and xenophobia prohibited in corporate multiculturalized domains of the commercial media, a warning to media theorists that not all oppositional discourse or new technologies are progressive.

Fluid Exchanges

A significant reorganization between the American independent film movement and the corporate entertainment industry happened in the 1990s as mergers created media corporations with economies larger than many nations. It is important to unpack the new relationship between the independent film sector and the transnational media sector in order to begin to see how this horizontal, flat business model has opened up the opportunity for more fluid exchanges among different economic sectors of media production. With the advent of digital video, it seemed that anyone could make a feature. This lightweight, small digital technology created the fantasy of a newly democratized realm of feature production that had been inaccessible.

In the early twenty-first century, the independent film scene in the United States has morphed into a multifaceted, diverse sector of the entertainment economy. In the decades since landmark indies like *The War at Home* (1979) and *Northern Lights* (1978), the independent film sector has grown exponentially. Currently, it defines American film and operates as a testing ground for new technologies like video, digital video, streaming, gaming, and digital interfaces. Digital video is viewed as providing low-cost access that democratizes the means of film production. Many feature-length narratives and documentaries were produced in this format and then dumped to 35mm for distribution, like Lars Van Triers's *Dancer in the Dark* (2000) or Mike Figgis's *Time Code* (1999). In the realm of the independent feature, digital video productions increased significantly; at the 2000 Independent Feature Film Market, 43 percent of the works were DV.[1]

Digital video is often described—at least in the DV magazines (see www.dv.com/magazine)—as a technology that lowers the barriers to making independents competitive with the studios and networks. However, the history of amateur media technologies suggests that although low-end technologies extend production beyond corporations, larger social and economic contexts interact with these technologies to create significant contradictions.[2] On the one hand, digital video is cheaper and lighter-weight than 35mm Panavision. On the other hand, the transnational media corporations exert a stranglehold on the industry: as global cartels, they cordon off access to distribution and exhibition because they own every form of interface from cable to DVD, theaters, video stores, and even internet portals.[3] No matter how many DV cameras circulate and how many new film festivals sprout up, the ability to compete against this massive global distribution oligopoly in terms of print costs, marketing, advertising and product tie-ins is minimal.

With international films and art cinemas in precipitous decline due to multiplexing and increased nationalization of exhibition, independent exhibitors call American indie films "art films without subtitles." According to Kenneth Turan, fewer foreign-language films are shown on American screens than at in any time in US history.[4] Yet, compared to two decades ago, independent films have proliferated in former art cinemas. Functioning as alternative exhibition networks, film festivals mushroomed in the 1990s, with almost every major city in the United States hosting one.[5] Rather than thinking in terms of a binary opposition of corporate entertainment versus indie films—a hangover from the 1970s vision of dominant and alternative media—it might be more analytically productive to move toward a metaphor of a three-dimensional integrated digital structure, with constantly moving, interdependent layers.

In a vertically and horizontally integrated entertainment economy in finance, organization, integration, and operation, indies serve a dual purpose. On the one hand, they are the farm team for entry into the majors of Hollywood cinema and to economic rewards as a director/producer. On the other hand, the discourse around independent film shrouds its acquisitive careerism in its outré status. Much indie narrative emphasizes character development and represses digital imaging that so defines the visual look of big-budget media even as these films use digital video, Avids, and Final Cut Pro. In opposition to the rapid-fire plotting, special-effects-heavy, blockbuster tentpole films with marketing tie-ins like *Minority Report* (2002) or *Spiderman* (2002), indie narrative film sustains the mythology that characters, dialogue, and complex narrative structures actually matter. They constitute a reactionary specter of the golden age of Hollywood where studio-based writers and directors created films with real actors, dialogue, and plot.

Despite increased access to the means of film production provided by new technologies, a digital divide remains in the entertainment industry between transnational corporate technological innovation for global market domination and independent feature production and distribution. Two kinds of digital deployment exist. On the one hand, all effects in major studio productions are digital. Cost savings and labor management factors offered by digital technologies for postproduction are attractive to studio financial analysts. On the studio end, digital technology has been deployed primarily for postproduction and special effects, solidifying corporate control and protecting their global market by maintaining high barriers to entry. Historically, studios viewed technological innovation as profit maximization, and digital special effects continue this trajectory. On the other hand, for independent features, digital video operates as a grassroots movement for access to low-budget narrative. Thomas Vinterberg (*The Celebration*) and Gary Winick (*Tadpole*) accentuate emotional realism with DV.[6]

In the early 1990s, transnational entertainment complexes reorganized into global distribution entities operating across technologies. In this context, independent narrative film provides a way to outsource production risk and to cultivate new talent and product without investment. A *Variety* article detailing the deal between James Schamus of Good Machine—an indie art film producer of *The Ice Storm* (1997) and *Crouching Tiger, Hidden Dragon* (2000)—and Universal to form a new entity called Focus points out that "major studios continue to invest in the specialty arena and not just for the prestige factor: At a time when production and marketing costs are spiraling upwards, they're nixing midrange pics in favor of event films that cost more than $80 million and nice films that cost less than $10 million, many of which come with foreign financing and minimal risk."[7] Because media transnationals hit niche markets through low-budget indie film and because no independent feature can recoup costs without corporate distribution, *Variety* mused that indies were the new "dependies."[8]

However, beyond distribution deals for niche films, a more variegated indie political economy has evolved since the early 1990s. This new ecosystem is not easy to track. The independent scene is more interdependent than trade papers suggest: it entails relationships between independent ventures and corporate media, emerging exhibition formations, new technologies, and the public media sector. Neither the valorization of incipient online democratic vistas nor "end of cinema as we know it" negativity sufficiently explain the relationship between digitality and independent cinema. In the early 2000s, digitalization solidified older transnational media formations but also offered new public media possibilities. As a result, the independent media sector changed significantly from the late 1970s. In the 1970s and 1980s, indies fought to gain access to public television and theater screens, public monies supported production and infrastructure, and independent meant opposition to dominant culture.

The indie sector that has emerged since the late 1970s has always combined both commercial and nonprofit media, ranging from films produced by celebrated art cinema directors like Jane Campion, Ang Lee, Todd Haynes, and Sam Mendes, to low-end digital video/streaming features like *The Last Broadcast* (1998), the first film to be digitally exhibited (www.tebweb.com/lastbroadcast). Political documentaries employing new digital technologies such as *Zapatista* (1999), *This Is What Democracy Looks Like* (2000), and *9/11* (2001) from the Big Noise Film Collective were self-distributed through websites. Short three-minute live action and Flash animation works crowd online film festivals. A range of political and experimental work in documentary, narrative, and hybrid forms migrated across technologies and distribution platforms. The lines of demarcation between different cinematic practices, however, are fluid. For example, the Independent Television Service (ITVS) and HBO, a subsidiary of AOL/Time Warner, financed a large number of award-winning features and documentaries at the prestigious 2002 Sundance Film Festival.

In this tangled environment, it is misleading to characterize the independent film scene with terms like profit/not-for-profit, film/video, or analog/digital. Emerging technologies, distribution platforms, political communities, and fluidity between formerly distinct sectors erase these binaries. The online film festival world provides a case study. Commercial media parodies of films ranging from *Star Wars* (1977) to almost any commercial release have emerged as a salient genre online, suggesting that binary oppositions are no longer descriptive. Instead, all media productions—even independent film—repurpose and remediate themselves across a range of formats and forms for various niche market segments in a multiplatformed media environment.

Retail

Exhibition emerges as an important node for an analysis of the shifting terrain of independent film in relation to digitality. Despite the mass-produced fantasies manufactured by most film schools and film magazines that production constitutes the most exciting and important part of the independent film world, exhibition—the place where profit is produced—has functioned as the economic powerhouse of the entertainment industry since the early days of the film studios. With the infusion of digital platforms in the 1990s and early twenty-first century, exhibition platforms multiplied beyond brick-and-mortar multiplex theaters into DVD, VCD, and web-based festivals that deliver point-to-point access to media. Although digital delivery within the context of the transnational media industry was in its formative period and still unclear, the industry's interest in broadband was directly connected to its awareness of the importance of multiple exhibition venues.

Film exhibition is the retail end of the film business. With twenty-first-century convergence and proliferating analog and digital platforms, film exhibition is no longer about selling movies in a theater. Rather, films are not the end product: they are nodal points of the circulation of many commodities. Film historian Tino Balio has elaborated this shift from cinema as text to cinema as a part of a commodity chain by analyzing the development of films that become franchise products. Large blockbusters with product tie-ins are dubbed tentpoles.[9] The difference between a studio production and an independent production no longer resides in production values, narrative structure, or casting but in distribution, exhibition, marketing, and product tie-ins. The major studios are massive marketing machines insuring global product domination and thousands of screens, while independent works are simply films-as-finite-texts, confined to limited distribution and exhibition. Within this economy, the late 1990s short film boom was simultaneously presenting calling-card films to get filmmakers access to the industry and doing eighteen- to thirty-four-year-old white males niche marketing.

Digital technologies like Flash animation, digital video, and streaming blur the borders between production, distribution, and exhibition. Although digital technologies lower distribution and exhibition barriers, they were plagued by moving image compression for streaming, limited broadband access, and slow downloads in the early 2000s. However, these technical limitations stimulated short film internet exhibition: three-minute films load faster and conform better to web surfing. The short film environment should not be confused with art cinema, the avant-garde, or underground film; it has more in common with pop songs and other popular culture formations.[10] As Dion Algeri of the now-defunct www.shortbuzz.com argued, internet films not only appealed to teenage boys, but served as anti-TV, focusing on sex, violence, and humor unsuitable for commercial television or cable.[11]

The online festival sector is also distinct from the independent film festival circuit. It focuses almost exclusively on shorts under three minutes, adapting to technological limitations and reception issues unique to computing and interfaces. Although the online sites primarily feature work by unknown directors without a studio affiliation, many feature film directors like James Brooks, Tom Burton, Mike Figgis, Spike Lee, David Lynch, and Barry Sonnenfield directed works specifically for the online environment, their cult status providing a marketing cachet to these sites.[12]

Most significantly, the online cinema business models illustrate the intertwining of independent work and commercial transnational studios as well as digital and analog exhibition. Atom Films is a prime example, as they not only ran shorts online, but also sold them to HBO, Warner Brothers OnLine, Continental Airlines, Blockbuster, and the Sundance Channel. The company worked with Lucasfilm to encourage fans to submit Star Wars spoofs on their site without fear of cease-and-desist letters.[13] However, it would be misleading to characterize Atom Films as a stand-alone independent. Although it functioned like an old media studio with distribution to a variety of markets, it operated more like a "dependie," with financial backing from merchant bank Allen and Company, Warner Brothers, and former Viacom and Universal Studios CEO Frank Biondi.[14] Ifilm (www.ifilm.com), a prominent online cinema site, moved from San Francisco to Los Angeles in 2000, financed by Microsoft Corporation billionaire Paul Allen; Kodak Corporation; Shamrock Capital Advisors, the investment vehicle for Roy Disney; and Sony.[15]

As mentioned earlier, exhibition constitutes the retail end of the film business, the point of sale where people meet the screen and money meets the film business. Film exhibition is a capitalist product where the customer pays in advance before using the commodity.[16] However, in the postmerger environments of the late 1990s, distribution and exhibition across different technologies, platforms, and spaces are the key to media transnational economic power, according to media political economist Janet Wasko.[17] On the one hand, digital technologies' capacity for lossless reproduction presents a major threat to copyright, the largest US export.[18] On the other hand, the digitalization of production in Hollywood big-budget film further empowered producers who could control the image in postproduction and reduce labor costs.

Aida Hozic argues that the historiography of the Hollywood entertainment industry can be reconceptualized as a relationship between space and power, rather than simply product differentiation. She identifies three periods/places of Hollywood hegemony: Hollywood in the studio, Hollywood on location, and Hollywood in cyberspace. Hozic's contribution to theorizing a political economy of the entertainment industry moves from an analysis of industry practices such as business operations, film aesthetics, marketing, and reception toward the specificity of spatial relations as material mappings of hegemonic power. The notion of spatial relations "defines the boundaries of what is private and what is public; what is visible and what is concealed; what is imagined and what is real" marking "the boundaries of politics."[19]

The studio period featured mass production, censorship, controlled environments, the Fordist structures of the vertically integrated studio, self-regulation, social control of actors, and surveillance. The location period after World War II signaled a shift toward more dispersed locales for more horizontally integrated companies due to factors such as the 1948 Paramount antitrust decrees, the crisis in export markets, increased labor costs, and the rise of talent agents in the 1950s and 1960s. For Hozic, the third period of Hollywood hegemony marks a distinctive shift away from location to cyberspace, where Hollywood and the military merge in digital technologies for special effects, now dubbed dual-purpose technologies for both civilian and military usage. She argues that the entertainment industry's digital conversion arose out of conflict between producers on the one hand and financiers, distributors, and agents on the other. For example, George Lucas and Steven Spielberg were early adopters of digital technologies in the science fiction realm, a genre the studios tended to ignore. They asserted producer's rights by replacing A-list stars with digital special effects. They led the way for industry digitalization by demonstrating how digital effects rendered the most expensive part of the production process such as sets, costumes, stunts, and location shooting unnecessary. Hozic emphasizes that the Hollywood in cyberspace period is organized around distribution rather than production technologies.[20]

Home digital projection advanced at record rates with the accelerated penetration of DVD. New technologies are not so much a threat to celluloid as they are indications of the multiplication of exhibition into many formats. Consequently, the much heralded possibilities of DV to lower barriers to entry into commercial production were most likely exaggerated, despite increasing numbers of DV works blown up to 35mm, as evidenced at the 2002 Sundance Film Festival. Despite the proliferation of DV, the large media transnationals continued to control the retail end of the business in all sectors, making it difficult for independent filmmakers to penetrate.[21]

Beyond the domains of the corporate media transnationals, a parallel world operated. Located in universities, media arts centers, museums, and film festivals, public media practices that promote public culture and artistic and intellectual exchange rather than commodity exchange and digital conversion challenged production, distribution, and exhibition. A major Ford Foundation study sponsored by the National Alliance for Media Arts and Culture called *Digital Directions: Conversion Planning for the Media Arts* convened independent producers and public media programmers from across the country to debate the impact of digital conversion on the independent sector.[22] With interfaces changing so rapidly and expensive start-up costs, technological change has threatened to destabilize the chronically underfunded public media sector.

Media arts organizations saw changes from their former mission to show work not typically accessible in commercial culture and to provide media services to the underserved. Their missions broadened from aesthetics and access to media to more hybrid sources of education and training in new technologies for underserved communities. The digital divide translated as more than access to equipment, but access to digital and computer knowledge and skills, an important part of twenty-first-century cultural capital. Collaboration became essential, and the emerging digital economies of the public media sector required development of public/private partnerships. Further, networked communication technologies created productive fluidities between local, national, and global organizations. New infrastructures for broadband, servers, and routes for interactive communications had to be developed. In the recalibrated independent media environment, the boundaries between public and private, between digital and analog, and between production and distribution became indistinct, creating unexplored territories for independent production.

In this media environment, the construct of the director making an artisanal work seemed as outdated as the feature film production line in Hollywood. Horizontally organized teams, cross-fertilization among people with different kinds of skills and knowledge, flexible and fluid organizational models, and multiple distribution and exhibition modes altered the independent media landscape from the film/video product to a multiplicity of iterations and interfaces in a range of exhibition environments.[23]

Because of limited broadband access, the media transnationals were slow to enter the online or on-demand digital sector. However, a major legislative and political battle unfolded between independent producers, media activists, and the Federal Communications Commission over two central issues: media concentration, which limited the diversity of voices and opportunities for independents as previous rulings on ownership were revoked; and media transnationals, particularly cable companies' entry into broadband, which threatened open access and unlimited, uncensored voices on the internet. The American Civil Liberties Union (ACLU) and the Center for Digital Democracy argued that "broadband is the free speech issue of the twenty-first century."[24] Independent producers, scholars, media reformers, and media activists formed broad-based coalitions to fight concentration and cable companies' broadband control, which advanced corporate monoculture but narrowed outlets for independents and inhibited a diversity of viewpoints.[25]

Flash Wars

While online festivals for digitized analog shorts presented a new exhibition formation within the digital networks for independent shorts producers, another digital formation in exhibition emerged that conflated production and distribution into a software created specifically to bypass slow downloads for moving images on the web: Flash. Flash appeared on virtually every website where images moved; it was one of the most pervasive software systems on the internet. The quick downloads of Flash works and their ability to circulate virally through email networks functioned as an important manifestation of the independent media rapid response to the war on terror that utilized point-to-point peer networks circulated through forwarded emails, websites, and online portals.

One to three minutes long to adjust to streaming capabilities, online films frequently used Flash animation with easily downloadable files. Atomfilms.com, ifilms.com, and madblast.com offered shockingly racist independently produced shorts about Osama Bin Laden, the war in Afghanistan, the war against terror, and Arabs. The war on terror and the commodification of patriotism became niche markets along with lesbian, gay, science fiction, comedy, spoofs, and other targeted works. Bin Laden, Al Qaeda, and the Taliban were not only enemies of the United States, but distinctive genres with identifiable characteristics and narrative patterns in these online environments. Many of these shorts mobilized a vengeful, jingoistic patriotism. They installed a dangerous binary opposition through a narrative structure featuring America versus the other. They demonized Arabs, the Middle East, the Taliban, and Osama Bin Laden as inept primitives. They made manifest President George W. Bush's and Donald Rumsfeld's covert racialized revenge fantasies that heads of state cannot state publicly.

Slow downloads, lack of general availability of broadband, and problems transferring between platforms and software applications challenged both studio websites pumping up blockbuster anticipation and independent online festivals. Flash animation software resolved the problem of creating moving-image media with sound in this transitional digital environment. Flash is vector based on mathematical formulas rather than pixels, facilitating easy download. It can transfer between web, mobile phones, movie screens, broadcast, and gaming platforms.[26]

Unlike video, Flash streamed better over a modem because it was not compressed and had infinite resolution. It was designed specifically for the web to provide the most television-like appearance.[27] It was initially shown at the 1995 Siggraph Conference, an annual gathering of computer artists and animators, and sold to Future Wave Software and then Macromedia in 1996. Macromedia Flash was the most distributed software in the history of the web, with 96 percent of web desktops using some Flash.[28] Flash appeared on many commercial websites, but it also attracted an underground cult following among college students, office workers, and political activists.

The software was designed to attract PC web surfers. Flash animations veered toward bawdy comedy and visual jokes. Using bold primary colors and simple drawings, Flash did not easily lend itself to social realist documentaries or complex argumentation. Its strength resided in making things move with a bare-boned narrative causality with music for effect. Much Flash animation on the web was humorous. More conceptual artistic work such as pieces produced by Freerangegraphics.com for progressive political groups like Greenpeace and the ACLU emerged with great impact and visibility. Many Flash animators such as freerangegraphics.com or Mark Fiore emerged from graphic design and political cartooning. Flash animation's flat images differed significantly from the commercial digital animation of *Toy Story* (1995) or *Antz* (1998), which continued tropes of cinematic realism and immediacy through 3D modeling, depth, texture, lighting, and an adherence to narrative cinematic language in shot design and story editing.[29] Instead, war on terror Flash animations represented an iteration of wartime Hollywood propaganda animation. During World War II when most studio production aligned with the US government, Warner Brothers animations applied a similar reductionist and simplistic schemata to mobilize patriotic goals in Bugs Bunny and Daffy Duck wartime cartoons. Frank Capra's *Prelude to War* (1942) utilized a Disney-style animation of black ink spreading across the globe to illustrate Axis expansion.[30]

Flash animations about the war on terror remediated historical propaganda modes to marshal nationalist sentiment. Defined by Jay David Bolter and Richard Grusin as reprocessing and incorporating legacy media into digital works for critical intervention or refashioning, remediation invokes the real with emotional responses and the repression of interface. Remediation resides less in postmodern surface play than in repurposing older analog media forms.[31] Flash animations about the war on terror repurposed nineteenth-century flat graphic newspaper-style cartoons and reenlisted classical Hollywood narrative structure from World War II–era cartoons. Although they addressed the war on terror, the films simplified complex geopolitics into a reductionist narrative, stimulating an emotional response by reprocessing historical propaganda forms from World War II. However, their interactive and privatized multimedia distribution platforms suggested that their exhibition interface rather than their software was what distinguished them as digital works.

The most prowar, anti-Arab narratives appeared on Madblast.com, a Flash animation portal. Unlike a conventional brick-and-mortar theater, Madblast Flash movies arrived on computers in viral interfaces to create wide market diffusion through personal networks. Each Flash piece ended with an option to forward to a friend by clicking a box and inserting an email address. Most Madblast Flash animations were extremely short two-minute-long visual jokes about sex, violence, bodily functions, or gender stereotypes with titles like *Beefcake for the Ladies, Mona Lisa's Naughty Secret, The Groovin' Granny Song, Sending You Some Crap, Let's Be Naughty like Adam and Eve*.

The war on terror supplied Madblast with a source for a cartoon cast of characters such as Osama Bin Laden, Al Qaeda, and the Taliban. Anti–Bin Laden and anti-Taliban Flash were featured prominently on the homepage after

September 11, 2001. These Flash animations portrayed stereotypical Arab iconography of beards and flowing robes. They linked these racialized, reductive, iconic representations to US military power; nearly every Flash on the war concluded with the destruction of Bin Laden or the Taliban. In a post-9/11 psychic landscape where out-of-control technology and terror loomed large and invisible, these works facilitated a compensational fantasy of control, revenge, and reimaging.

Dubbed "classic Flash" and featured in an NPR story and many online festival web sites, *Bin Laden Nowhere to Run, Nowhere to Hide* emerged as a notorious response to the war on terror. The three-minute Flash animation spliced the Calypso-inspired Harry Belafonte song *Day-O* with new prowar lyrics. The narrative offered a racialized binary opposition. In the Flash, we see Bush playing congas while Colin Powell croons about the war, intercut with Osama Bin Laden hopping between hills and caves. Cartoon-like images of George W. Bush, Colin Powell and Osama Bin Laden were created by splicing analog photos to digital bodies. Parallel editing between Colin Powell/Bush and Bin Laden in Afghanistan mapped binary oppositions between the United States and Afghanistan, Bush and Bin Laden, high technology and primitive caves.

The storyline purges psychoanalytic repression with a single objective: kill Bin Laden. The song exclaims: "George Bush say revenge come, daylight come and we drop the bomb. Come Mr. Taliban hand over Bin Laden, Colin Powell going to bomb his home, cruise missile knocking at your door." The narrative concludes with obliteration of the other; in the final image, a missile destroys the earth. Afterward, a box pops up to forward the Flash animation. *Nowhere to Run, Nowhere to Hide* visualized, popularized, and animated Bush's war on terror. It channeled hatred into fantasies of active agency and control over the future, nationalizing psychic economics of military superiority. *Nowhere to Run, Nowhere to Hide* conflated narrative resolution, sexual climax, mouse movement, violence, and xenophobic patriotism into one large blast.

The Madblast Flash animations demonstrate how independent cinema in the new media era can splice together old media screens with new media screens as a way to create stability within the flux of multiple windows, constant interaction, and the migration of data across computers and databases. Lev Manovich argues that the construct of the screen has undergone three periods of change: the classical screen of perspectival painting, the dynamic screen of the first one hundred years of cinema, and the interactive screen of the computer with its emphasis on interface and multiple screens.[32] These Flash animations straddled the classical screen and the interactive screen. On the one hand, their visual design and narrative structures deployed binary oppositions and invoked American nationalism, evoking classical Hollywood narrative to suggest a more stable and predictable historical modality. Similarly, their short form recalled the early years of primitive cinema with its short one-reel structure. On the other hand, their interface operated as a node within the new media environment of networked, circulatory media, where images migrate between multiple screens. Their narrative structures connoted the historical past of classical cinema while their interface traced the historical present of interactive networked computer media. Finally, their imaginary ironic scenarios project a history of the future.

Streaming Indies

While online festivals served as clearing houses for a range of analog and digital video shorts, and Flash operated as a way to present moving images without the download problems latent in networks, streaming technologies presented another sector of exhibition that offered new and different possibilities for independents, particularly in the context of the war on terror because they mixed analog and digital, cyberspace and real space. For antiwar and antiracist media activists, streaming offered a way to traverse different sectors of the media environment to address different kinds of audiences and communities without resorting to broadcasting or more traditional exhibition.

As exemplified in *Nowhere to Run, Nowhere to Hide* as well as myriad other sites with shorts on the nationalistic response to the war on terror, the utilization of the linear, resolved, transparent storyline, a form of condensed classical Hollywood narrative cinema, drove most of the online screen world in Flash and gaming sites. These works projected a US-dominated future of infinite war. They expressed the revenge and hatred that mass media's distanced discourse of sobriety suppressed. While CNN and Fox News ran 3D digitally composited layers of flags and weaponry, they did not openly express racialized hatreds. However, the online independent environment was not confined to militaristic, nationalistic, racism—which might have led theorists and analysts to link digitality to regressive reactionary politics—but also included investigative journalism, interrogations into racism, and alternative news and documentaries, modes that recouped the potentialities of the digital for democratization of media access and the pluralization of discourses.

In response to the war on terror, a plethora of independent media projects in the documentary and muckraking journalism genre emerged. This work employed a realist documentary aesthetic rather than imaginary narrative projections. Its epistemological structure deemphasized unity, hatred, racism, and binary oppositions. Instead, it elaborated the complexities and pluralities of difference through regions, ethnic groups, national identities, and histories. Rather than focusing on an imaginary future, these works threaded historical understanding into the present.

These projects were streamed video rather than Flash animation. Streaming refers to the conversion of analog media (movies or audio) for internet communications. Due to the large file size of moving images, files must be compressed to be viewed, converting information into the smallest files to reduce the size of artifacts. Streaming allows a file to be played before the download is completed. Although constantly confronting lost image parts, slow downloads, and length, streaming provided independent media a distribution and exhibition advantage as it moved toward a model of narrowcasting.[33] Streaming could show moving images and audio on the internet for wider distribution. In the 1990s and early 2000s, 80 percent of computer users used dial-up, with lower capacity for larger image and sound files than broadband on T1, DSL, or cable modem. Rather than shipping video to venues, streaming allowed users to sample independent media. As John Carr from www.konscious.com, an independent media site, explained, "Streaming allows you to bypass the traditional means of distribution."[34]

Three different initiatives emerging in the post-9/11 environment pointed to streaming's potential to create viral environments for antiwar, antiracist work outside mass media distribution. Streaming had the potential to generate political consciousness and action by producing networked exhibition. As an interface, it offered an expandable archive of accessible, downloadable, and mutable media.

In 2002, the Independent Television Service (ITVS), one of the largest funders for independent film in the United States, commissioned nine independent producers (Dan Bergin, Lena Carr, Hector Galan, Joan Mandell, Louis Massiah, Sam Pollard, Ellen Spiro/Karen Bernstein, Termite TV Collective, and Kyung Sun Yu) to produce minute-long responses to September 11 titled *A 9/11 Moment*. The press release noted, "We are redefining ways of looking at ourselves as American and at others in our global community. To promote understanding and compassion in our communities around the country, we look to independent media producers to speak about the sudden changes in our lives."[35] Thirty-four sixty-second spots were offered to PBS stations to air by November 23, 2002. The spots were also streamed on the ITVS website.

The 9/11 moments project offered a variety of voices across the United States who expressed outrage, fear, sadness, pain, loss, mapping a complexity of responses. Navajo filmmaker Lena Carr produced *Quintera Yazzie*, where an eleven-year-old Navajo girl reflects on the events she witnessed at school. Joan Mandell, an artist with extensive experience collaborating with Arab communities, made *Scout Leader*, where a Michigan Boy Scout leader, Khalil Baydoun, and his teenage scouts describe being unjustly accused of being suspicious characters. In *This Is Not a John Wayne Movie*, Ellen Spiro and Karen Bernstein filmed columnist Molly Ivins commenting on the support of America's European allies around 9/11, despite the vast cultural differences between Texans and the French. Louis Massiah's *Flag* interviewed Philadelphians pondering the varied meanings of flags displayed after 9/11. These spots elaborated the multicultural pluralities of

American responses in contrast to nationalist cable and network responses. They functioned as historical records of the multiplicity of voices responding to these events. The short form facilitated streaming for a web-distribution system traveling between digital and analog: the spots were available online for preview, and could also be broadcast on public television between programs.

The www.konsicous.com site called *9/11 and Beyond: Independent Voices Speak*, identified as "voices of the people, from the streets," included twenty-five streamed pieces ranging from two minutes to twenty-eight minutes from groups such as Konscious, the War and Peace D Word Collaborative Project, and the Third World Newsreel Call to Media Action. Downtown Community Television's trailer, *Afghanistan: From Ground Zero to Ground Zero*, tracks a young Afghani woman who travels from New York to Afghanistan in the aftermath of her family's death in US raids. *Invisible Girl*, by Angela Alston, looks at how a Palestinian American girl in New York confronts the aftereffects of the World Trade Center bombings. From the Third World Newsreel collection, Kevin Lee's *New York Chinatown 9/11* looks at how the World Trade Center bombings affected Chinatown.

Konscious.com functioned as a portal (a gateway for other related sites) for works in response to the war on terror. Their special feature on 9/11 attracted the most hits of any project on their alternative progressive web site. However, like ITVS, the Konscious strategy was not limited to the internet. It included a move to real spaces. Konscious curated selections from their website for Anthology Film Archives, the Culture Project, and Manhattan Neighborhood Network. They shared programs with the Free Speech network to upload the videos to satellite. Unlike the more rabid prowar Flash animations that survived only in the privatized internet netherworld, these antiwar works migrated between screens and exhibition venues and between digital and analog to build multiple public spatialities.

Stories from the ground that counteracted commercial news-media war hysteria provided an exposé of the proposed war. Www.iraqjournal.org, a project by independent journalists Jeremy Scahill and Jacquie Soohen in conjunction with WORT in Madison, Wisconsin, collapsed distinctions between production, distribution, exhibition, and reception. As the world community debated war in Iraq, and Congress authorized war, iraqjournal.org webcasted from inside Iraq. The project supplied a different kind of storytelling than the anti-Osama Flash animations that mobilized hatred; it concentrated on specifics of everyday life in Iraq as a result of the sanctions. The site featured downloadable text-based news stories, deep background, audio reports, and video reports.

An evidentiary cinema, these handheld DV videos wove an alternative archive to the images of weapons inspection. They created representations from inside so-called enemy territory, dislodging nationalistic revenge fantasies. With iraqjournal.org, digital warfare occupied networks, circulating stories that connected people across the globe using viral marketing techniques like passing on links to websites and Flash animations via email—a political agency-provoking assault against the mobilization of hatred in other online environments. Iraqjournal.org suggested that information, documentary visions, and new technologies could function as instruments of hope rather than machines of death.

Targets

Digital technologies simultaneously fortified old patterns in the entertainment industry that secure profit through the control of exhibition *and* created new spaces for a different kind of independent producer to create different discourses within different interfaces. Digital technologies solidified concentration in the exhibition sector at the same time that they opened up and expanded the exhibition sector with online festivals, Flash, and streaming. The interdependent relationship between independent film and the media transnationals suggests that media critics need to more closely examine the economic structures and business models of these new entertainment-industry behemoths that feed on indie work as they look at narrative and theoretical models to analyze the films themselves. It is no longer possible to talk about the film industry as a stand-alone entity, nor is it possible to conflate independent film with feature-length filmmaking. Digital technologies such as DV, Flash, streaming, online festivals, and web portals demonstrate the importance of thinking *across* technologies, sectors, industries, and audience formations. In other words, the transindustrial media environment of multiple platforms and repurposed remediated media migrating across and between different formations requires that indie media be reconceptualized within a variety of production and exhibition interfaces and forms. To understand the significance of independent film in both its analog and digital formations of features and shorts and in its prowar and antiwar standpoints, it is necessary to see that the multiple sectors of indie production are now in constant movement, migration, and mixing, rather than in a single location of opposition.

In the context of the war on terror, digitality offered a means of rapid response formerly reserved for the vast resources commanded by commercial networks. Rather than broadcasting, digitality also presented a different model of exhibition in point-to-point narrowcasting that circulated through its viral marketing. However, it is important to be sober about the possibilities that digitality offered indies. Although the oppositions between dominant and oppositional media that fueled the antiwar movements during Vietnam, the incursions in Central America, and the Gulf War no longer help us to triangulate and to map the much more variegated and complex indie media scene of the twenty-first century, their histories of successes and failures to mobilize public opinion and widen debate sustain serious reminders that in the end, technologies are only as significant as the social and political movements that deploy and then reimagine them as means to produce spaces for critique and resistance.

Notes

1. Bart Cheever, "D-Film and Internet Distribution," Digital Cinema Symposium, Massachusetts Institute of Technology, Cambridge, MA, November 6, 2000.
2. For a discussion and analysis of the development of amateur film and its ideology of democratic liberation and competitive possibilities, see Patricia R. Zimmermann, *Reel Families: A Social History of Amateur Film* (Bloomington: Indiana University Press, 1995).
3. For a detailed analysis of the power of the media transnational in the areas of distribution, exhibition, and acquisitions of new technologies, see Toby Miller, Nitin Govil, John McMurria, and Richard Maxwell, *Global Hollywood* (London: British Film Institute Publishing, 2001), 146–171.
4. Kenneth Turan, *Sundance to Sarajevo: Film Festivals and the World They Made* (Berkeley: University of California Press, 2002), 31–48, 160–168.
5. Turan, *Sundance to Sarajevo*, 31–48.
6. Jonathon Bing, "H'W'D's Old Spool Ties," *Variety*, August 19–25, 2002, 1, 24.
7. Jonathon Bing, "Will U's Focus Prove Blurry?" *Variety*, July 1–14, 2002, 1.
8. Charles Lyons, "New Machine Comes into Focus," *Variety*, May 13–19, 1, 11.
9. Tino Balio, *Hollywood in the New Millennium* (London: Palgrave Macmillan, 2013), 25–60.
10. David Sterritt, "Short Film Festival Quick Flicks Are No Longer Getting the Short End of the Stick Thanks to Internet Exposure," *Christian Science Monitor*, August 11, 2000, 13.
11. Dion Algeri,"Economics of Short Film Distribution on the Internet," Digital Cinema Conference, Massachusetts Institute of Technology, Cambridge, MA, November 3, 2000.
12. Frank Houston, "Hollywood Flirts with Short Films on the Web," *New York Times*, June 15, 2000, G13.
13. Jonathon Webdale, "Atom Film Hopes to Deliver a Shock to the Media System," *New Media Age*, March 1, 2001, 36.
14. Mary Louis Harding, "Now Showing: Shorts," *New Media Age*, September 30, 1999, 3.
15. Greg Miller, "Internet Movie Firm Shifts Focus to LA: New Media Flush with $35 Million in New Investment Capital," *Los Angeles Times*, January 25, 2000, c1.
16. See Gregory A. Waller, ed., *Moviegoing in America* (Malden, MA: Blackwell, 2002), and Douglas Gomery, *Shared Pleasures: A History of Movie Presentation in the United States* (Madison: University of Wisconsin Press, 1992).
17. For an analysis of how new technologies in the Hollywood film industry have multiplied distribution venues, see Janet Wasko, *Hollywood in Information Age* (Austin: University Texas Press, 1994).
18. Stephen E. Siwek, *Copyright Industries in the US Economy: The 2000 Report* (Washington, DC: International Intellectual Property Alliance, 2000).
19. Aida Hozic, *Hollyworld: Space, Power and Fantasy in the American Economy* (Ithaca, NY: Cornell University Press, 2001), 27.
20. Hozic, *Hollyworld*, 133–163.
21. Miller, McMurria, and Maxwell, *Global Hollywood*, 146–170.
22. National Association for Media Arts and Culture, *Digital Directions: Conversion Planning for the Media Arts* (San Francisco, California: National Association for Media Arts and Culture and the Ford Foundation, 2000).
23. National Association for Media Arts and Culture, *Digital Directions*, 69–81.
24. Patricia R. Zimmermann, "Media Democracy Day(s)," *The Independent*, September 2002, 7, and Priscilla Grim, Association of Independent Film and Video Media Advocacy Day Coordinator, interview with the author, July 25, 2002.

25. Organizations engaged in political advocacy working against rollbacks in Federal Communications Regulation on media concentration and broadband internet included Reclaim the Media (www.reclaimthemedia.org) and the Center for Digital Democracy (www.democraticmedia.org).

26. Lisa Delgado, "Lots of Flash, Even More Sizzle," *Wired*, July 25, 2002, accessed January 2018, https://www.wired.com/2002/07/lots-of-flash-even-more-sizzle/.

27. Jonah Sachs and Lewis Fox, partners of www.freerangegraphics.com, interview with the author, August 1, 2002.

28. Jonathon Gay, "The History of Flash," Untold History, accessed January 18, 2018, http://untoldhistory.weblogs.com.

29. Lev Manovich, "Reality Effects in Computer Animation," in *A Reader in Animation Studies*, ed. Jayne Piling (London: John Libbey, 1997), 5–15.

30. For a historical analysis of Hollywood studio interaction with wartime propaganda efforts during World War II, see Thomas Schatz, *The Genius of the System: Hollywood Filmmaking in the Studio Era* (New York: Pantheon Books, 1988), 297–407; and Erik Barnouw, *Documentary: A History of the Non Fiction Film* (Oxford: Oxford University Press, 1983), 139–172.

31. Jay David Bolter and Richard Grusin, *Remediation: Understanding New Media* (Cambridge: MIT Press, 2000), 20–80.

32. See Lev Manovich, *The Language of New Media* (Cambridge: MIT Press, 2001).

33. James Monaco, *The Dictionary of New Media* (New York: Harbor Electronic Publishing, 1999), 237.

34. John Carr, founder of www.konscious.com, interview with the author, October 19, 2002.

35. Press Release, "ITVS Presents a 9/11 Moment," Independent Television Service, January 14, 2002.

Figure 10.1. Still from *Evil 8: Unseen* (Tony Cokes, US, 2004). Courtesy Tony Cokes, Greene Naftali Gallery, and Electronic Arts Intermix.

10

PUBLIC DOMAINS: ENGAGING IRAQ THROUGH EXPERIMENTAL DIGITALITIES*

Public Domains

Public domain crosses through the new media ecology—works without copyright, that is, an archive with no doors and no rules. Public domain presents the open text that is able to commingle with other texts. Public domain means works exempt from proprietary interests that form our common aesthetic, cultural, and

---

*This article emerged from research, programming, and invited lectures in the mid-2000s during the war on terror and the war in Iraq. Tom Shevory and I, as codirectors and programmers for the Finger Lakes Environmental Film Festival (FLEFF) at Ithaca College, were searching for media works that addressed Iraq and the war on terror. We wanted to open up a critical discourse through public convenings that widened ways of thinking about the war that went beyond the spectacles on CNN. We programmed Big Noise Films' *Fallujah* on campus, and watched it with different kinds of audiences and listened to the discussions. We had also programmed various forms of new media, from websites to gaming, as a way to explore the expanding independent media ecologies, and in this context, I saw the computer game *Airport Insecurities* with festival audiences rather than alone on a computer. We also programmed Naeem Mohaiemen from Shobak.org as a guest speaker and heard his impassioned and urgent arguments for combatting reductionist Islamaphobia through a plurality of interfaces and critical discourses. Another guest was Tony Cokes, who brought his *Evil Series*, which we programmed across different interfaces infiltrating public spaces: an installation with multiple monitors at a party, on video monitors across campus that normally advertised alumni news and special events, and as trailers before feature films. Charles Musser invited me to present on new media and the war on terror at an event called "Iraq and the Media Symposium" he was mounting at Yale University in February of 2007. I started to think about how these works all used various digital interfaces and documentary strategies in experimental ways to complicate the simplistic unities of Bush's war on terror with multiplicities. I also thought about how I had seen most of these works and artists with audiences, small publics where a different kind of critique of the war on terror and the war in Iraq seemed to emerge in a more complex alternative to the reductionist mainstream news. From these experiences of seeing work with audiences, I took the concept of public domain and expanded it beyond its typical positioning as a work outside of copyright into a way to consider how these works created publics. Drake Stutesman, the editor of the academic film journal *Framework*, was at the Yale conference and later published this piece developed from my talk there, "Public Domains: Engaging Iraq through Experimental Digitalities," *Framework: The Journal of Film and Video* 48, no. 2 (Fall 2007): 66–83.

intellectual landscape.[1] This category is not stable: works change their passport status and migrate from proprietary to public domain continually, rapidly, and fluidly. Nor is this category universal, as public domain often implies countries of the global North that comply with the Berne Convention.

The word domain suggests the internet, a virtual space where cyberactivity coagulates, coalesces, and convenes. However, in this quest for free culture unfettered by capitalist exchange and intellectual property, lawyers, hackers, remixers, copyright pirates, mash-uppers, clubbers, found footage artists—often white male cybercowboys hacking and whacking on their Macs—focus on the image, fetishizing and eroticizing its acquisition and capture as though it were an endless high.[2]

In a time of war and empire, however, public domain needs a new definition, more pluralist, beyond an exclusive focus on the fixity of the image and the artifact. This time necessitates a definition that moves into transitional zones and provisional places and interrupts dominant discourses and positions. A rewired conception of public domain must consider a new kind of media politics within this new media ecology: it must create places where publics can emerge. Public domains materialize new publics and actualize new spaces. Some forms of new media circumvent the theatrical setting and instead adopt a strategy of infiltration into consumer grade technologies to produce critiques of the war on terror and the ways that it wedges into everyday life. For example, an online satirical game called *Airport Insecurity* asked the player to inspect airline passengers and luggage for forbidden items like toothpaste and hair gels, but the list changes each moment, making it difficult to detect contraband. Some of the items on the prohibited list include pants and hummus. The game developed in response to the Fall 2006 US security agency change in policies regarding what could be brought onto flights. The game is downloadable for cellphones from a website called Persuasive Games.

Public domains activate new ways of thinking, acting, and connecting with others across difference.[3] Empire and war no longer exert power solely through force, embedded reporters, or press restrictions. They enact and inscribe power through the production of panic: they replace the freedom of messy interaction implied in the inventive ideas and concrete practices of public domains with a systematic incarceration of imagination and mobility: border patrols, data mining, learning objectives, packet sniffing, passports, pay for view, news blackouts, silence, surveillance, and teaching outcomes.

Empire and war no longer just provide a field of operations to achieve national objectives. They are now in the manufacturing business. They produce endless product lines of panic, amnesia, and anaesthesia.[4] Empire and war have migrated into the mass production of chaos and incomprehensibility. As a result, the classical construct of the public sphere—a place for the open discussion of ideas among equals to create and sustain civil society—has become a chimera, a collective hallucination, a fantasy concocted by theory to enforce the science fiction of democracy. It does not, in the age of empire and war, exist a priori. Rather, the current conditions of massive media mergers and concentration make understanding the war in Iraq remote, continually rendering it invisible despite the endless visibility of soldiers and improvised explosive devices (IEDs). Therefore, it is critical to consider how to produce viable public domains. Public domains suggest plural pasts, collaborative histories and practices, and a refusal to separate the past, present, and future.[5] It means decentering the white male unities of empire and instead mobilizing the polyvocalities of multiple others that can dismantle it. It means reverse engineering ideas about independent and oppositional media into a new concept of public media.[6] It means no longer adopting a media model of pushing back—make it and they will come and they will learn the truth. It means adopting a different strategy and tactic of pulling in—create a space with, by, together, side by side for people to enter.

The Production of Panic

Panic is the operating system of the war on terror. Panic is produced and mobilized. The pope's comment about Islam in 2006 coincided with the E. coli bacteria spinach outbreak in the United States. Both create a phantasmatic of panic, with fear of the unknown shutting down borders everywhere, between countries, between difference, between ideas, between people.

Islamophobia exhibited distinct visual markers in the commercial mass media, visually shaping panic. In September 2006, Pope Benedict XVI delivered a speech at a university in Germany, a country with 1.9 million Muslim Turkish guest workers and Turks born in Germany. Pope Benedict said, "Show me just what Mohammed brought that was new, and there will you find things only evil and inhuman, such his command to spread by the sword the faith he preached."[7]

On CNN, a white male news anchor in a business suit occupied the center of the frame, flatly describing the reaction around the globe to the pope's speech. Behind him, digitally composited images formed four quadrants from Indonesia, Gaza, Sudan, and Pakistan. These images showed large groups of angry people with picket signs in different—but untranslated—languages. These were images of chaos and nameless, undifferentiated crowds.

Translation: white male anchor equals calm rational discourse, while swarming masses of Muslims equals incomprehensibility and violence. These images erased the significant cultural, political, and religious differences of these populations, promoting a visual geography that equated Islam and Muslims with panic. By extension, the images served as a justification of the US exportation of war, its cyberwarfare tactics clean, direct, and immutable in comparison to the messiness of others erupting in hysterics.

CNN and Fox News represented the response in what they termed the "Muslim world" as a visual iconography of racialized panic from an image without location, history, or specificity. Pakistan is Indonesia, Indonesia is Morroco, Morroco is Malaysia, and Malaysia is Saudi Arabia in this orientalized cartography. Panic here functioned as a projection of all that was unspoken about the war, all that could not be said but erupted in endless repetition; that which seemed to defy understanding by the transnational media outlets but burst out with threats to kill, maim, destroy.

However, beyond American cable news, a very different kind of public media practice charting the war on terror and the politics of Muslim identity emerged. For example, far beyond CNN, Muslim intellectuals and journalists from all over the globe populate the blogosphere, analyzing everything from the pope, to Zidane's head butt, to racial profiling on airline flights in a radical online space. Altmuslim.com features penetrating writing and news coverage from an alternative vantage point.

Shobak.org, a blog and listserv, features the snappy, gutsy analysis of postconceptual artist Naeem Mohaeimen. Mohaeimen is a member of the Visible Collective, whose website, performances, and installations called disappearedinamerica .org track the politics of detained migrants. Independent public media from around the globe have resisted this production of panic, amnesia, and anesthesia. They operate in what theorist Arjun Appadurai has called cellular convergences. He writes, "It is also the organizational style of the most interesting progressive movements in global society, those movements which seek to construct a third space of circulation, independent of the spaces of state and market, and which we may call movements for grassroots globalization."[8] These collaborations across difference and nations mobilize larger transnational goals and solidarities. They combine analog, digital, and embodied practices that are multiplatformed and migratory.

New Media Ecologies for New Public Domains

Public media looks different in the twenty-first century than it did in the 1970s, 1980s, and 1990s. Since these earlier periods of independent media, significant structural, political economy, and aesthetic reorganizations have offered new technological affordances as well as different aesthetic articulations of the domains of public media. In these decades, filmmakers were saying, "We will reveal it; we will speak the unspeakable, show the unshown; we will make it, and they will come and gain consciousness," a collective philosophy that has largely disintegrated. Flows have been reversed, formats have multiplied, participating producers have increased, and authorship is dispersed, multiple, and horizontal. The old binary oppositions between commercial and nonprofit as well as between amateur and professional have dissolved in exciting, problematic, confusing, and productive ways.

Thus, public domains constitute transitional, provisional, pluralized, and fluid zones constantly created and mobilized through interaction among many creators rather than made by one producer or producing one media object. As elaborated in the *Deep Focus* report produced by the National Association of Media Arts and Culture (NAMAC), the new media ecology differs dramatically from older media formations that pitted independent media against commercial/for-profit media. As *Deep Focus* argues, the new media ecology is layered, multiplatformed, mutable, and constantly reconfiguring audiences and outreach. It alters the relationships between production, distribution, and exhibition with long-tail marketing and niche markets blurring the boundaries between professional and amateur, and among new economic models and emerging sectors of public media such as clubs, Flash, installation, the internet, iPods, mobile media, remix, RFID, viral media, and beyond.[9] Apart from the market, public media can now be conceptualized as the creation and mobilization of public domains rather than as the production of singular static objects.

The public domain does not represent one entity, but many. Open source, then, can be reconfigured in this model not as a single strategy of open access to code, but rather as an active process of opening multiple sources.[10] Open source, then, is not just simply a way to access code democratically and in a transparent, collective way. Instead, open sourcing can be reformulated as a metaphor and model to navigate the emerging complex media environment. This process requires thinking through new strategies to open up access, distribution, ideas, and platforms. Public domains activate rather than function as an activist object. They shift from content to process, from what is on the screen to the screen as one nodal point around which communities can form. In other words, open sourcing and public domains entail moving away from one screen to multiple screens and platforms that facilitate communities: the production of publics and the opening of sources.

This strategy suggests a participatory model of public media that shifts from making works *for* communities, and instead proposes making works *with* communities that form around practices, contradictions, and openings. This collaborative work is frequently invisible in the commercial, feature film, independent media sector that propagates major international film festivals like Sundance and Tribeca. It entails being invited into someone else's space for a shared exploration of ideas and practices, rather than maintaining a differential in experience with media tools and representations. It means embracing the heterogeneous array of practices and technologies reshaping the media landscape. It suggests movement away from an auteurist model of media production as artisanal self-expression toward a model of media activating participation in the production of new collaborative knowledges.[11]

Collaborative Knowledges to Say No to War

A diverse range of groundbreaking public media works counter the hystericized CNN view of Muslims, Islam, and the occupation of Iraq by expanding the kinds of voices within the works and specifying place and history. In this way, these works create and open up public domains.

The *Shocking and Awful* series (2004), executive produced by Deep Dish Television, involved over one hundred independent media producers from around the globe to chart the war in Iraq from the ground up. Deep Dish is a pathbreaking public media collective marshalling satellite distribution for public media. *Shocking and Awful* featured the voices of Iraqis, international antiwar activists, and US military personnel speaking off the record to nonimbedded, independent journalists. The series featured twelve half-hour episodes ranging from occupation, women, cultural destruction, economics, oil, and resistance.

Code Pink, the feminist antiwar group, partnered with the Iraqi indie media collective to produce *Fallujah* (2005), a searing expose of the destruction of that city by US troops in November 2004, a major offensive that went largely unreported in the US commercial media. Over 2,000 Iraqis died; 250,000 people lost their homes. In the film, displaced Iraqis describe the military assault and their current living conditions in refugee camps. Comparing the siege of Fallujah to Guernica, the piece was screened at the prestigious Whitney Biennial. That screening spurred over one thousand university and public library purchases.

In contrast to the mass-mediated panics that commercial media propagated and promoted, independent public media deactivated the volatile manufacture of panic, fury, and fear. Public media on Islam, Muslims, and the occupation in Iraq opened up a transnational public space for a larger, more expansive, and more complicated conversation. As borders close and panic spreads like a virus, maintaining a vigorous, analytical, and resistant public domain sustains a necessary inoculation against and antidote to mainstream media news.

Historiography and Public Domains

Heterogeneity forms a central distinguishing characteristic of public domains that are in a continual process of construction, reactivation, and mobilization. Public domains loosen up rigid unities of discourse that produce panic, amnesia, and anesthesia. This vast untapped domain of imagining and creating public domains requires many approaches and tactics to move beyond the artifact or the text into historical understanding of the significance of these tactics, critical engagement with the forms of knowledge they yield, and development of a strategy to enact an antiwar epistemology. In his *Beyond the Great Story: History as Text and Discourse*, Robert F. Berkhofer Jr. argues that advances in the philosophy of history have moved history away from a single metanarrative and omniscient viewpoint based on referentiality, realism, and facts. This form of historiography represses heterogeneity. Instead, historiography needs to shift away from omniscience and the metanarrative toward a more particularlized multicultural construct of plural pasts that layer into and intersect each other in dynamic ways. Berkhofer identifies the construction of these plural pasts as polyvocalities: more than one viewpoint is presented, and contradictions and disjunctures abound. This marshalling of polyvocalities not only multiplies the voices and agents of historical processes, but necessitates opening up historical analysis to multiple explanatory models that can account for these complexities.[12]

In his *History and the Limit of World-History*, Ranajit Guha argues that the complicity between history and imperialism should not be reduced to an "expropriation of the pasts of the colonized by the colonizers." Instead, these complicities operate as a necessary component of globalization, which installs Europeanized development on the rest of the world by disconnecting stories and histories from the everyday. The state and history become intertwined. This process redefines temporality as a linear causal narrative that progresses in a one-way trajectory from the storyteller down to the listener. This process circumvents, silences, and marginalizes histories that emerged in more horizontal and open structures, such as interaction with listeners gathered to hear a story that repeats, changes, moves, alters, adapts.[13] These open constructs of listeners gathering and stories continually modifying contribute to an understanding of how the public domain materializes. Thus, the concept of the public domain differs from the public sphere: it is not abstract discourse, but rather, it is enacted, embodied, and produced outside of dominant power relations. Elaborating this move from centers of power to multiple dispersed stories, Guha observes that "the noise of world history and its statist concerns has made historiography insensitive to the sighs and whispers of everyday life."[14]

Guha advances that history requires regrounding in the specifics of everyday life through a creative engagement with the human condition: "No continent, no culture, no mark or condition of social being would be considered too small or too simple for its prose."[15] This shift to everyday life moves historiography from the grand to the granular and from the unified to the multiple. For Guha, the elite histories of Indian nationalism narrated history from the point of view of the colonizer. Thus, they were incomplete: they ignored the subaltern, defined as the people who were colonized, and the everyday. Partha Chatterjee has also elaborated on subaltern history as a more "intricately differentiated and layered" process to restore active agency to the everyday. His historiography involves rejecting unities through a "constant process of interrogation and contestation, modifying, transforming and enriching."[16] Subaltern history is not a practice that seeks a unified subject or analysis. Instead, it mines "living contradictions" by focusing on the overlaps, contacts, struggles, and accommodations between elites and subalterns. Guha advocates an opening up of all the pasts to dismantle unities. This process of moving from the colonizer to the subaltern and from unities to multiplicities facilitates retrieval of retellings, reperceptions, and remakings, acts of invention of possible futures emerging out of layered polyvocal histories.

Guha's critique of colonialist historiography and his vision for a historical practice renewed and revitalized through a grounding in everyday life offers a methodology to examine the forms and functions of oppositional independent media within emerging media ecologies surrounded by war and empire. Employing Guha's ideas, public domain media practices can be analyzed as multiple respositionings of historiography away from the storytellers and toward stories from the listeners.

Evil and Panic

Postconceptual artist Tony Cokes produced a series of shorts called the *Evil Series* (2001–ongoing). Rejecting the image as the focal point of the war on terror, Cokes animates text from Bush's speeches, news stories on bombings and Abu Ghraib, antiterrorism websites, and *New York Times* op-ed pieces against changing red, white, and blue backgrounds to unpack the semiotics of the war on terror. Postrock soundtracks generate disjunctions between the horrific discourse of war and the pleasures and latent erotics of rock music.

Challenging previous configurations of video art as a museum object, Cokes's *Evil Series* opens up new territories in not only artistic practice and conceptual design but also in exhibition. The *Evil Series* rethinks and rewires collaboration, distribution, exhibition, and production. Its process is to create and generate new forms of public space for critical engagement. Cokes produces migratory works that craft public domains. They move, morph, and adapt across formats and interactions. They screen as single-channel pieces, shorts before features, works on plasma screens in public environments, installations, and curated groupings of multiple pieces.

The *Evil Series* situates the video image as a space of conjecture and disjuncture rather than as representation. These various short pieces construct provisional zones that jettison the unities of realism. Instead, they produce a dialectic of possibilities and unsettlings. In the *Evil Series*, the production of space for contemplation and metacommunication is more important than the representation of the content or the plasticity of the image. The *Evil Series* creates liminal zones between advertising, club culture, critical theory, fine art practice, popular music, postconceptual art, and remix culture. It assembles a public domain where ideas and layered contradictions between discourses and practices replace panic, amnesia, and anesthesia.

Rather than a postmodern pastiche or a twenty-first-century-style remix or mash-up of pirated material, Cokes's work builds arguments about Abu Ghraib,

George Bush, pop music, and the post-9/11 world by layering these different cultural modalities into each other to facilitate new polyvocal structures that generate historiographic explanation and disjunctures about the war on terror. Cokes's work disturbs unexamined normative thinking and rewires assumptions about cultural production and consumption. This task is conceptually and artistically complex. These tactics have a long tradition in conceptual art, practices derived from an idea rather than from the internalized state of the artist's subjectivity or the artist's interaction with the materiality of the object. Cokes interrogates the distanced approach of conceptual art by linking concepts with more sensuous and embodied pop cultural modes of spectatorial positioning. For example, he employs graphic design from advertising a pared down minimalist aesthetic that rejects the congestion of much postmodernist art and montage, an emphasis on text imbedded within the works from print ads, and postrock soundtracks (rock music without the typical verse/chorus structure and 4/4 beat, operating as popular culture renditions of minimalism).

The *Evil Series* functions as a series of interventions into the transparency of the image, ideology, and narratives of nations and their fantasied others. Their conceptual design reconfigures expectations centered on the "reading" of media, artistic or experimental, or mass media. Most importantly, Cokes's work functions as a theoretical exercise to reorganize expectations about how to read media discourses by layering texts in such a way as to generate contradictions and fissures. Many works in the *Evil Series* challenge and confuse the very notion of a "readable" text through the multiple layers of scrolling text from sources as diverse as presidential speeches and *New York Times* editorials. Rather than simply blurring the borders between fine art, mass culture, popular culture, and theory, the *Evil Series* layers plural pasts to generate contradictory heterogeneities, a historiographic rather than representational tactic.

The *Evil Series* is the most significant work that Cokes has produced to date, and, in the increasingly cluttered landscape of post-9/11 war on terror art and media projects, the most politically and intellectually rigorous. By disposing of images of war and destruction almost entirely, the *Evil Series* questions the colonizing power politics of representation. Instead, it focuses on discursive structures and visual design as public domains for plugging ideas into different conceptual categories and activating them into new vectors of epistemological action and political critique. The multiple pieces in this series engage postrock soundtracks, igniting disjunctive readings of the text; discussions of Abu Ghraib are juxtaposed with the lightness of smooth pop music.

Much activist media chronicling the war in Iraq or activist mobilizations in the United States and Europe used realist representational tropes and focused on giving voice to the voiceless or images to the image-less, strategies identified with 1980s and 1990s political documentary media. In this aesthetic and political context, the *Evil Series* represents a significant historiographic intervention because it focuses on exhuming the latent contradictory epistemological structures of the post-9/11 environment and the ensuing war on terror. These multiple short video works that comprise the ongoing *Evil Series* are conceptually rigorous, beautifully designed, and elegantly presented, a counterpoint to more traditional realist images of war and terror typical in photojournalism. Most importantly, their political urgency emerges from how they develop a multiplicity of design strategies, layering contradictions to decipher the conceptual gridlock in the United States post-9/11. These works formulate a liminal zone where a variety of different modes and strategies from advertising, fine art, mass culture, music, and pop culture elaborate plural pasts, multiple dispersions, and polyvocalities. The *Evil Series* proposes a public domain of unsettled meditation and contemplation of contradictions that refuse to be resolved or unified.

Transformative History

Hayden White argues that history is an imaginative and transformative act, where fiction and fact endlessly flow in and out of each other. He sees the historian's work as a process of active engagement to transform archival materials through emplotment and explanation rather than the reductionist delivery of facts and evidence. Projects such as *Shocking and Awful, Airport Insecurities, Fallujah, Shobak*, and the *Evil Series* engage these various historiographic strategies to craft provisional public domains. The wide swathe of conceptual strategies utilized in these various works that range from conceptual art and new media gaming to realist documentary all share an interest in a historiography of multiplicity, polyvocality, and contradiction. They offer acts of reimagination, public domains for reconsideration of dominant power relations. White argues that historiographic practice needs to be reimagined: "I think the problem now, at the end of the twentieth century, is how we re-imagine history outside of the categories that we inherited from the nineteenth century."[17] Part of the strategy of moving historiography beyond its origins in the romantic era entails thinking through how to elaborate multiplicities and contradictions through juxtapositions. Highlighting the political function of history, Tzvetan Todorov advances that "totalitarian regimes of the twentieth century have revealed the existence of a danger never before imagined: the blotting out of memory. These twentieth century tyrannies have understood that the conquest of men and territories could be accomplished through information and communication and have created a systematic and complete takeover of memory, hoping to control it even in its most hidden excesses."[18] The takeover of memory in the post-9/11 environment of the war on terror entails narrowing multiplicities and contradictions down into false unities. By exposing contradictions and mapping multiplicities, the works discussed in this essay dismantle false unities through a variety of historiographic strategies.

F. K. Ankersmit argues for a critical historiography that does not accept the past or the archive as neutral.[19] Resonating with Guha and White, Ankersmit reconceptualizes history as an interrogation of the incongruities between the past and the present and the invention of new languages for speaking about their juxtaposition. He argues that the idea of an inert, immobile past derived solely from the evidentiary and empirical constitutes a fallacy. White parallels Ankersmit's claims about history as interrogation: "It is impossible to legislate the way people are going to relate to the past because, above all the past is a place of fantasy. It does not exist anymore. You can't replicate, by definition, historical events."[20] In considering independent media not as representations but as public domains, it is necessary to develop a new language for thinking about how these new media formations as exemplified in *Airport Insecurities*, *Fallujah*, and the *Evil Series* function. As historiographic interventions into the takeover of memory by those in power, they open up spaces for multiplicities and contradictions. These works enact public domains because they interact with the present and the future, looking backward and forward simultaneously in endless recombinations and mutations. Different temporalities and categories of evidence are remixed into new combinations to activate contradictions, provoke new explanatory models, and thread new connections.[21]

Collaborative Histories

Anthropologist and filmmaker David MacDougall moves ethnographic film away from making a film "about" toward making a film "with." Rather than an omniscient, monologic filmmaking strategy, he proposes that the act of cinema is a contemplative and participatory act that always enacts a relation and an encounter, an act of collaboration and dialogue between the subject and the person filming. MacDougall argues for interconnection rather than separation to produce a compound work and an elaborative embodied knowledge.[22] He explains that the goal of collaborative ethnography and compound work is "to see social behavior and indeed culture, as a continual process of interpretation and invention."[23]

Contemporary critical theory dissects this problem of how to construct historical models engaging heterogeneity, plurality, and polyvocality from one set of evidentiary groups to many different registers and kinds of evidence. Commenting on the need for a transcultural ethnography that takes into account multiple interstices and disjunctions, David MacDougall has observed that "the transcultural makes possible an overlapping of experiential horizons, where certain indirect and interpretive leaps of understanding can take place."[24] Dipesh Chakrabarty advances a similar argument about overlapping and plural histories. Arguing that the politics of including minorities in the history of India goes far beyond the embrace of a new set of archives and instead raises questions of explanatory models, he claims that the past is disjointed in nature and always plural: "thus the writing of history must implicitly assume a plurality of times existing together, a disjuncture of the present with itself. Making visible this disjuncture is what subaltern pasts allow us to do."[25] Robert Berkhofer points out that critical historiography has worked to minimize coherency, continuity, and univocality. Instead, historiography focuses on fragmentation, difference, and polyvocality in order to highlight the importance of the local and the contingent. Heterogeneity and discontinuity displace traditional notions of historical continuity.[26] In cinema studies, Phil Rosen also advocates for a model of temporal hybridity counterposed to the linear coherences of historiography and the pursuit of an authentic, transcendent "pastness."[27]

In historiography, the process of explaining an event by gathering together multiple forms of evidence and a plurality of discourses that appear to be disparate and disconnected is called colligation. In the arts, the connection of different kinds of materials and forms to create collisions and new ideas is called collage. Montage, the cinematic form of collage, has a long history in cinema as well, derived from the theories of Dziga Vertov and Sergei Eisenstein that advocated for different ideas operating in collision to create new synthesis and conceptual ideas.[28] Works as varied as *Airport Insecurities, Shobak, Shocking and Awful, Fallujah*, and the *Evil Series* can be analyzed as colligations, working to produce public domains through creating compound encounters, knowledges, and temporal hybridities.

The End of Empire and War: A Fantasy

The era of empire, infinite war, and massive media consolidation poses enormous obstacles to collectivity, freedom, heterogeneity, and imagination. The public spaces for an interventionist, argumentative public media shrink daily. Public domains seem elusive, lost, phantasmatic, and theoretical. These variegated and diffuse practices of engaged and interventionist digitality in works such as *Fallujah, Shocking and Awful, Evil Series, DisappearedinAmerica.com, Shobak*, and the *Airport Insecurity* game may offer a way to reclaim and reinvent transient public domains beyond the strangleholds of corporate media.

These digital environments are collaborative, contingent, and malleable. They are situated in material lived spaces. They resolutely intervene into power relations and consciousness in sensuous and affective ways. These engaged digitalities offer possibilities to assemble, conjure, galvanize, and imagine the key components that define and form the foundations of public domains as an oppositional media practice: a raucous convergence of like-minded partisans that dismantles convention and disassembles power through multiplicity.

Notes

1. For useful discussions of the concept of public domain, see special issue of the Sarai Reader, *The Public Domain* 01 (Amsterdam: Society for Old and New Media, 2001).

2. For a substantive and thorough discussion of the battles between intellectual property and anticopyright artists and activists, see Kembrew McLeod, *Freedom of Expression: Overzealous Copyright Bozos and Other Enemies of Creativity* (New York: Doubleday, 2005).

3. For a discussion of tactical media as a way to generate connections across difference, see Nato Thompson, "Trespassing Relevance," in *The Interventionist: Users' Manual for the Creative Disruption of Everyday Life* (Cambridge, MA: MIT Press, 2004), 13–22.

4. For an analysis of how panic blurs the borders between the political, the institutional, the psychic and the pharmaceutical, see Jackie Orr, *Panic Diaries: A Genealogy of Panic Disorder* (Durham, NC: Duke University Press, 2006), 33–78. For an analysis of how panic is always racialized, see *"Race" Panic and the Memory of Migration*, ed. Meaghan Morris and Brett de Bary (Hong Kong: Hong Kong University Press, 2001).

5. Robert Berkhofer Jr., *Beyond the Great Story: History as Text and Discourse* (Cambridge, MA: Harvard University Press, 1995), 170–201.

6. Patricia R. Zimmermann, "Public Domains for Public Media," Media Channel, www.mediachannel.org, May 2005.

7. "Pope Benedict XVI and Islam," September 16, 2006, accessed January 2, 2018, http://news.bbc.co.uk/2/hi/europe/5349808.stm.

8. Arjun Appadurai, *Fear of Small Numbers: An Essay on the Geography of Anger* (Durham, NC: Duke University Press, 2006), 131.

9. National Association of Media Arts and Culture, *Deep Focus: A Report on the Future of Independent Media* (San Francisco: National Association of Media Arts and Culture, 2004).

10. For a cogent analysis of open source culture and its relationship to old media forms of licensing, patenting, and copyright, see Lawrence Lessig, *Free Culture: How Big Media Uses Technology and the Law to Lock Down Culture and Control Creativity* (New York: Penguin, 2004), 264–280; Mark Poster, *Information Please: Culture and Politics in the Age of Digital Machines* (Durham, NC: Duke University Press, 2006), 122–138.

11. Critical ethnography has been interested in countering the orientalism of representation by offering a model of collaborative ethnographies where both the maker and the subject enter into the practice of media to produce new knowledge. For a discussion of collaborative knowledge production, see David MacDougall, *Transcultural Cinema* (Princeton, NJ: Princeton University Press, 1998).

12. Berkhofer, *Beyond the Great Story*, 263–283.

13. Ranajit Guha, *History at the Limit of World-History* (New York: Columbia University Press, 2002), 48–75.

14. Guha, *History at the Limit*, 22.

15. Guha, *History at the Limit*, 22.

16. Partha Chatterjee, "The Nation and Its Peasants," in *Mapping Subaltern Studies and the Postcolonial*, ed. Vinayak Chaturvedi (London: Verso, 2000), 18.

17. Interview with Hayden White, in *Encounters: Philosophy of History after Postmodernism*, ed. Ewa Domanska, (Charlottesville: University of Virginia Press, 1998), 16.

18. Tzvetan Todorov, "The Uses and Abuses of Memory," in *What Happens to History: The Renewal of Ethics in Contemporary Thought*, ed. Howard Marchitello (New York: Routledge, 2001), 11.

19. Ankersmit in Domanska, *Encounters*, 73.

20. White in Domanska, *Encounters*, 24.

21. For discussions of how strategies of historical collage can remedy the epistemological and political problems of linear causality in historiography, see Berkhofer, *Beyond the Great Story*, 245–270. See also Dipesh Chakrabarty, *Provincializing Europe: Postcolonial Thought and Historical Difference* (Princeton, NJ: Princeton University Press, 2000), 97–113.

22. MacDougall, *Transcultural Cinema*, 75.
23. MacDougall, *Transcultural Cinema*, 131.
24. MacDougall. *Transcultural Cinema*, 142.
25. Chakrabarty, *Provincializing Europe*, 109.
26. Berkhofer, *Beyond the Great Story*, 171–191.
27. Phil Rosen, *Change Mummified: Cinema, Historicity, Theory* (Minneapolis: University of Minnesota Press, 2001), 107–144.
28. See Sergei Eisenstein, *Film Form: Essays in Film Theory* (New York: Harvest Books, 1969); Dziga Vertov, *Kino-Eye: The Writings of Dziga Vertov*, ed. Annette Michelsen, (Berkeley: University of California Press, 1985).

Figure 11.1. Image of Cambodian Buddha. Photo by Patricia R. Zimmermann and Hend Alawadhi.

# 11

CAMBODIAN DIGITAL IMAGINARY ARCHIVE

*Genocide, Lara Croft, and Crafts**

Mithona

My closest friend, Anne, asked me to bring her back a Cambodian Buddha from Southeast Asia.

Anne forms part of our extended, nonbiological family—a sister, comrade, feminist, and my oldest friend. Using my global satellite phone card, I had called her at her home in Boston asking what I could bring her back from Cambodia. It was June, and the so-called SARS (severe acute respiratory syndrome) epidemic had hit China, Hong Kong, Singapore, and parts of north Vietnam in Spring 2003. As a result, it was difficult for Anne and her daughter to travel with us to Cambodia as we had hoped months before when we were all stateside.

---

* In 2002–2003, I was on sabbatical from Ithaca College. In September 2002, my treasured colleague and mentor John Keshishgolou took me out for breakfast at a local spot near Ithaca College called Sunset Grill. Recently retired, he was just getting ready to go teach communications at a university in Singapore. Over sunny-side-up eggs and toast with strawberry jam, he asked me if I might want to teach in Southeast Asia, as the university with which he was affiliated through many stints as a visiting professor might be in need of someone to teach film studies. A media historian and theorist trained in American-focused work, I said I had never thought about going to Asia or Southeast Asia. He insisted that I send him my CV, which I did, and a few weeks later the School of Communications at Nanyang Technological University contacted me about joining them as a visiting professor in the Spring of 2003, to teach courses on documentary history and theory and introductory international film aesthetics. I had never been to Asia before. My partner, Stewart Auyash, and my son, Sean Zimmermann Auyash, came with me. My friend Gina Marchetti had also taught at the same university a few years earlier. She provided many useful tips for living in Singapore, the most important of which was to read as many books as possible on the historical, political, and social relations of Southeast Asia, since the region held a very complex, variegated history. That semester, I was lucky to team teach with Sharon Lin Tay, a Singaporean PhD student back from her university in the United Kingdom to finish her dissertation. We quickly became close friends, and she helped me to navigate all the cultural and linguistic complexities of Singapore. Our family had a goal: we would end our time in Southeast Asia by traveling to

Anne was explicit in her directions: no fat Chinese Buddhas with their flowing robes and goofy grins, no faux hand-carved Thai machine-made Buddhas varnished to look old and hustled in street markets. If possible, the Buddha needed to be bought from a nongovernmental organization that retrained Cambodians. This process ensured that the money went to them as a form of war reparations. She did not want the money to go to American, Thai, or Vietnamese middlemen trafficking in Westerners' orientalist fantasies that framed Buddhism as a new-age remedy for the work speed-ups of globalization, devoid of specificity and location. She wanted the money to remit to the craftspeople themselves; Cambodia is one of the poorest countries in the world. The United Nations classifies it as a least-developed country (LDC).

Anne, a single mom raised Irish Catholic in Indiana in the heart of the American Midwest, wanted the Cambodian Buddha for her daughter, Mithona. In the Cambodian language, Mithona translates as June, the month her daughter was born. Mithona's Cambodian parents had given her up to an orphanage because they could not afford to raise her. In July 1998, two days before the first democratic election in Cambodia, when strongman Hun Sen was voted into power, Anne traveled on short notice to Cambodia to adopt Mithona.

Holed up in the Sunway Hotel—the famous outpost for adoptive parents—with other single moms and couples, both heterosexual and gay, who wanted children, she found herself in the middle of volatile political instabilities between three rival candidates. There was shooting in the streets. There were guns. If someone other than Hun Sen won the election, the agencies worried that adoptions by the West would be closed off.

Adoption in Cambodia is often a life-or-death issue for children: the country has one of the highest infant mortality rates in the world, a high level of child labor in sweatshops, and child sex trafficking to other parts of Southeast Asia. As Dr. Beat Richner pointed out during a June 2003 fundraising concert in Siem

---

Angkor Wat, the famous complex of temples in Cambodia, one of the poorest countries in the world. Besides our interest in these temples and in learning more about the horrific genocide in Cambodia, we were also driven by a family matter. One of my closest friends had adopted a child from Cambodia a few years before. With this new child in our lives, my family developed an interest in Cambodian history, the legacy of the Khmer Rouge, and the legendary crafts of the region. I took copious notes during our stay in Cambodia, trying to anchor myself when I was overwhelmed by the horror of Cambodia's history juxtaposed with the sublimities of Angkor Wat and the stories its walls revealed. I bought a lot of pirated books about the history of Cambodia, Buddhism, and Cambodian crafts in the night markets, their pages photocopied and often crooked. Eventually, I presented a few conference papers on Cambodia, and later wrote a more analytical and scholarly article for an Asian communications journal. The final version of this work evolved into this more lyrical essay written for my friend and her daughter. For privacy reasons, their names have been changed in this piece. The original, scholarly version of this essay was initially published as "The Cambodian Digital Imaginary Archive: Moving between East and West," *Media Asia: An Asian Communications Quarterly* 32, no. 2 (2005): 15–16.

Reap for Jayavarman VII Children's Hospital, the number of children who died from dengue fever and tuberculosis that week far exceeded the number of people who died across the globe from SARS. After the concert, my family and I donated money to the hospital in Mithona's name.

Buddhas and DVD Pirates

I spent seven months of 2003 living in Singapore with my partner and our son. I had never been to Asia before I was invited to teach cinema and digital theory at Nanyang Technological University in Singapore during my sabbatical. With my partner, a public health professor, and our ten-year-old son, I traveled throughout Southeast Asia to Indonesia, Malaysia, Thailand, and Vietnam. We made a trip to Nepal to see the Himalayas. We visited tropical islands in the South China Sea. In each place, we focused on visiting nongovernmental organizations so that our flurry of sightseeing at temples and shopping for crafts would be anchored in some kind of localized, social, and political reality that was not so much about objects to bring back to Singapore and the states, but about people. In most of the places we visited, tourism constituted the major industry. Every tour guide, whether in Bali, Bangkok, Chiang Mai, Ho Chi Minh City, or Katmandu, escorted us to collectively organized craft workshops or NGO-sponsored shops for handicrafts and artifacts.

However, these traditional crafts must be viewed in a dialectic with the more contemporary and high-tech craft of media piracy that stands in opposition to global capital. The Motion Picture Association of America, formerly under the helm of Jack Valenti, functions as the major police agency to protect US copyrighted products. It identifies Southeast and South Asia as posing the largest threat to intellectual property after China. Copyright products—films, games, music, software, and videos—now constitute the largest US export, exceeding aerospace and military products. The transnational media corporations have shifted from the business of producing media toward the business of advancing and protecting intellectual property rights across the globe.

In virtually every city in Southeast Asia except Singapore, where international copyright conventions are strictly adhered to, pirated copies of *The Matrix* (1999), *Tomb Raider* (2001), various computer games, Hong Kong *wuxia* films, and Adobe Photoshop programs abound, sold for the equivalent of one US dollar. In Johor Bahru across the straits from Singapore in Malaysia, shopping malls openly hawk DVDs of pirated Hollywood films and music, with aggressive salespeople listing genres and actors with the acumen of a Ph.D. in cinema studies.

In each place, we shopped in markets overflowing with the most gorgeous, evocative handicrafts cascading from makeshift stalls like a waterfall of color, design, and general excess: batik, bead work, carpets, hand-carved chopsticks, embroidery, intricately woven fabric, figurines, folk art and fine art paintings, gems, hand-woven baskets, lacquer ware, masks, mango wood vases, shadow puppets, silk, silver, and *thangka* paintings, Every market was filled with expats from around the world, living in global capital entrepôt like Bangkok, Hong Kong, Jakarta, Kuala Lumpur, Singapore. They earned high salaries with subsidized housing that allowed them to travel extensively and shop with an abandon unknown to middle-class professionals back in the countries they called home. In Europe, the United States, and Australia, the economy had plummeted: the cost of living was triple, even quadruple what it was in Southeast Asia.

This new colonial imaginary combined global capital in the high-tech and financial sectors of the knowledge economy, travel to least-developed countries, and acquisition of crafts and art to materialize the difference of living overseas when one returned. In these global cities, cell phones, fast computers, MP3 players, and wireless internet were commonplace. Many expat families, whether from Australia, Europe, India, or the United States, didn't bother to ship much to their new temporary homes in Singapore. Hardly anyone stays too long. It's a kind of tour of duty in one of the most high-tech and safest places in the world that has functioned as a global center of trade and transport for hundreds of years. Singapore is a point on the map through which all manner of goods and crafts circulate: Vietnamese beaded purses, Thai silk, Afghani kilims, Indian cotton tablecloths, Malaysian batik, and computer hardware pieced together in digital sweatshops in Indonesia, Malaysia, and Singapore.

The acquisition of crafts and artifacts from Southeast Asia for business or academic expats should not be read as a simple colonial revival. The handcarved Buddha heads from Bali, hand-knotted Persian rugs, and meticulously detailed Vietnamese lacquerware signify the localized, historical other of the digitized placeless transnational capital sectors in which the expats operate. These material artifacts marked by folk culture, the hand, and place serve as a displacement of all that the dematerialized, transnational digital flows of data, information, and money repress.

This dialectic between the material and the dematerialized is important: it travels across the psychic and economic, fantasy and reality, local and global. On one hand, these artifacts and crafts represent the bounty acquired through the largesse and mobility provided by transnational capital. On the other hand, international nongovernmental organizations have advocated for development initiatives that revitalize traditional crafts for export to the global markets throughout South and Southeast Asia as a way to assist people, especially women, the poorest of the world's poor, to achieve self-sufficiency.

Handicrafts as well as these NGO-sponsored workshops need to be situated within two larger racialized and gendered global flows, particularly in Cambodia. At one level, Cambodia suffers from a huge sex slave industry, with an estimated 15,000 children trafficked to Thailand. Back in Cambodia, 23 percent of children between the ages of ten through fourteen work. The NGO workshops that revive lost artisanal skills like stone and wood carving or lacquerware through training for young people provide income and operate as a deterrent from entering the sex trade.

On another level, textile sweatshops have multiplied in Cambodia, growing from thirty in 1996 to 110 within one year. This explosive growth of US apparel exports has escalated labor and human rights abuses, with two protesting textile workers shot dead in June 2003 in Phnom Penh. Since 1997, Cambodia's low wages in one of the poorest countries of the world and quota-free access attract European Union, US, Malaysian, Hong Kong, Chinese, and Singaporean outsourced manufacturing. Within these two flows, the global circulation of Cambodian handicrafts serves a quite different function than simply tourism's orientalist appropriation of otherness.

Make Me an Offer

In their air-conditioned condos, expats love to point out and share stories about their carpets, crafts, and folk art paintings. They purchase these items on family trips during school holidays, weekend getaways to Bangkok or Bali, or at auctions and what are called fancy faires at various clubs and hotels in Singapore. The pieces hold a story of contact between expats from the developed world navigating language and cultural differences with craftspeople, shop owners, or stall salespeople, and each piece they show is more beautiful and more artistically complex than the last. Each requires retelling the story of the contact and also entails explaining the Buddhist, Hindu, or Muslim religious story or folktale inscribed into the shape of the object: the Barung story, dragons, Garuda, Hanuman, mermaids, phoenixes, and the Ramayana. These narratives unfold a complex interplay of cultural encodings, re-codings, deconstructions, and interpretations.

A tale of capital in its most undiluted form doubles each story: bargaining aggressively with the hawkers for lower prices on intricate, high-quality, detailed textiles, carvings, rugs, and paintings. Will you take less *bhat*? What about only 200 *rupiah*? What about less *ringgit* for this batik? Each of these crafts cost less than a ticket to *Tomb Raider* in a stateside multiplex. The bargaining is literally about pennies.

But cultural differences about economic exchange complicate this bargaining. My partner and I tried to buy a carved Buddha head from a woodcarving workshop in Bali without bargaining. We were embarrassed by our relative privilege compared to the hardships of the Balinese in the aftermath of the 2002 bombing that drove all the tourists—the major source of revenue for the island—away. The young saleswoman explained that she could not accept that we agreed to the first price. She explained that we must fight about the price so we can learn about each other and share something. Perhaps fixed prices represent the static cultural hegemony of corporate capital where exchange is reduced exclusively to money rather than exchanges between people, where things transform into commodities rather than crafts. In Southeast Asia, prices were debated, fluid, and social. They required time. They had a rhythm. They were not a transaction: they were a shared narrative of cultural difference.

Genocide and Crafts

In Cambodia, the Khmer Rouge (red Khmer) held power from 1975 to 1979. They murdered approximately 1.7 million people, roughly 21 percent of the population. Prior to the Khmer Rouge, Cambodia was one of the largest exporters of raw silk in Southeast Asia. The Khmer Rouge killed engineers, farmers, professionals, students, and teachers. They also murdered dancers, musicians, silversmiths, and woodcarvers. Because they considered arts and crafts elitist, they forced craftspeople into the fields.

Besides murder, the Khmer Rouge's major craft practice consisted of photographing its victims, producing documents for an archive of death. In this context of genocide, the revival of traditional crafts like textile weaving, carving, and silver by international nongovernmental organizations, especially from France and Germany, represents something more than the colonialist trope of trafficking in Southeast Asian artifacts and tomb raiding.

The adoption agency gave Anne and the other soon-to-be parents a list of NGOs in so-called safe areas where they could buy Cambodian crafts like carvings, fabric, and silver. The parents wanted some artifacts of Cambodian culture to bring back with them to the states. From an NGO workshop that retrained land-mine amputees in woodcarving, Anne bought two wood carvings: a mermaid from the Ramayana, and an image of the monkey king, Hanuman.

Among parents with adopted children from Asia, there is a strong ethos to support their children's cultural identity of origin. In the 1970s and 1980s, with a wave of Korean and Chinese adoptions, families raised their children as white, eradicating their Asian identities and histories. This parenting model, which deleted history and difference, created a posttraumatic sense of loss in these children regarding their identities and their location between two different worlds of East and West.

Anne, however, was in Cambodia for less than forty-eight hours. She spent most of her time sitting in the United States Embassy waiting for the visa to bring home her daughter. Mithona suffered from malnutrition: at thirteen months, she weighed only eleven pounds. She had an ear infection and a 102-degree temperature.

In the twenty-first century, the history of the United States, with military interventions, bombings, and land mines in the countries of Southeast Asia, weighs heavily on adoptive parents, who often feel a moral imperative to promote peace and reconciliation. Among international peace activists, the atrocities of the Khmer Rouge are only the second phase of the Cambodian genocide. President Nixon's secret bombing of Cambodia during the Vietnam War (or American War, as it is called in Southeast Asia), which commenced in 1969, killed six hundred thousand Cambodians and produced over two million refugees. Similarly, many adoptive parents work to think through and materialize the interrelationships between the personal and political by inventing ways of raising their children within a mixed-race family that recognizes their Southeast Asian origins.

The Water festival, Cambodian New Year, and Khmer crafts like Buddhas, textiles, and temple rubbings play a major role in extending the adoptive family beyond its privatized realms into a more social and hybrid sense of family. Within this transnationalized sphere, family traditions and identities are imagined differently, continually reinvented, and concretely forged, never defaulting to a racialized white patriarchal familialism. For example, north of Boston, the town of Lowell, formerly the site of women's labor union organizing around the textile mills, now houses the second-largest Cambodian refugee population in the United States after Long Beach, California. Cambodians who fled the Khmer Rouge and then the Vietnamese occupation that followed were resettled in Lowell from the refugee camps in Thailand.

This Cambodian community has close ties with various organizations for parents who have adopted Cambodian children. Each summer in New Hampshire, they sponsor a Cambodian Jamboree featuring *apsara* dancers, traditional Cambodian music, and crafts vendors. On the Silk Air flight returning from Siem Reap, Cambodia, to Singapore, I met a Cambodian woman from Lowell returning from a buying trip to stock her store with Khmer crafts. When I asked her who bought these crafts, she replied: adoptive families, Cambodian immigrants, and collectors.

The Psychic Economies of the Global Circulation of Craft

Cambodian crafts in this social/political/familial construct forging adoptive, interracial families do not simply function as an orientalist artifact of the Southeast Asian exotic imaginary. Instead, they move within a much more transnational fluid arena where artifacts and crafts, as my friend Anne describes it, "aid children in the understanding that it is normative to be different." Anne's daughter Mithona was one of only two children of color in her first-grade class in a private Boston elementary school, the only child in a nonnuclear, nontraditional family, and the only adopted child. Mithona brought a small, slim Khmer-style Buddha with a bell hanging from his feet to her class show-and-tell. In her mostly white class, the Buddha's bell rang out her difference without words, the sound creating space for her own racialized identity in a different kind of family. As Anne explains it, some parents see an adopted child from China easier to negotiate culturally than a child from Cambodia simply because the Chinese diaspora is more visible in the United States in Chinatowns, museums, and contemporary multicultural revisionist American history. Most US museums almost exclusively focus on Chinese artifacts and art, perhaps replicating the hegemonic influence, power, and size of China.

The Museum of Fine Arts in Boston dedicates an entire wing to China, with not one piece of Khmer art despite the large population of Cambodians in nearby Lowell. At the Metropolitan Museum in New York, the Southeast Asian collection features only eight Khmer pieces, many more Thai pieces, and thousands of works from China. Very limited Cambodian and Khmer crafts are sold on eBay. Khmer art and Cambodian artifacts lack visibility and space in the United States, in contrast to the many important and moving web-based projects documenting the genocide committed by the Khmer Rouge, such as Yale University's Cambodian Genocide Project.

For my friend Anne, Khmer crafts and Buddhist folk art insist on a presence as an intervention into the absences in high-art museums. This activation of presence becomes part of daily life, with incense to the Cambodian Buddha lit every day in her home. Mithona often asks her playmates to light incense to the Buddha.

Lara Croft

Cambodia has no movie theaters. They have been converted into warehouses or shops. In the late 1960s, King Norodom Sihanouk made films often starring himself, various Cambodian ministers and officials, and the country's military. His films, which historians note lack any redeeming artistic merit, epitomize the conflation of total control over the narration of the nation and absolute state power. Representation and nation blur into one.

However, another history of Cambodian cinematic imaging also exists, one that moves across borders to form the Cambodian traumatic imaginary for global consumption. At one end is Roland Joffe's *The Killing Fields* (1984), a Hollywood studio production shot in Thailand that chronicled the relationship between *New York Times* reporter Sydney Schanberg and his translator Dith Pran as they covered the brutal civil war in Cambodia. It won several Academy Awards. At the other end, Rithy Panh, a Cambodian living in Paris, directed the documentary *S21: The Khmer Rouge Death Machine* (2003) which interviews prisoners and guards at the Khmer Rouge's notorious and deadly S21 camp. Coproduced by Franco-German TV Arte and France's National Broadcast Institute, the 2003 Cannes Film Festival bestowed the Un Certain Regard award on the film. These works situate the Cambodian cinematic imaginary as marked by a collective political trauma that must circulate in realist visual modalities across the globe. On one end, a Hollywood action film, on the other, a modest documentary using reenactment.

The relationship between Cambodia's craft heritage in the temples of Angkor Wat with their intricate stone carvings of Apsaras, Vishnu, Kali, and Buddha, and the global entertainment industry with its digital imaging and special effects converged in the filming of Paramount's *Lara Croft Tomb Raider* (2001) starring Angelina Jolie. Filmed at the temples of Angkor Wat and featuring scenes of Ta Prohm, the deteriorating temple overgrown with large tree limbs, *Tomb Raider* was the first commercial film to be shot in Cambodia since 1964. The Angkor Wat conservation authority charged Paramount $10,000 US a day for shooting at the temples, a fortune in Cambodia. Based on a popular computer game produced by Eidos, *Tomb Raider* suggests the constant shuttle of the transnational media corporate product between the digital and the analog, each vampires of the other.

At Angkor Wat, I asked our guide Phailim, a former lawyer who earned more escorting English-speaking tourists around the temples than working as a lawyer in a country where laws change incessantly, what he thought about the filming of *Tomb Raider* in Angkor Wat. His reply surprised me. He replied that Angelina Jolie was a great woman, a heroine in Cambodia because she adopted a Cambodian child, bought a house in Cambodia, and advocated for Cambodian human rights across the globe as a Goodwill Ambassador for the United Nations High Commission for Refugees.

Shopping for Mithona's Buddha

In Siem Reap, my family and I searched for the perfect Cambodian Buddha for Mithona and Anne. Several weeks before, my partner and I had read Jeff Greenwald's *Shopping for Buddhas* (1996). Greenwald had lived as an expat journalist in Nepal in the 1980s. He describes his search for the perfect Buddha in Katmandu. The story mixes a Western consumerist quest for the perfect art object with a journey into Nepalese Buddhism and the saga of the illegal trade in antiquities. The book fueled us to find the perfect Buddha for Mithona.

A colleague in Singapore instructed us to look for the most seductive, all-knowing smile. Another colleague suggested analyzing the eyes. Our family scoured the Psar Chas Market souvenir stalls, where bronze, clay, silver, and wood Buddhas in every pose and every shape were stacked from floor to ceiling. We debated each Buddha. We needed a Buddha made in Cambodian by Cambodians. The market Buddhas were of unknown origin. My son Sean, then ten years old, insisted that we think of Mithona during our shopping. He bought her elephant toys, rings, temple rubbings, textile hangings.

We bought Mithona's Buddha from the French NGO-supported Artisans D'Angkor, a retail shop in the center of Siem Reap that also trained young adults to learn stone carving, woodworking, and lacquerware. We found a Buddha in the teaching Buddha pose, with one hand down and the other raised. This pose seemed appropriate, since our friend Anne was a college professor. Carved from wood and then lacquered, craft workers copied the design from snapshots of the Buddhas at Angkor Wat. It was also signed, a rarity in Southeast Asian folk art. We toured the workshops and took photos of the artisans carving the Buddhas for Mithona. We also bought one for ourselves.

Because Anne and Mithona were coming to visit us when we repatriated, we decided to pack the two Buddhas in our suitcases rather than ship them back to the states via sea with our other possessions. After going through customs in Detroit, all our suitcases where searched and then scanned in a high-tech security system. The security guards yanked the two Buddhas out and checked out their pointy heads. In Southeast Asia, snails on the Buddha's head signified how these animals protected the Buddha from sunstroke during meditation. In George W. Bush's national security state of the early 2000s, the scanners interpreted them as a potential threat or a weapon.

From Beads to Pixels

Amidst and beyond the gripping, realist, epic films exposing genocide to the world looms a Cambodian digital imaginary threaded into transnational capital. Neo-Hollywood is a transnationalized, intensely concentrated entertainment industry that spans the globe in multiplatformed modes that transform what was once called cinema into "franchises" and "tentpoles" for the distribution of various forms of repurposed intellectual property, products, and tie-ins. Neo-Hollywood no longer has a center of production or a studio in a specific location: it is nowhere and everywhere, constantly reorganizing capital and information. Theorist Aida Hozic has identified the entertainment industry's new economy as "Hollywood in Cyberspace," where special effects, computer generated imaging (CGI), compositing, and manipulation of bitmap images replace cameras and studios. This transformation has shifted commercial filmmaking from a craft-centered practice of cinematography, costuming, lighting, and mise-en-scène focused on production to algorithm-based computer engineering located in postproduction.

Further, as many communication political economists have noted, neo-Hollywood operates as a studio without walls, constantly searching for economies of scale by outsourcing digital effects and location shooting to regions with weak currencies against the US dollar such as Asia, Australia, Canada, Eastern Europe, and Mexico. Since the economic crisis of 1997, countries in Southeast Asia such as Thailand, Malaysia, and Vietnam have aggressively cashed in on the West's orientalist cinematic fantasmatics, offering exotic locations and cheap labor for drivers, extras, and helpers to the global entertainment industry. Throughout Thailand and Malaysia, one can find beaches, cities, islands, and jungles sold to international tourists as the sites of various Hollywood films. For example, remnants from the TV show *Survivor* sets litter the group of tropical islands called Sibu in Malaysia in the South China Sea, the leftover debris decomposing from sun and sea.

East and Southeast Asia produce over 80 percent of the analog and digital animation broadcast in the United States in operations often nicknamed "digital sweatshops." One Singaporean observer of new media policy told me that "there is not that much of a jump between intricate Southeast Asian beadwork and embroidery and pixels on a computer bitmap. Both require detailed manipulations on a minute scale and both require enormous time." In 1999, the Association of Southeast Asian Nations (ASEAN) developed a comprehensive plan for member countries to compete in the global information networked economy. In a special report on the particular challenges for Cambodia, it argued that the development of an information economy is critical for economic competitiveness, advocating "leapfrogging" technologies to build a network of broadband multipurpose networks around the country. Digitization and networking will form the basis for industrial reorganization.

Yet it is important to remember the other side of the digital divide, even in the context of public regional economic policy that advocates leapfrogging. Cambodia has the lowest number of telephone lines per person, the lowest number of mobile phones, the lowest number of personal computers, and nearly the lowest number of internet hosts of any of the ten nations of the Association of South East Asian Nations (ASEAN), Northeast Asia, and India. As a postconflict nation, Cambodia lacks a viable physical infrastructure; most rural areas have limited access to roads, a water supply, and electricity. It is one of the poorest countries on the globe, with the highest infant- and child-mortality rates in the world. According to The Sharing Foundation, a NGO supporting children, the average GDP in the early to mid-2000s was $300USD. Forty percent of the children are malnourished. Only 36 percent of the population has access to safe drinking water. Much of Cambodia is literally off the grid.

Evil Is Easy; Goodness Is Hard

We asked our guide, Phaillim, why the steps to the main temple at Angkor Wat were so steep as we gingerly climbed up using our hands and our feet. He replied that for Cambodian Buddhists, "evil is easy; goodness is hard."

When I ask my son what he remembers most about being in Cambodia, he does not say shopping for Buddhas or witnessing the magnificent Angkor Wat temples. He says, the bones in the *stupa*, which made him so sad. Outside Siem Reap on the road to the temples of Angkor Wat, we found a small Buddhist stupa made of glass. It recognizes the victims of the killing fields. The Buddhist monastery that occupies this site was once a school where the Khmer Rouge killed all the teachers. The stupa is filled with skulls and bones recovered from the killing fields around Siem Reap, a makeshift memorial and historical reclamation of artifacts of bodies and memories of a community. A sign in English explained that the people of Cambodia endured a genocide of massive proportions on this site.

It said that the people of this community were too poor to build a proper memorial to the dead; they ask for donations in a box. Under a pavilion next to the stupa, children played soccer with a makeshift ball of crumpled cloth. My family and I put money into the box.

For Cambodians, the US secret bombings and the Khmer Rouge are not over. This history continues, marking bodies, handicrafts, psyches. Cambodia has the largest number of amputees in the world, a result of land mines abandoned by France, Thailand, the United States, and Vietnam. There are no maps of where these land mines are buried. Nearly every Cambodian we met had a relative murdered by the Khmer Rouge. To buy a Buddha carved in Cambodia is to remember this history, and to carry it home with you.

My friend Anne told me that Mithona invented a game. In her bedroom or on the kitchen table, she makes what she calls museums out of the pictures we took in Cambodia and the little Buddhas we gave her. Mithona's miniature installations conjure an act of history, an act of secular spirituality, an assertion of a racialized and located identity. As a form of folk art, Mithona's museums resonate with the bones in the stupa outside Siem Reap. These little shrines insist that craft embodies an action mobilized by the living in order to remember that what has been considered lost actually still lives.

PART III
HISTORIES

Figure 12.1. Film still from the Lynette Frazier Collection, circa 1960. Courtesy of the South Side Home Movie Project, Chicago, Illinois.

12

THE HOME MOVIE ARCHIVE LIVE*

Overture

The live music, multimedia, and spoken-word project, *Memescapes* (USA 2007), produced by Ann Michel and Phil Wilde in collaboration with the Human Studies Film Archives (HSFA) of the Smithsonian Institution, was a special commission of the Finger Lakes Environmental Film Festival in Ithaca, New York.[1]

Memescapes explored the notion of a meme, a concept or idea that changes and reconfigures as it migrates through different platforms and spaces. With an original postrock, postminimalist score by electronic violinist and composer Judy Hyman, the project digitally manipulated amateur films from Africa, Asia,

---

* This piece was originally delivered as a keynote address for the Saving Private Reels Symposium in Ireland at the University of Cork in September of 2010. Faculty members and fellow screen studies scholars Barry Monahan and Laura Rascaroli had invited me to this international gathering of scholars working on home movies and amateur film. For this talk, instead of presenting a scholarly argument based on my historical research, I wanted the audience to consider the possibilities the home movie archive offers to activate new meanings through live performance and remix.

I did not offer this talk as an intervention into more traditional scholarship. Since 2003, I had written and produced projects with archival film, live music, remix, and scripted spoken word at Ithaca College. I returned to archives I had used for my scholarly books, such as the Human Studies Film Archive of the Smithsonian Institution in Washington, DC, and Northeast Historic Film in Maine. I established large collaborative teams of archivists, filmmakers, musicians, and scholars to mount these projects, partly because Ithaca College houses accomplished artists in an internationally recognized school of music and has many active scholars in disciplines across the campus, all of whom were looking to undertake something more unconventional in community with others. In 2005, to celebrate the fiftieth anniversary of the Robert Flaherty Film Seminar, I produced a large collaborative project with an electronic musician, three percussionists, and an opera singer performing live to *Nanook of the North* (1922).

By 2004, Ithaca College had assumed primary sponsorship of the Finger Lakes Environmental Film Festival and named me codirector with Thomas Shevory, a scholar of environmental studies in the Department of Politics. The college provost asked us to broaden the scope of the festival beyond film, saying that it needed to engage all the different schools and disciplines at Ithaca College. The idea to produce live performances with archival material solved several problems: archives needed their works to be shown, classical musicians wanted to fill concert halls, local producers wanted meaningful contexts in community for their films, scholars wanted to work

Europe, and Latin America, slowing down and repeating the image to echo the repetition in the music. Actress Cynthia Henderson performed a spoken-word script describing four memes—maps, metropolis, panic, and soundscaping.

A suite in four parts, the section entitled "Soundscaping" featured an intricately layered sound design by a second composer, Robby Aceto. A close-up of a wooden water wheel from an amateur travel film shot in Cambodia in the late 1960s, before the ravages of the Khmer Rouge, was slowed down by more than half its original speed—and repeated. The wooden wheel suggested a dreamscape of daily life in pre–Khmer Rouge Cambodia, a visual compendium of Buddhism, water, and wheels. The repetitive sensuous electronic music combined with analog violin and banjo evoked a trance-like state in which to contemplate amateur film and history.

Constructing live performance as a dialectic between the present of the layered electronic music and the past of amateur film, *Memescapes* raises an epistemological question.

What happens when the home movie archive goes live?

The question of the "live" and cinema is embedded in the origins of exhibition. Many histories of silent film and music have analyzed their interactive, kinetic, and responsive exhibition practices.[2] Now, what we think of as live encompasses both similar and different functions. The inclusion of live elements revitalizes public exhibition in film festivals, museums, theaters, and universities—and has increased audience numbers for challenging and obscure works. Classical music venues like Carnegie Hall can sell out demanding contemporary music concerts when media artists like Bill Morrison build archival projections for experimental composers like Michael Gordon.[3] Groups such as Alloy Orchestra who perform original live music for classic silent films play to overflow crowds at art houses, festival venues, and repertory cinemas such as Cornell Cinema at Cornell University.[4]

In contrast, home movies often evoke that which is dead, decayed, ghostly, or inert. In response, this essay proposes an opposite, seemingly counterintuitive move toward our ideas of live: alive, lively, enliven, living, to live. I advocate the home movie archive live, which is intended neither to discount nor trivialize decades of important scholarly work analyzing home movies as economic

---

collaboratively with artists and people from other disciplines, Ithaca College wanted to showcase all of its schools, and I was committed to revitalizing amateur film in more public ways. Since these early forays, I have written and produced more than fifty live music/archival/spoken-word film performances in large collaborative teams that continue to work together, all based in Ithaca, New York. My keynote from the symposium in Ireland was later revised and published as "The Home Movie Archive Live" in Laura Rascaroli and Gwen Young with Barry Monahan, *Amateur Filmmaking: The Home Movies, The Archive, The Web* (London: Bloomsbury, 2014), 282–301. This piece represents a revision of that original essay.

relations, historical evidence, indexes of trauma, marginalized social and political histories, or texts. Nor does it critique the use of amateur films or home movies in documentary, experimental, and narrative films.[5] Rather, this essay ponders how linking the home movie archive with the practices of live performance can function proactively in order to examine how reconsidering historiographic strategies might generate new thinking and new spaces through a principle of juxtaposition.

Because film and cultural studies often consider home movies as artifacts, this essay proposes a friendly countermove to reframe home movies as dynamic vectors. Although scholars often position home movies as evidentiary and referential, my argument shifts the conceptualization of the home movie into a system of resonating polyvocalities. Embodied, multisensory, performative, responsive, and sensual qualities underwrite the home movie archive live. Because "live" implies spectacles of the senses and bodies in material spaces that feel different from daily life,[6] it is marked by the provisional, transitive, and transitory. We can begin to chart the shape-shifting landscapes of the home movie archive live with an analysis of works such as remix projects with classical and experimental live music, installations that require the audience to walk through and around images, shows in clubs with multiple projections on the walls, and guided bus tours with home movies on monitors. These diverse works typically engage a specific location, operating from a place-based ethos rather than from a text-based position.

Projects subsumed under the designation of home movie archive live share similar components and concepts: analog home movie images, digital interfaces, embodied spectatorship, historiography, mobility, multiple screens, and space. They activate a pull-in rather than a push-out model of spectatorship. Although projections of classic silent narratives and amateur movies with live musical accompaniment represents a vital, popular arena of archival exhibition, projects where the sound/music is subservient to the projected image will not be included in my argument here. In contrast, this essay examines projects that combine the home movie archive with live performance to craft a sensorium through disjunction and contradiction, a strategy that amplifies place and space. Thus, the home movie archive live serves as both a concept to reconfigure the archive as fluid and as a practice to enact dynamic historiographic embodiments.

This essay is limited to collaborative projects that use archives with large holdings of amateur films. These projects position spectators' bodies in different relationships to images through additive structures such as altered exhibition spaces, live music, and reconfigured screens. Spatial rather than temporal, these various live projects reconceive images as mobile architectures rather than as artifacts.[7] Postcolonial historiography and relational aesthetics provide a way to situate the significance as well as the function of home movie archive live projects. All the projects under discussion represent collaborations between archives, artists, performers, and scholars. The images utilized in these projects have not been downloaded from internet sites, illegally copied, hacked, or pirated. Indeed, these projects propose a third way, a middle ground between intellectual property and free culture: a commons established by collaboration between archives and performers/producers in one-off situations.

How do conceptual models change when the archive shifts from a fixed, immobilized place into migrations and movements across and between iterations, people, platforms, and spaces? Can the archival image be reshaped as malleable and mutating? How does it migrate from the private and quarantined toward a more collaborative, embodied, and public encounter? As the home movie archive shifts away from its focus on the fetishized and monumentalized image, how can we understand its migration into these new materialized performative spaces that propel the "live"?

Once home movies are recovered and deposited in archives, a default position emerges: their acquisition generally constitutes the end zone in the reclamation process. The thing itself—the celluloid reels, deteriorating color, metal cans—becomes fetishized as a fixed representation and an artifact. However, the home movie artifact can be repositioned as open and active, no longer a mortuary of historic images shrouded in desire, longing, and idiosyncrasy. Instead, the archive can be reconsidered as a partner in dialogue with specific histories; an interruption, relocation, and transformation of nostalgia into transversals of aesthetic, historical, political, and social contexts. Thus, the home movie archive live is dynamic: not a product but a process, not a text but an encounter, not a representation but a collaborative space.[8]

Relational Aesthetics and the Archive Live

The case supporting the home movie archive live describes an alternate path through representations of the real and trauma. Rather than a politics of representation or a fixed archival practice, the home movie archive live reimagines a sense of place through the active production of convenings among people. Rather than a singular auteurist vision, it improvises through horizontally designed collaborations. Unexpected encounters and productive contingencies displace linear reasoning. Home movie archive live projects can establish provisional microterritories by combining a variety of performances, platforms, and technologies. These projects emphasize processes of recombination across films, media texts, music, and speech rather than the fixity of the image.

Live performance with archival images is neither a new development nor unique to the digital era. It has a long ancestry in twentieth-century experimental arts, from conceptual art, Dada and Futurist performances, to feminist art, Fluxus happenings, minimalism, and a variety of art practices that required the audience to participate or activate the work. In his book *Conversation Pieces,* art historian Grant Kester explains that contemporary socially engaged arts practices share similar conceptual strategies: they refute individual artistry, shock value, and the specularities of modernism and postmodernism. They also jettison abstractions and ambiguities. Instead, these newly emerging forms of art practice emphasize accessibility, conviviality, and the everyday, opening up to audiences as an invitation to contribute or participate. Kester posits that socially engaged arts practices inaugurate a "collaborative and dialogical model" that catalyzes participants into conversations with unpredictable outcomes. These creative encounters instigate shared experiences and amplify multiple ways of knowing.[9]

In *Relational Aesthetics,* French theorist and curator Nicolas Bourriaud has also charted new forms of participatory art organized around producing collaboration, contingencies, and encounters for a transitory production of microcommunities. For him, social practice art proposes a convivial shared world of new generative relations, which he calls a micro-utopia. For him, it is not distance, but proximity that defines this move from the visual to the tactile and the interactive.[10] Bourriaud contends that these works produce interstitial spaces offering openness and possibilities. "Art . . . is attempting to construct concrete spaces," argues Bourriaud.[11] Thus, relational aesthetics, shifting toward new arrangements of agency, ideas, and space, introduce pluralities extending beyond families, institutions, and technologies. Relational aesthetics elaborate polyphonic formations by binding together arenas of social and political life that are often separated.[12]

These tactics of engagement, multiple knowledges, performative encounters, polyphony, and relational convenings can open up the home movie archive into a live dimension grounded in a variety of specific locations. As a result, the concept of the home movie archive live extends the archive into other sets of relations and other kinds of spaces beyond movie theaters.

Dialogic Historiography and the Home Movie Live

Cinephilia represses history and immobilizes images as rarefied objects. Cinephilia—and its correlative, archive-philia—are founded on desire for the authentic and the uncontaminated. The historical that signifies and marks changes is abandoned, replaced with a fantasized, inert, and monumentalized construct of history.[13] Tzvetan Todorov argues, for example, that the monumental in historical discourse almost always suggests authoritarian ideologies and impulses.[14] Todorov's assertion describes cinephilia and archive-philia, which can conceal problematic politics and centralized power relations.

A more radical historiography removes the object from its monumentalizing position and opens it to multiple vectors of recirculation that contain the possibility of forging new connections and meanings. This historiography rejects linear argument, causal explanation, the fetishized object, and the monolithic story. Instead, a radical historiography reanimates artifacts within polyphonic frameworks, excising both the unitary object and the unified history it suggests.

Historiographers like Robert F. Berkhofer, Dipesh Chakrabarty, Ranajit Guha, and Philip Rosen have argued for a fluid, plural, and polyphonic historical practice in order to develop new explanatory models.[15]

Heterogeneity, then, offers the possibility to reconceptualize historiography. It functions as an antidote to the isolating immobilizations of cinephilia, focusing on the creation of new knowledge production and explanatory models. Berkhofer advances that this historiography shifts from a unitary history toward reconstructing multicultural plural pasts.[16] Charkrabarty and Rosen have also advocated for explanatory models that layer multiple temporalities to dislodge linear causality.[17] Their conceptualizations foreground contradictions and disjunctures. The home movie archive live then, mobilizes multiple temporalities as a historiographic strategy of dispersals.

The home movie archive live operates on a vector of generative fluidity: open and recombinant, active rather than static, evolving instead of fixed, opening to new tactics where it can be energized and mobilized. As a result, the home movie archive needs to be reconceptualized as a process rather than a collection of artifacts. In this conceptualization, the archive is dialogic and transversal. It produces new forms of explanation and relation.

Ordinarily, once home movies are recovered and deposited in archives, a default position emerges: their acquisition becomes all that matters. The thing itself—the celluloid reels, metal cans, damaged white leader—becomes more and more fetishized. The images become anchored in their referents and aesthetic form. The archive and its images are thus immobilized, an inert repository of nostalgia shrouded in longing and singularity. Regardless, the home movie artifact must be repositioned as open and active so that it may engage in dialogic relationships with specific social and political histories that push beyond the confines of nostalgia, a transversal movement across aesthetic, historical, political, and social relations.

In *History and the Limit of World-History*, Ranajit Guha argues that imperialist history disconnects narratives and events from the everyday and the locally situated. As state-centered history, it marshals a unified linear chronology that centers on institutions holding power, rather than harvesting the multiplicities comprising everyday life.[18] Guha suggests that the new historiography requires a reorientation to smaller arenas of social life, rather than larger institutions.[19] This historical strategy maps the multiple accommodations and struggles between elites and subalterns and restores active agency to those without state power, who may not be the subject of written records, either their own or by others. For Guha historiography necessitates reformulating historical processes as contestations, interrogations, modifications, and transformations. If state-centered historiography represses multiplicity, then this more localized historiography opens up many pasts.[20]

In this historiography, the home movie archive live can be reconfigured as a migratory system of multiple processes that summon everyday publics. Home movie archival objects need not be inert, catalogued within fossilized, monumentalized, sacralized categories. Assumptions about the fixed archival object must be replaced with reconceptualizations of the artifact as provisional. These fluidly-conceived artifacts can create a collaborative performative space to imagine histories as truly public works—an instantiation of the migratory home movie archive live.

Multimedia artists Art Jones and Simon Tarr created a live remix with dual-screen projection called *Dismantling War* (USA 2005). Collaborating with the Human Studies Film Archives of the Smithsonian Institution, Jones and Tarr fashioned loops out of amateur films shot in places that have been infiltrated in various ways by the US empire: Bolivia, Brooklyn, Cambodia, Ecuador, Florida, France, Germany, India, Iraq, Mexico, and the former Yugoslavia. Jones and Tarr loaded these loops on their laptops. During the live performance, they responded to each other's images, each screen in dialogue and responsive to the other. Different images—a digital soldier, planes, and bombs, created in 3D animation by Jones—were superimposed over the amateur footage. Although the archive's footage was originally produced by ethnographers, explorers, lecturers, missionaries, and travelers, the collaborative live performance exhumed the traces of empire imbedded in the images. Shot from the 1920s through the 1960s during the expansion of global capital, these images entered a new future with a hip-hop music track remixed live by Jones. The loops were also manipulated live on the laptops, the images colorized, slowed down, and repeated, with the subjects' minute movements and gestures emphasized. Through image, music, performance, and sound, *Dismantling War* inserted live into the archive.

Movement in Space and Making Space

Histories and stories are always told and retold differently, moving from the individual to others, from the private to the public, from the speaker to the listener, from the virtuoso to the amateur.

In his book and installation, *Images Cachées*, made for the Centre national de l'audiovisuel in Luxembourg, visual artist Yves Dorme pulled stills from amateur films deposited in the archive.[21] The resulting images exemplify this movement toward the amateur, the body, the everyday, the listener, and the public. Each still image, taken from the films, captures an incomplete gesture. The still images function as a retelling of the amateur film, probing what it means to be an ineffable image that moves. The images meditate on movement itself, its ambiguities, details, and textures. Women in high heels with bare legs walk in unison down a pavement away from the camera, a woman in a two-piece black bathing suit standing behind a camper bends backward and pops a grape into her mouth, a woman sits by a window looking up from her knitting, two women in black-and-gray patterned dresses kiss each other. These images capture small gestures that in juxtaposition reveal the grace and ineffability of leisure time.

Images Cachées was not just a book, but also an installation in the Centre national de l'audiovisuel. It took over an entire gallery. Stills from the images were printed and placed on waist-level shelves that formed a grid in the room. Monitors hung from the ceiling, each showing different reels of amateur film. Against one wall, spectators could sit and search a computer database for concepts and places in the amateur film archive. The installation, then, invited the spectator to collaborate in considering the amateur as a spatial proposition within a live framework. The screen space of the home movie was multiplied: appearing on computers, in photographs, in film projection. Multiple screens and images at different levels evoked movement in the architecture of the home movie exhibition. The spectator was asked to look, but also to move, the body redeployed as an editing device through form, motion, shape, and texture.

Once archives acquire amateur films, they are confronted with the enormous conceptual and logistical problems of use and access: are these movies simply records that can be used as evidence in future compilation films and as fetishized objects of preservation? In 2002, the Miami International Film Festival produced the Magical History Film and Video Bus, organized by the Lynn and Louis Wolfson II Florida Moving Image Archive (FMIA), a kind of twenty-first-century reinvention of the early Soviet kino-trains.

The city of Miami is known for its aggressive development and complicated history. Artists, entertainers, entrepreneurs, exiles, gangsters, and retirees have contributed to massive changes in its environmental landscape. Rather than inviting the public to come to the archive, FMIA brought the archive to the public by putting it on wheels in an air-conditioned tour bus equipped with video monitors and a DVD deck, with the footage driving the routes. The amateur film footage is never from one decade; it is scrambled to show the dynamic relationships between all layers of urban life and many different historical periods invisibly imbedded in streets and buildings. The tours are performative and improvisational rather than scripted and canned.

This bus tour exemplified a model of historiographic contiguity, the idea that combinations may explain more than causality and linearity. On the tour, juxtaposed with images of news, history, and specific places, the home movies acquired an urgency and depth as historical documents. The manner of exhibition instantiates ideology in a way that watching them alone as single-channel screenings could never sustain; inserting these images into an analogic documentary would render them one-dimensional. Images from the past on the screen contrasted with images out the windows of the bus in a dynamic, constantly shifting montage of impingement.

Since the postwar period, Miami has been a major tourist destination, a cultural phenomenon that provides a larger context for the tour and offers fertile ground to tap the history of popular entertainment in nightclubs, television shows, and movies. During the film festival, the bus tour featured Paul George, an urban historian specializing in South Florida. George—a human encyclopedia of South Florida history, politics, and culture—linked the past in the home movies on the bus monitors with the present rolling by outside the windows. Home movies of families playing on the relatively undeveloped beachfront in the 1950s contrasted starkly with the fashion models and beautiful people parading down a clogged Ocean Drive in Miami Beach.

When the bus passed the site of the Red Carpet Club, a well-known gay bar in Miami Beach, images of police raids appeared on the screens. George explained that the gay community, while marginalized in the 1950s, contributed in important ways to the evolution of Miami Beach, which had been largely a family vacation site, with the addition of movie star performers to add some glamor when the kids were asleep. When people started to go elsewhere for vacation, the neighborhoods deteriorated, with hotels past their prime populated primarily by retirees. In the 1980s, following a massive influx of cocaine money, it became a slick, polished area of exclusive restaurants, shops, and nightclubs. Investment in the new Miami became an effective method of money laundering. With cost no object, buildings were rapidly refurbished and replaced, displacing the elderly residents of South Beach. Passing Mt. Sinai Hospital, home movies of its former incarnation as the Carl Fisher–designed Nautilus Hotel exemplified this historical change. Fisher was the legendary developer known as Mr. Miami Beach. George noted that before World War II, the hotel and many country clubs were restricted; it did not permit Jews. Later, the bus drove to Temple Emanu-El, one of the oldest synagogues in Miami Beach while passengers watched home movies shot outside the temple.

FMIA's location in Miami—often referred to as the point where North and South American cultures converge—offers enormous potential to excavate unknown histories and the images that map them. Miami has large African American, Cuban, Haitian, Jewish, and Latin American communities as well as a full panoply of displaced snowbirds, people from the Northern United States and Canada who live in Florida during the winter months. The city has been a destination for Cuban exiles since 1959. Haitians who moved to Miami were both political and economic refugees, while many South Americans who moved there were generally more well-off.

The tour, for example, often travels through a neighborhood called Overtown, a once thriving African American community now in decline, screening home movies of daily life on the streets and in local businesses before the expressway cut through, dividing and nearly destroying the neighborhood. At the famous Fontainebleau Hotel, images of Sammy Davis Jr. showed him performing for happy white families cavorting by the pool. During segregation, Davis was not allowed to stay at the hotel, so he stayed in Overtown.

Although specialists in the culture of South Florida in areas like architecture, archival film, and Florida history have narrated the tours, some of the most compelling Magical History bus tours have been narrated by longtime local residents. These bus tours with archival films frequently spark riders to share their stories and memories, underscoring how amateur footage can mobilize what historians call "history from below," the memories of everyday people rather than official histories. FMIA staff often change the images they put up on the screens in response to riders' observations and queries. Thus, the bus tours and their screenings exhibit an improvisational and performative vitality that distinguishes them from more formal screenings valorizing the image. The Magical History Film and Video Bus Tour exemplifies what an interactive historical encounter might look like situated within a matrix of historical reclamation, live performance, and movable space. The home movie archive is live, and, in this case, on the bus.

Plural and Provisional Contiguities

Temporality in the home movie archive live is relentlessly plural: not one historical period, but many. This concept hinges on a notion of contiguities—the placement of artifacts, evidence, and specific historical moments side by side rather than in linear progression. Heterogeneity constitutes a central feature of migratory archives; it dislodges the unities of discourse and practice that reproduce dominant power relations and with them, historical amnesia. Migratory archives require a variety of tactics to push beyond the artifact into a critical engagement with a historiography of contiguous multiplicities. Berkhofer posits that this consideration of historiography transitions history away from an omniscient metanarrative repressing heterogeneity toward the recovery of a multicultural plural past. He defines these plural pasts as polyvocalities, an explanatory historiographic methodology engaging contradictions and disjunctures.[22]

An example of polyvocalities as performance, Astor Piazzolla's music mixes European classical music's formal structures with rhythmic and polyphonic African music and the emotional address of Argentine folk music. A multimedia live performance of *Cuatro Estaciones Porteñas* (*Four Seasons of Buenos Aires,* performed in Austin, Texas, in 2007) combined two pianists, Jairo Geronymo and Jeffrey Meyer, two *tangueros* (tango dancers), and live video mixing multiscreen projections of rare archival amateur footage from Europe, Latin America, and the United States, a collaboration with the Human Studies Film Archives of the Smithsonian Institution. Juxtaposing different art forms, media projections, and aural, tactile, and visual sensory experiences, the performance physicalized the conceptual and musical layers in *Cuatro Estaciones Porteñas* as it enacted contiguities among its elements. The two screens also alluded to Piazzolla's involvement as a composer of film scores. The home movie projections generated new contiguities with the Piazzolla music, foregrounding plural temporalities in the score.

The two screens of the *Cuatro Estaciones Porteñas* multimedia project allude to the displacements of immigration. These amateur travelogues shot between 1915 and 1936 from Bolivia, Brazil, Ecuador, London, New York, Peru, Rome, Spain, and Venice reveal how tango is grounded in transnational experiences and identities. Signifying unofficial histories of Latin America and Europe, these home movie images counter dominant and official representations as an area of natural resources to extract and for investment from the global north. The visual design of this project accentuated the propinquities of its constituent parts rather than emphasizing the continuities of an imposed narrative and resonated with the layers and references in Piazzola's music.

Coda: Live Is Polyphonic

The home movie archive live can never be unified: it is relentlessly polyvocal and polyphonic. It is infinitely and resolutely combustible: collisions among elements open new explanations, unanticipated relations, and collaborative spaces. The home movie archive live proposes pulling in people, rather than pushing out to audiences. The home movie archive live presents a dynamic archival practice where exhibition features the responsiveness and agency of spectatorial relationships to images and space.

The conceptualization of the home movie archive live presents one very provisional attempt to think through some significant challenges. What happens with all this home movie footage that gets collected and processed? What is the social role of the archive? What possibilities reside in recovered material? Can digital interfaces and platforms offer new ways to open up this material and to create new pathways into it? How do we connect communities with archival materials? The home movie archive live considers the movement of artifacts as a journey across multiple interfaces, a complex system comprised of collaborations, convenings, encounters, hybrid temporalities, and migrations. To investigate how to enact these kinds of historiographic practices, archivists, artists, musicians, and scholars could collaborate to produce transitory places of engagement with others.

In the end, what movements, propositions, strategies, tactics, and vectors can be deployed to imagine the home movie archive live? In closing, I propose eight provisional speculations to begin an exploration into these significant questions. What follows are suggestions for modifications in conceptualizing the home movie archive live:

- From a phantasmatic of the past and the archival artifact as a fixed object to be revered and decoded to an engagement of home movies with urgent issues and imbedded matrices of the present that can converge and be foregrounded in a live environment

- From nostalgia for the material artifacts of home movies and amateur film as precious objects of cinephilia to the construction of new translocal spaces building contiguities between history, the present, and the future to craft more intuitive, multisensory environments
- From closed circuits of auteurs, connoisseurs, cultural elites, historians, and theorists engaging with home movies and amateur films to releasing the repressed potentialities of these films into more open circuits of collaboration, embodied organized encounters, and networked distribution, located somewhere, everywhere, elsewhere
- From considering the archive as a place to collect and store images to reconceptualizing the archive as a facilitator for the creation of new spaces for collaboration, interaction, and the formation of public works
- From the fixity of reclaimed national imaginaries into which home movies and amateur films are inserted to the fluidities of transversal and polyvocal vectors of movement that are locally situated
- From a text-based position to a place-based ethos
- From the archive as a brick-and-mortar institution to the archive as an experimental and experiential encounter
- From the home movie archive conceived as a repository of images to reimagining the archive as a mobilizer of communities, histories, multisensory environments, resonances, sensualities, and spaces that expose unknown territories

Notes

1. Full disclosure: as the codirector of the Finger Lakes Environmental Film Festival, I commissioned, wrote, and directed *Memescapes* in a collaborative team with the artists identified in this essay.

2. See Rick Altman, *Silent Film Sound* (New York: Columbia University Press, 2004); *Celluloid Symphonies: Texts and Contexts in Film Music History*, ed. Julie Hubbert (Berkeley: University of California Press, 2011).

3. For descriptions of Bill Morrison's live music/archival film performances, see his website, http://www.billmorrisonfilm.com.

4. For descriptions of Alloy Orchestra projects, see their website, http://www.alloyorchestra.com; Lacy Landre, "Alloy Orchestra Returns to the Oriental Theater," *Third Coast Digest*, accessed on May 2, 2018, http://thirdcoastdigest.com/2012/10/alloy-orchestra-returns-to-the-oriental-theatre/.

5. For example, *The Moving Image*, the journal of the Association of Moving Image Archivists, has been on the forefront of publishing groundbreaking research in home movie studies.

6. For a discussion of performance and "liveness" as a key component in the avant-garde, see Peggy Phelan, *Unmarked: The Politics of Performance* (London: Routledge, 1993).

7. For a thorough historical exploration of this shift from the temporal to the spatial in new media performance, see Steve Dixon, *Digital Performance: A History of New Media in Theater, Dance, Performance Art and Installation* (Cambridge, MA, MIT Press, 2007).

8. For a theorization of live performance and archival film, see Anna Siomopoulos and Patricia Zimmermann, "Silent Film Exhibition and Peformative Historiography: The *Within Our Gates* Project," *The Moving Image* 6, no. 2 (Fall 2006): 111–118.

9. Grant Kester, *Conversation Pieces: Community and Communication in Modern Art* (Berkeley: University of California Press, 2004), 14, 17.

10. Nicolas Bourriaud, *Relational Aesthetics* (Paris: Les presses du reel, 2002), 22.

11. Bourriaud, *Relational Aesthetics*, 46.

12. Bourriaud, *Relational Aesthetics*, 94.

13. Dale Hudson and Patricia R. Zimmermann, "Cinephilia, Technophilia, and Collaborative Remix Zones," *Screen* 50, no. 1 (Spring 2009): 135–146.

14. Tzvetan Todorov, "The Use and Abuse of Memory," in *What Happens to History: The Renewal of Ethics in Contemporary Thought*," ed. Howard Machitello, (London: Routledge, 2001), 11.

15. For an example of subaltern historiography advancing these ideas, see Ranajit Guha, *History at the Limit of World-History* (New York: Columbia University Press, 2002). For a discussion of how historiography has shifted away from narrative linearity and artifacts, see Alun Munslow, *Deconstructing History* (London; Routledge, 1997).

16. Robert Berkhofer Jr. *Beyond the Great Story: History as Text and Discourse* (Cambridge, MA: Harvard University Press, 1995), 170–275.

17. Philip Rosen, *Change Mummified: Cinema, Historicity, Theory* (Minneapolis: University of Minnesota Press, 2001), 265–359. See also Dipesh Chakrabarty, *Provincializing Europe: Postcolonial Thought and Historical Difference* (Princeton: Princeton University Press, 2000).

18. Guha, *History at the Limit*, 68.

19. Guha, *History at the Limit*, 22.

20. Guha, *History at the Limit*, 45–52.

21. Yves Dorme, *Image Cachees* (Luxembourg: Center national de l'audiovisuel au Luxembourg, 2007).

22. Berkhofer, *Beyond the Great Story*, 61–139.

Figure 13.1. Still from *Dramatically Repeating Lawrence of Arabia* (Les LeVeque, US, 2004). Image courtesy of Les LeVeque.

13

THROBS AND PULSATIONS

Les LeVeque and the Digitizing of Desire*

L ES LEVEQUE, A NEW YORK CITY-BASED SCULPTOR TURNED video artist, has spent at least two decades exploring the idea of machine interface by mathematically reprocessing a variety of mass media forms, such as Hollywood films, advertisements, presidential broadcasts, and publicly televised hearings. His use of algorithm and computer interface demonstrates how new technologies reposition

---

*I first discovered the work of video artist Les LeVeque through Video Data Bank, the well-known distributor of video art and activist video located in Chicago. I was searching for more experimental shorts to pair with feature films for my two-hundred-person lecture course, Introduction to Film Aesthetics and Analysis, at Ithaca College. The class is programmed around a concept of heterogeneity, mixing together narrative, documentary, and experimental films at each screening to produce resonances and combustions, a strategy that I pirated from many years of attending the Robert Flaherty Film Seminars and from talking to my friend and colleague Scott MacDonald, who employs a similar programming system for his introductory film studies courses at Hamilton College. When I found LeVeque's *4 Vertigo* (2000) on Video Data Bank's website, I immediately thought of showing it with Alfred Hitchcock's *Vertigo* (1958). It proved to be a productive pairing for students, a collision between the invisibility of classical Hollywood narrative editing and the visibility of an experimental deconstruction of those strategies, which pulled out the deeper psychoanalytic meanings disguised by causality and adherence to unities of time and space. In 2003, I moved to Singapore to teach film in the School of Communications at Nanyang Technological University for a semester, where I team taught with a Singaporean graduate student named Sharon Lin Tay, who studied the theories of Gilles Deleuze. Back in Singapore to write and to teach, Sharon assigned to team teach the introductory survey course with me. She was a devotee of Hitchcock, Sadie Plant, and Gilles Deleuze. We paired *4 Vertigo* and *Vertigo* together for the class and found ourselves talking endlessly about pedagogical strategies of creating conceptual mosaics between narrative and experimental film as a way to help students enter into more complex thinking about both. We then ended up presenting our ideas on LeVeque's strategies of remixing and unpacking classical Hollywood cinema at the Visible Evidence Conference in Montreal, programmed by Thomas Waugh from Concordia University in August of 2005, as a joint presentation where Sharon read our paper and I did a remix of LeVeque's projects. Our goal was to argue for this form of aggressive deconstruction of commercial films with new technologies and systems as an example of what is possible with the merger between documentary and digitality. The original version of this essay before it was revised for this volume was published as a coauthored piece with Sharon Lin Tay, "Throbs and Pulsations: Les LeVeque and the Digitalization of Desire," *Afterimage* 34, no. 3 (2006): 31–45.

the cinema imaginary and provoke complex issues of political and theoretical urgency for media practices and activism. Reverse engineering old technologies like analog film with mathematics, LeVeque fashions a high-tech aura through low-tech means, a conjuring of the interstitial zones between the old and the new, the psychoanalytically inscribed past and the technologically crafted future.

In place of the spectatorial relations and psychic control that govern much of our understanding of the cinema, LeVeque's works produce an alternative field charged with different coordinates that mobilize the use of gaps and fissures, durational strategies, rhythms, and soundscapes. LeVeque's artistic process is to reflect on how the contemporary mediascape presents a series of theoretical and political provocations that unsettle how we consider copyright, the image, interface, and spectatorship. The rising uncertainty over the status of the indexical sign where the signifier is caused by the signified shifts discussions of the image from representation and meaning to that of interface and materiality. This process modifies conceptualizations of spectatorship and desire by allowing the possibility of freedom from authority, whether psychoanalytic, political, or proprietary.

Influenced by Situationist politics, LeVeque's video projects digitize desire. They stage an often explosive contradictory movement between algorithms as controlled experimental systems and desire as uncontrolled, inchoate, ineffable, and immaterial. Digital media can be considered from the perspective of Gilles Deleuze's conceptual model of contingency as a way to develop a theory of the unexpected: moving from a model of an inert theory and practice of control of a stabilized imagescape to a model of a mobile media interface that produces unexpected and unpredictable results. It also moves media practice from the question, "What does it mean?" to "What would happen if?" These moves constitute not so much interpretations of meanings as much as they suggest tentative speculations of reordering image and sound as landscapes. This essay explores the key conceptual and political nodal points in a vast network of relations that comprise the new challenging mediascapes that LeVeque's video works invoke.

Materialities and Operation

The early film theorists Rudolph Arnheim and Siegfried Kracauer represent opposing approaches to the cinema. While Arnheim privileges the medium's inherent ability to manipulate images, Kracauer considers the machine's ability to record reality as a definitive aspect of the cinema. Fortified by inclinations toward realism and the generation of psychoanalytic meanings, Kracauer's approach dominates discourses on Hollywood cinema, while placing filmic materiality and specificity second. However, within the context of the contemporary explosion in digitality and new media technologies, the significance of cinematic materiality becomes much more salient and urgent to sustain a political imperative when considerable political autonomy has been lost by the imposition of an eroticized psychical economy on film theory and criticism. It is, therefore, both productive and necessary to shift analytical attention toward the interface rather than to the images that digital tools produce.

In LeVeque's works, algorithms strip and then shred psychoanalytic auras from the image. They investigate and then release its materiality from the immobilized shrouds of identification systems and eroticized models. Often producing a visual field that is not in the original films, algorithms function not as deconstructive devices, but rather as an alchemy to release the unexpected, the unpredictable, and the unacknowledged.

By digitally remediating classic Hollywood films, LeVeque subverts the dominance of psychoanalysis in cinematic discourse. In *2 Spellbound* (1999), LeVeque condenses Alfred Hitchcock's *Spellbound* (1945) into a 7 1/2 minute flickering Rorschach test by extracting a single frame from every second of the original film in a linear fashion—from Hitchcock's opening sequence to the copyright warning. LeVeque then reedits these frames into a series of flickering patterns that appear split down the middle, accompanied by an electronic dance track punctuated by voices repeating phrases articulating desires and mental states taken from the original *Spellbound*'s dialogue. *2 Spellbound* reconfigures the menacing and irrational desires of the gothic romance, which, in Hitchcock's film, focus on finding an identity for Ingrid Bergman's amnesiac lover. It then transforms these coded cravings into pulsating desires that thrive and proliferate on the surface of the image in nonsexually differentiated terms.

While some artists inscribe desire onto the material surface of their projects to expose or evade the psychoanalytic codification of desire, LeVeque challenges the dominance of psychoanalytic interpretations. His project operates in a different modality; he aims to reconfigure desire in order to free it from reductive codifications. In his multiple projects, desire resides in the machine, not the image. These exorcised materialities summon different theoretical considerations, such as flow, fluidity, and immersive embodiment. As a result, LeVeque's projects turn from the eye of cinema toward an exploration of the politics of the immersive body of the digital.

In LeVeque's films, the algorithm functions as the spine which supports the visual field. Rather than being embedded in the machine, these processes expose its operations, gears, and systems. In *4 Vertigo* (2000) and *2 Spellbound*, LeVeque employs algorithmic procedures by hand-cutting and pasting one frame per minute of screen time into the editing software Premiere. In these earlier works, he deployed a time-based corrector, a jitter patch, and old Amiga computers to manipulate the materials systematically exported from the original films. *2 Spellbound* reverses every other frame, disposing of the psychoanalytic desires embedded in *Spellbound* through speed, symmetry, and music. In *Dramatically Repeating Lawrence of Arabia* (2004), a work demonstrating the link between orientalism and stasis, a more complicated algorithm changes sequences between one and four. It produces convergences and divergences, *mise en abîme*, endless mirrorings that are then pulled apart. Temporality is not condensed through algorithmic sampling but instead transmuted into spatiality and surface, a zone of tactility and sensory excess.

From Images to Interfaces

Interface—the physicalized relational structure between user and machine—constitutes a key mode in theories and practices of digitality. It prompts a reconsideration of the image as no longer fixed and immutable but constantly changing and manipulated in order to generate new meanings and social spaces. *A Song from the Cultural Revolution* (1998) is a frame-by-frame capture of hand gestures Bill Gates made during his testimony before the United States Senate committee on the American Standard Code for Information Interchange (ASCII). The gestures are then reedited to spell out text from *Quotations from Chairman Mao Tse-Tung* (1967). In this piece, questions of interface move theory away from the relationships between images to an interrogation of the zones between machine, image, and user. This strategy suggests rejection of the image as representation and an exploration of the interface as tactile relation. Although manipulating Gates's hand gestures expresses LeVeque's antiauthoritarian stance, the objective of *A Song from the Cultural Revolution* is not to enact parody but rather to reconfigure the relationship between image and signification by inscribing the user on the surface materiality. Similarly, *Notes from the Underground* (2003) manipulates the blinks of President George W. Bush during a televised speech to spell out in Morse code a statement made in 1969 by the Weather Underground—another case where parody blends with tactility on the interface.

LeVeque's project shifts reception from conceptualizations of the spectator and interpretations of texts toward interface, which is elaborated as a productive, physicalized, and always changing coordination between user, machine, and image. In *Doubling Forbidden Planet* (2003), a ninety-nine-minute experiment in the durational, every image from the film is doubled and thus removes chiaroscuro and depth. It generates a conceptual shift from narrative to abstraction while it simultaneously emphasizes shapes, forms, colors, and textures as the interface of the work. This doubling enacts a conceptual pun: the original story chronicles a machine where users manifest their conscious and unconscious desires. LeVeque's piece doubles the machine in the film with the machine of the digital. This move proposes that the subconscious and conscious can be remapped as the analog and the digital, centered on the physical as an interface. A theorization of interfaces shifts analysis from the visual spaces within the screen to the idea of the screen as one vector within a larger social and physical space.

Charging the Space through Relay

LeVeque's contortions and manipulations transform Hollywood cinema from a narrativized psychic zone into a social space constructed out of a series of visual relays. Codes of economics, gender, power, and race deeply mark these films, which are imbued with a cultural presence overdetermined with ideological baggage. *The Birth of a Nation* (D. W. Griffith, 1915), *Gone with the Wind* (Victor Fleming, 1939), *Forbidden Planet* (Fred Wilcox, 1956), *Vertigo* (Alfred Hitchcock, 1958), and *The Sound of Music* (Robert Wise, 1965) are films that LeVeque grew up with as a child and teenager. As he explains their impact on him, they function as much as psychic landscapes and imprints of personal history as they operate as narrative stories and fantasies. Although LeVeque's video works engage the psychic and imaginary desires inherent in the cinematic apparatus, they inscribe the spectator's archive of desires and memories back onto the film's surface. This strategy signifies resistance to the otherwise predetermined spectatorial, psychic, and ideological space mapped out for the boxed-in spectator.

The algorithms transpose the unconscious of cinema into a material object. Jacques Derrida writes that the archivist "produces more archives ... and that is why the archive is never closed."[1] LeVeque's work actualizes a conceptual model of the archive as open, moving, and transforming rather than inert. Mobilizing a collision between the archive of cinema as a materiality and its psychoanalytic analog residue, LeVeque reconfigures established meanings and forms of authority in Hollywood films through displacement, materialization, and layering. Algorithms, then, animate, produce, and release contingent meanings, politics, and desire.

By configuring the archive as a problem worked on and investigated through algorithms, LeVeque's videos open a field of the unexpected. They produce an aleatory space *between* the images rather than *on top of* the images themselves. These projects conceive of the archive as not only a physical place but also as an imaginary field. For LeVeque, the archive is always an open source to be mined, which operates without walls, an endlessly mutating and material field. Beyond the material possession of the celluloid object, the archive possesses an unconscious dimension as a repository of repression. LeVeque's archive is comprised of Hollywood films and media images as well as his own subjective relationship with them as memory machines. This figuration of the archive resonates with Deleuze's concept of the brain as a screen that tracks a cinematic lapse from active extension into the intensity of the brain, memory, and thought. It discovers "subjective images, memories of childhood, sound, visual dreams and fantasies."[2] LeVeque's works represent an onslaught and an assault on the ideologically laden films and media images that he engages. They open up the epistemological possibility of conceiving the cinematically contingent through physicalized temporal hybridities.

LeVeque's video works juxtapose the archival analog object with mathematical logics. They jam the original narrative into a specter of flicker and rhythm that plays with persistence of vision, a nineteenth-century scientific trope that forms the foundational visuality of cinema. Also, to shear away the psychoanalytic, they also jettison the characters and narrative structures imbedded in Hollywood films. *4 Vertigo* (2000) poses the conceptual problem of the consequences of deleting the male gaze, a psychoanalytic model coursing through most scholarly writing on Hitchcock's films. The video condenses the film by grabbing one frame every two seconds and duplicating it four times. It thus inscribes a new digital gaze that exists in more of a public social exhibition rather than in a psychic space. LeVeque's works refuse the iconic and representational; they reject rearranging examples, excerpts, or fragments. Each video runs the source film from start to conclusion while continually dropping frames. They operate as experiments in the various forms of shifting the temporal into the durational.

LeVeque's digital practice charges the spaces of exhibition. It activates a conceptual zone through the physicality of watching and experiencing rhythmic patterns. This intensive physicality experientially exhumes the political valences in the works as they screen in the present tense. For example, *Backwards Birth of a Nation* (2000) reverses racism and *Dramatically Repeating Lawrence of Arabia* (2004) reveals the essentializing of the Middle East as a static masculinized landscape, with all movement removed in the reprocessing of the images. The works transform the operations of Hollywood cinema from a space of transference to multiple spaces of dissonance.

Hallucinations

Dipesh Chakrabarty argues that realism and rationality block minor histories that require "plural ways of being in the world."[3] However, the poetic, the dream-like, and the phantasmatic "pierces the veil of the real," transports beyond and transcends the "mere thingness of things," reconstituting but not denying the real.[4] The aesthetic and imaginary moment "creates a certain irreducible heterogeneity in the constitution of the political" by interrupting the one definition of the political aligned with the realist and prosaic, "to introduce unannounced the political change that only poetry can deliver."[5]

The political, then, must be reconstituted into a plurality of layers from dreams, ghosts, lived material reality, and nightmares, an enactment of a minoritarian politic that differs significantly from constructing oppositional or peripheral positions. Deleuze and Félix Guattari observe that "in erecting the figure of a universal minoritarian consciousness," one becomes revolutionary "by using a number of minority elements, by connecting, conjugating them, [inventing] a specific, unforeseen, autonomous becoming."[6] Whether working with classical realist texts, such as *Lawrence of Arabia* (1962, by David Lean), *Spellbound*, and

Vertigo, or genre-driven works like *The Sound of Music* and *Forbidden Planet*, LeVeque destabilizes the embedded realism by conjugating plurality as a conceptual model within the digital reprocessing. These works reverse the repression of incoherence, as though the hallucinations of Scottie in the original *Vertigo* were privileged moments rather than aberrations. This destabilizing operation alludes to Deleuze and Guattari's assertion that a "schizophrenic out for a walk is a better model than a neurotic lying on the analyst's couch," a rejection of prescribed psychical equilibrium.[7]

LeVeque produces hallucinations through erecting polarities between the original narrative and the persistence of vision. This process exemplifies the relationship Sadie Plant discerns between drugs and the cinema, the two "chemical responses to the speeding changes of the nineteenth century." Invoking Paul Virilio, she argues that the contemporary mediascape bases itself "on psychotropic derangement and chronological disturbance."[8] The soundscapes of many of LeVeque's videos elaborate this hallucinatory aesthetic. The dance music of *2 Spellbound*, the remixed sound track of *4 Vertigo*, and the pulsations of *16xTheHillsAreAliveWithTheSoundOfMusic* (2005) serve to modify "states of mind, perceptions, bodies, and brains; [and are] music that become[s] almost as immediate as drugs themselves."[9] These soundscapes "let the body escape the structures and boundaries that keep it organized" and allow an exit point from ideological baggage and the spectatorial regime.[10]

Produced through algorithms, works like *2 Spellbound* and *4 Vertigo* engage a kaleidoscopic effect by doubling and flipping the image. These abstract patterns shift with scene changes and underscore the image as a spatialized zone. These two works in particular, and LeVeque's video exploration of the historical hysteria around bioterror, *Strained Andromeda Strain* (2002), function as epistemological puns on the digital. Although the images appear digitally composited and layered, each frame is actually only one image extracted from the original film. The layering effect results from persistence of vision, a move that suggests an additional conceptual pun of an embodied virtuality.

Copyright and Dislodging Authority

LeVeque emblazons all of his work with an anticopyright sign, indicating his allegiance to expanding and redefining the threatened public domain of the free circulation of media imagery. However, one must not position his oeuvre within the embattled sector of collage, cut-up, and pirate media genres, even though it shares with these works a political stance that embraces archives without borders, rejects intellectual property as part of corporate relations of exchange, and advances an aggressive antiauthoritarianism. In the range of cut-up work that remixes and reedits speeches by President George Bush and British Prime Minister Tony Blair on the Iraq war, reedits of image and sound depend on reorganizing the level of the denotational to generate readable ideological interventions. In contrast, LeVeque's videos unfold differently from works that critique political hegemony and transnational corporate power solidified around issues of intellectual property and information technologies. Situationist artistic practices have contended that "detournment is less effective the more it approaches a rational reply."[11] In this context, LeVeque's projects veer away from the "rational reply" and instead unleash the irrational.

For LeVeque, the practice of doing digital seances on Hollywood films is a practice of dislodging authority on multiple levels: the authority of desire, the authority of linear coherence, and the authority of the narrative. These videos activate a Deleuzean network of flows and contingencies: they reconfigure the dynamics of power and the politics of media activism in the face of globalized corporate power. Graham Meikle observes that the impact of tactical media "often comes through highjacking the agenda of mainstream media."[12] LeVeque's video works do more. They corrupt the integrity of mainstream visual images, open up a struggle for interpretations, and assert the power of the irrational and the unconstructed. Such tactical protest and resistance suggests a strategy not of direct rational confrontation but of a set of infiltrations that eat into the authority and established meanings of the cinematic object. This strategy presents, perhaps, a more formidable model for media activism than opposition through hijacking.

Appropriation and collage juxtapositions often function on the level of the rational and the indexical. Unlike these devices, LeVeque's works are suspended between a double movement. While their reprocessing seems to argue that intellectual property in the context of transnational corporate media exists within deeply embedded social, historical, and psychic networks, they also examine the possibility of restoring physicality to both the cinematic object and spectator. LeVeque's pieces disengage the denotative, connotative, and legal from the image. Each functions as much more than an interrogation of what the image represents or how its meaning can be twisted into new subversive meanings. Rather, these works propose that Hollywood films are not proprietary property but circulatory, etherealized phantasms that lodge within us as a parasitic psychic fungus occupying brain and sensory cells. Rather than considering these films property or evidence, LeVeque deploys the digital to reposition Hollywood films as a shared psychic and political zone requiring exorcism through mathematics. The algorithmic cycles produce a visual and political yield exceeding the source film to arouse conceptual ideas through the incessant production of the unexpected.

Tensional Zones

LeVeque's exploration concentrates on engineering tensional zones through machine interface. In geology, a compressive zone piles materials on top of each other vertically, while a tensional zone pulls materials apart horizontally. LeVeque describes his process as "pulling a string of images taut and then plucking it to see what field of waves emanate."[13]

These works do not function within the conceptual framework of montage editing, with its reliance on generative dialectical collisions between images, formal structures, and ideas. Instead, they propose an exploration of cinema as surfaces, where algorithmic structures generate tensional zones. A kind of digital alchemy, LeVeque's project proposes a challenge for contemporary media practices: how to make something new beyond the location of cinema, in order to charge and open up its space.

Notes

1. Jacques Derrida, *Archive Fever: A Freudian Impression* (Chicago: University of Chicago Press, 1998), 68.

2. Gregory Flaxman, ed., *The Brain Is the Screen: Deleuze and the Philosophy of the Cinema* (Minneapolis: Minnesota University Press, 2000), 6.

3. Dipesh Chakrabarty, *Provincializing Europe* (Princeton, NJ: Princeton University Press, 2000), 101.

4. Chakrabarty, *Provincializing Europe*, 170–2.

5. Chakrabarty, *Provincializing Europe*, 178.

6. Gilles Deleuze and Felix Guattari, *A Thousand Plateaus: Capitalism and Schizophrenia* (London: Athlone, 1987), 106.

7. Gilles Deleuze and Felix Guattari, *Anti-Oedipus: Capitalism and Schizophrenia* (London: Athlone, 1983), 2.

8. Sadie Plant, *Writing on Drugs* (London: Faber and Faber, 1999), 48, 51.

9. Plant, *Writing on Drugs*, 166.

10. Plant, *Writing on Drugs*, 167.

11. Les LeVeque, interview with Sharon Lin Tay and Patricia R. Zimmermann, July 15, 2005.

12. Graham Meikle, *Future Active: Media Activism and the Internet* (London: Routledge, 2002), 124.

13. Les LeVeque, interview with Sharon Lin Tay and Patricia R. Zimmermann, July 15, 2005.

Figure 14.1. *No Business* cover design by Sean Tejaratchi/Negativland (2005).

14

JUST SAY NO

Negativland's No Business*

A HIGH STAKES CIVIL WAR RAGES ON YOUR PC. But it's not on the *Counterstrike* computer game or through the US government's secret Echelon surveillance program. It is between the ever-expanding proprietary commercial music industry empire and the file sharing, grassroots freedom fighters who transform old sound into new ideas. It's a war between intellectual property and fair use. It's also one of the central contradictions of transnational capital in the digital age: proprietary code or open source. It dives right into a central issue about democracy and artistic practice in the era of transnational media corporations that circle the globe like empires: to appropriate or not to appropriate commercially produced images and sound.

The audio collage art collective Negativland describes their multimedia project, *No Business* (Seeland, 2005) as a compendium of anticopyright strategies.

Ganesh, the Hindu god of wisdom with the body of a man and the head of an elephant, occupies the center of the inside jacket cover of the CD. Ganesh is the destroyer of evils and obstacles: he is the deity who pursues knowledge and

---

* I first encountered Mark Hosler, the iconoclastic partisan of anticopyright and one of the founding members of the remix band Negativland, at a conference titled "Collage as Cultural Practice" at the University of Iowa, March 2005. He gave one of the keynote speeches on his new project, *No Business*, a CD and manifesto making a militant case for anticopyright practices. Conference organizers Ruedi Kuenzli and Kembrew McLeod had assembled a dynamic, daring, and wide array of artists, scholars, and activists across many disciplines to probe questions of appropriation, collage practices, fair use, the history of art, and piracy. I gave another keynote at the conference, where I analyzed a range of new-media artists who mobilized collage practices. The conference held special meaning for me, since I was an alumna of the university's English and film departments. The classes, late-night screenings, poetry readings, and protests catapulted me into charged political and experimental worlds. At this conference, Hosler gifted me a copy of the *No Business* project. I had never written about sound art before and found the questions of collage and remix to be similar to questions in documentary compilation projects. I wrote a review essay that was published as "Just Say No: Negativland's *No Business*," *Afterimage* 34, no.1 (2006): 66–72. This essay is somewhat revised from the original, with an eye toward more precision in the arguments.

serves as a sort of mascot for the playful combinings of Negativland. This image suggests that collage represents nothing new at all. Or that perhaps collage has its own god—Ganesh.

A multiplatformed, anticorporate, prodemocratic media manifesto, *No Business* provides an operations manual to mobilize people to use their computers to burn, intervene, mash, recycle, and rip into mass culture. A twenty-first-century manifesto for audio collage, public domain, reuse, and sampling, the multimedia project—consisting of a fifty-six-page essay on public domain, the 5x11 die-cut outer sleeve art, the audio CD, and a DVD copy of their video *Gimme the Mermaid*—advances sly, subversive, and often brilliant polemics against propriety corporate culture and copyright.

Like special operations undercover agents, Negativland camouflages their hard-hitting anticapitalist, ignite-the-masses radical politics with fun, satire, and popular culture references ranging form Ethel Merman to the Beatles to Rosie O'Donnell. But underneath the guffaws and endless audio jump cuts lurks an uncompromising, sharp-as-a-laser surprise attack of unrelenting artistic civil disobedience.

Every image and sound on *No Business* is resolutely illegal—an aggressive no-holds-barred attack of civil disobedience, a kind of audio-visual sit-in against the transnational media corporations (TMCs). In the early decades of the twenty-first-century, the TMCs have shifted out of production and into global distribution across platforms, an economics that depends less on original productions than on the control of copyright and intellectual property as the most mobile form of real estate and power. Controlling intellectual property and archives represents the equivalent of printing money. The TMCs themselves recycle and remix their intellectual property, reducing the high financial investment and corresponding risks of production and reaping enormous financial gains.

As the outer sleeve slyly proclaims, "no elements original to Negativland were used to make these recordings." In a word, everything on the CD is illegal—not one of the tracks is copyright cleared. This avowedly illegal approach contributes to Negativland's outlaw status in the world of cultural production, a position that has often dumped their highly conceptual and political art work into the shadowy realms of the novelty category in record stores and pranksterism in the art world.

No Business is not exactly an easy-listening CD to pop on while chopping onions and carrots for the evening's pilaf. Instead, it functions more like a conceptual art piece for headphones—it's a form of portable audio art more often found in museum installations than on CDs. It mines the interstitial zones between popular culture, activism, music, and complex conceptual art.

Listener, beware: *No Business* is no cute mash-up combining incongruous tracks for ironic effect. Under the cover of zany, seemingly tangential cacophony lurks a compelling, logical, and surprisingly deductive argument to liberate the public domain from corporate colonization. It advocates multiple weaponry: computers, creativity, file sharing, grassroots defiance, law, online activism, and stealing music. And it insists culture should be free and shared—a vibrant dose of optimism.

Celebrating their twenty-fifth anniversary, the music press has crowned Negativland the "elder statesmen" and "merry pranksters" of anticopyright audio collage with found sound. However, Negativland is more than a rock band, although they slyly teeter on the edge of the indie music scene. They reject rock star auteurism, operating as an artists' collective rather than as individual personalities, rarely identifying the group's members by name—a refutation of the cult of personality imbedded in the commercial music business. They have worked as a collaborative group of audio and visual artists across a variety of platforms.

A hybrid between an artists' collective, a punk rock band, and a satirical performance art team, Negativland's subversive antics have helped to define interventionist art in the last two decades. They coined the term "culture jammer" in 1984. They provoked an infamous copyright lawsuit in 1991, when Island Records sued them for sampling U2 and remixing it with outtakes from a swearing Casey Kasem. Filmmaker Craig Baldwin's 1995 rollicking collage documentary film, *Sonic Outlaws*, released on DVD in 2005, unpacks the case and provides one of the best entrees for the uninitiated into the radical insurgency of Negativland. They have wrangled in legal skirmishes with the Recording Industry Association of America (RIAA), Pepsi, Geffen Records, and even Phillip Glass. Their densely collaged weekly live improvisational KPFA radio show, *Over the Edge*, has aired continuously since 1981.

In 2004, Negativland collaborated with Creative Commons (www.creativecommons.org) to develop a sampling license as an alternative to existing copyright laws. They served as project leads, working with the Creative Commons team of lawyers to develop a middle ground between copyright and unbounded fair use that would protect noncommercial creative music sampling. They were instrumental in instituting the "no use in advertising" clause into the Creative Commons sampling license.

Negativland's unique aesthetic, a kind of caffeinated, torqued-out version of Prairie Home Companion on shuffle mode, forges a combustive sonic landscape out of tangents, interceptions, and juxtapositions in such CDs as *Escape from Noise* (1987), *Helter Stupid* (1989) *U2* (1991), and *Dispepsi* (1997). Drawing on the long traditions of Dada's juxtapositions of the everyday for political intervention and the kind of intricate sonic mindscapes produced by Orson Welles and Firesign Theater, Negativland illuminates the power relations imbedded in the media that surrounds us. They perform exorcisms into the inane surfaces and sounds of popular music and audio culture, attempting to release polemics through the aggressive production of gaps and breaks. They ransack and then shred popular culture to craft arguments about artistic freedom. Besides records, they have produced books, fine art, live performances, and videos from appropriated images, sound, and text.

Designed in bright yellow and black, the *No Business* CD sleeve evokes a warning zone or police tape, alluding to the dangerous trespass they advocate. The visual iconography catalogs the trickster and boundary-crossing gods and goddesses of spliced and collaged entities from mythology to consumer culture: Batman, centaur, Elsie the Cow, Frankenstein, the Little Mermaid, Medusa, Mickey Mouse, minotaur, Smokey the Bear, sphinx, unicorn, and wolfman. Unlike so much of postmodern art practice, Negativland eschews a distanced irony and instead advances a political argument to promote action and intervention. Some commentators have linked their art practice with postmodernism's mixing of high and low culture, its collaged aesthetic, and its irreverent mix of genres. However, Negativland veers away from postmodernism's dispassionate, ironic exploration of surface and instead attempts to mobilize its listeners to free the cultural productions and expressions that surround and engulf them.

More political in terms of intervention into mass culture and more conceptual in terms of moving beyond surface into abstraction, Negativland actually operates more in the realm of rational argumentation than is immediately apparent from the wild graphics and aggressive sound recompositions. The images and sounds in the *No Business* project are assembled not as surface manifestations of a bankrupt commercial culture, but instead as available archival evidence to be reorganized into new arguments and explanatory models aimed at changing the listener's own conceptual grids. It operates as an art practice that works to shift the spectators' notional models and reframe the world of popular culture as evidence to be deployed in new arguments—a very ambitious and risky undertaking.

Intriguingly, the CD functions as short form study notes, illustrating and explaining the free culture arguments in the fifty-six page booklet, "Two Relationships to a Cultural Public Domain." Negativland advances two worlds at war. The first—and clearly the most dangerous—advances the idea that all cultural work is proprietary and requires financial compensation, a position identified with the five transnational media corporations that control most of the music industry. The second—and for Negativland the most creative and democratic—engages a culture that is endlessly reproducing, redistributing, and remaking itself in free and open creative exchange.

Negativland contends that digital technology has rendered copyright an outmoded legal form. Self-ownership and free exchange may be the future of music on the internet and a new frontier of possibilities. The booklet refutes the music industry's standard argument that file sharing eats market shares, pointing out the effects of the decline in long-form album production, of Clear Channel, and of consumer migrations to DVD and gaming. The music industry attempts to control the internet, but its open, sharing, decentralized technology of easy exchange subverts industry control. Negativland argues that the internet's library-like structure, which facilitates sharing and spreading ideas, reverses the one-way communication of other mass media. This argument is only the latest iteration in radical communication theory of advocacy for two-way communication. From Brecht through the twentieth century, artists and scholars have argued for an exchange model of communication, but Negativland points out that it is worth revisiting and reemphasizing as a call to arms. Most importantly, they advocate for free and open access, as well as for a legal redefinition of fair use to include transformative use.

Negativland emphasizes that the home computer functions as "the ultimate collage and appropriation box," a tool for creative recycling that requires free access for free expression. Outdated copyright restrictions constitute prior restraints, a censoring of creative practice inhibiting social commentary, satire, and criticism. Negativland agitates for an expansion of fair use and public domain to redress laws biased in favor of commercial media. The essay argues for a politics and aesthetics of transformation and recomposition—"the logical and inalienable right of artists"—to "enlarge all of our brains in a less intellectually constructed environment."

The eight soundscapes on the CD counter the serious arguments of "Two Relations" with a wryly ribald and irreverently gutsy sound design—another strategy to make the same argument about fair use, but more inductively, with quirky, offbeat tactics. The multitrack process of layering sound resembles multiple layers of film soundtracks more than it does recorded music, a form of recomposition that works to create arguments imbedded in dense soundscapes that envelop the listener. This process plunders virtually every mass media genre—award shows, commercials, film noir, musicals—with disconcerting aural juxtapositions and jujitsu editing.

"Old Is New" creates an eerie, horror-film-like environment by layering and pitch shifting voices from the Beatles track "Because" into a Greek chorus, a sort of opening anthem for collage as a central feature of the collective aesthetic legacy. The title cut of the album features Ethel Merman's 1954 ode to the entertainment industry "There's No Business like Show Business" recut to say "there's no business like stealing." And in "Favorite Things," Julie Andrews, from *The Sound of Music*, chortles that her favorite things are dog bites, nose cream, and bee stings—a sound prank that works as a metaphor, perhaps, for Negativland's modus operandi, the art of inversion and subversion.

The almost ten-minute-long "Downloading" is the political tour de force of the CD. It interrupts and intercepts Michael Green, president/CEO of the National Academy of Recording Arts and Sciences, speaking at a Grammy Awards broadcast against file sharing and downloading, with layers of sound dissonance from

BBC News, NPR, Elton John, and others. Green's choice phrases, like "downloading," "worldwide theft and indifference," "rip, rip, rip," and "entire music food chain" are repeated, tweaked, and morphed into what amounts to a town hall of voices from the opposition. "Downloading" disturbs the seamlessness of music industry propaganda with debate and disjunctures, hijacking space for more utopian discourse by inserting openings and fissures into smooth corporatized soundscapes. The monologue of transnational capital, epitomized in the production of sound jump cuts and gaps, is replaced with a dialectic of struggle over the ideas of file sharing, now a central battleground

In the 1990s, an era when the object itself was the point of contention and artists pilloried by court cases could gain fame, corporations sued a variety of visual and audio artists (including Negativland) for copyright infringement. In fact, Negativland has often joked that they are the band not with a hit record, but with a hit lawsuit. Now, the TMCs have moved their attention away from the artistic object to the networks of circulation, like downloading, encryption, and P2P, a historical shift that *No Business* recognizes and engages.

No Business also includes a video called *Gimme the Mermaid*, rendered at night on Disney's own computers. The piece features elaborate and also beautiful digital compositing and visual layering that echoes almost Baroque layers of audio. A male voice replaces the mermaid's, an act of remixing gender. The *No Business* project also includes an anticopyright whoopee cushion just in case, after taking in the booklet and CD, you still need to be convinced that copyright strangles creativity.

Negativland's artistic strategy over many decades has been to problematize the readability of popular culture and loosen up the locations of artistic production, always mining the liminal zones between pop culture, art, and politics. It constitutes a process of endless unsettling rather than categorization, where the bits and pieces in the continuing mass culture surround are reassembled into new arguments.

One problem with this somewhat wild west cowboy tactic is that despite the populism inherent in Negativland's idea of collage as democratizing creativity, it devolves into a US-centric, white male world of technological utopianism, music industry insider jokes, and civil libertarianism. At the 2005 Collage as Cultural Practice Symposium at the University of Iowa, Negativland's charismatic, articulate, and funny Mark Hosler related the group's saga and discussed their audio projects to a packed house comprised of a mostly under-thirty, white male audience, a fan base derived from college radio and audio cognescenti dedicated to file sharing in their dorm rooms.

Collage practice has largely shifted into the digital, with mash-ups and cut-ups flooding the internet in a variety of viral marketing forms that appear daily in our email forwards. And with this shift to the internet and new technologies has come a regendering of collage as a form of ribald, adolescent male fun where George Bush's speeches are cut up but a political analysis of war, gender, and empire are absent, as evidenced by the fact that the majority of attendees at the collage conference were white and male. The world of hacking and manipulating digital technologies appears to be gendered male, echoing the rock and roll and the indie music scene.

Beyond the US file sharing and music sampling scene, however, collage looks quite different. A variety of postcolonial visual and media artists such as Ximena Cuevas (Mexico), Péter Forgács (Hungary), Leandro Katz, (Argentina/US), Jean-Marie Téno (Cameroon), and digital media collectives such as Sarai in India have shifted the vectors of collage toward linking the national imaginary, social struggle, and gender with more international vectors. Bhangra remixers like A. R. Rahman, Asian Dub Foundation, and Bally Sagoo have deployed recomposition of sound and music to link the East with the West in a critique of imperialism that infiltrates clubs and embodies politics in pleasure to danceable beats.

One wonders where the creative and political potential of talents like Negativland might go if they shifted their vectors away from the United States, popular culture, and male technogeeks to a larger conversation—and intervention—with the world of empire, war, gender, and race. A hint of what these new coordinates might yield and open up for a truly radical, more transnational engagement with the world occurred at the Deep Wireless Festival, a celebration of Radio Art, held in Toronto in May of 2005. Negativland performed a live radio show that boldly took on the discomfiting question of fundamentalism in both East and West and used audio of an Arab woman discussing Islam in Canada—a daring intervention during a time of war, border policing, and racism.

However, perhaps Negativland, which emanated from the suburbs of San Francisco, understands how to provoke the radical potential of suburban white male file sharers through insider humor about the record industry, a way to materialize the vast power of the TMCs for those who want music on demand and do not want to submit to the strangleholds of copyright-dependent political economies. Whatever their fan base, Negativland has taken up one of the most radical positions on fair use around. On the other hand, their defense of creativity and free expression veers uneasily toward civil libertarianism and rugged individualism disengaged from other significant social struggles or economic analysis.

No Business's idealism about the unique radical potentialities of the internet as a democratic rejection of top-down communication is not historically grounded and reads like hyperbole rather than a careful analysis of the complexities of digitality. They err on the side of optimism and hope, which may be their own way of disengaging from the immobilizing politics of inertia and despair. One could argue that Negativland deploys hope and fun as a form of performance art, functioning like shamans to exorcise corporatized thinking about intellectual property from listeners.

Perhaps one can forgive the overstatement in the context of Negativland's quest to reach a wider audience that may not be interested in scholarly research on the contradictory political economies and ecologies of new technologies. Virtually every new media technology to appear in the twentieth century has been imagined as a radical liberation of the masses by artists, engineers, entrepreneurs, and intellectuals alike. Bertolt Brecht, for example, wrote an influential essay seeing the potential of radio as a two-way form of communication in the 1920s; the Film and Photo League saw film as a way to mobilize workers in the 1930s; and early Portapak video activists in the 1970s argued for a new radical empowerment through media.

But these critiques are not arguments against the Negativland project to position intellectual property as a major political battleground for activists and artists, nor do they take away from the complexity of the conceptual artwork they produce. The power of *No Business* and the entire Negativland project resides in the fact that their strategy of appropriation does not end with the recomposition of images and sounds into clever diatribes against corporate control of culture. In addition, *No Business* and Negativland build spaces for polemics about cultural practice, creativity, and politics, spaces getting smaller and smaller day by day.

No Business exemplifies a form of radical cultural practice occupying the liminal zones between analog and digital, arguments and tangents, political polemics and multilayered mass culture humor, proprietary and open source, and between Mickey Mouse and Ganesh. Plundering the psychic and political unconscious of mass culture, *No Business* propels the reader and listener to refuse and refute culture as property—and to make something new out of the old.

Figure 15.1. Screenshot from *Within Our Gates* (Oscar Micheaux, USA, 1920).

15

REMIXED AND REVISITED BLACK CINEMA

Oscar Micheaux's Within Our Gates *Live Project**

W*ITHIN OUR GATES: REVISITED AND REMIXED* LAUNCHED BLACK History Month in 2004 at Ithaca College (Ithaca, New York, USA) with a newly commissioned score by Ithaca-based jazz pianist Fe Nunn for Oscar Micheaux's *Within Our Gates* (USA, 1920), a landmark silent film and the first African American feature film to be included on the United States National Film Registry. The performance featured live music from a jazz quartet, a Baroque clarinet solo, and gospel singing. It also featured digital live mixes and spoken-word performances by the Body and Soul Ensemble and the Ida B. Wells Spoken Word Ensemble, comprised of faculty from across the Roy H. Park School of Communications and the School of Music on the Ithaca College campus. On a conceptual level, the project and the performance engaged four central ideas: critical historiography, the new film history, digital culture theory, and collaborative ethnography. This

---

* In fall 2003, a group of Ithaca College administrators approached me about doing some programming for Black History Month in February 2004. This group included administrators from student affairs such as Roger Richardson and Stephanie Adams, and the assistant provost of Ithaca College, Tanya Saunders. They wanted to focus on music and wanted programming that would be something more than simply showing films with postscreening discussions. They also suggested an interdisciplinary program, bringing faculty together from across the campus. The renowned School of Music at Ithaca College, the impressive local music scene of Americana and jazz, and several film and communication scholars in the Roy H. Park School of Communications were looking for a way to collaborate on a project for this college-wide celebration. My colleague and fellow film historian Anna Siomopolous had the idea to screen *Within Our Gates* by Oscar Michaeux, inspired by new research being published on this early African American producer. Our group developed the idea of creating a spectacle to kick off Black History Month by combining our research into the history of racism in America and the history of the film into a spoken-word script we performed as a group. We invited a local jazz musician, Fe Nunn, to play, and he reached out to faculty in the School of Music such as oboist Baruch Whitehead. This production was one of the first of many projects combining silent film with live music and spoken word that I produced as collaborative participatory projects focused on enlivening archival objects and expanding audiences for this work. An earlier version of this essay was published as "Remixing and Revisiting *Within Our Gates*," *The Moving Image: The Journal of the Association of Moving Image Archivists* (Fall 2006): 118–124.

collaborative project posed a central question: how could music and spoken word mobilize and animate a reconceptualization of a silent film in a way that functioned as an intervention into the classical Hollywood model of music driving the narrative and supplying emotion?[1]

Drawing on conceptual models from critical historiography, the project sought to reroute the linear drive of the narrative of the film (problematized by Micheaux's somewhat fragmented and polemical intercutting in the first instance) with a more spatialized configuration. This would connect the historical context of the film and the contemporary historical moment with musical references from a range of African American musical traditions in order to intervene into the temporality of the film's narrative progression. In the critical historiographic theory of writers like Jacques Derrida, Runajit Guha, Tzvetan Todorov, and Hayden White the question of how to narrate histories as multiple and multilinear, as opposed to traditional metanarratives that are singular, unified, and immutable, has been interrogated as a central epistemological issue.[2] These concerns drove the creative and research work to mount this live performance project.

Developing out of these writers' arguments about the formation of the archive and its privileging and marginalization of particular discourses and practices are questions about the distribution and structure of primary source material, interrogating the very formation of the archive. Critical historiography counters the linear unity and immobility of traditional historiographic models of explanation with an emphasis on creating new explanatory models that conceive an interplay of multiple, contested meanings, expanded archival sources, an emphasis on polyvocalities, and an interest in inventing new forms and models of explanation that recognize and engage difference.

Within the context of the new film history that seeks to move the historical project away from the dominance of classical Hollywood texts and corporate archives toward a recovery of marginalized historical practices and spaces, *Within Our Gates Revisited and Remixed* intended to create a way to embody theoretical concepts of an archive that opened, as Derrida explained it, toward the future. Because Micheaux's film was only recently recovered in the 1990s and entered the US National Film Registry after that, many film scholars or programmers did not regard it as a canonical text. The development of the new film history has not only expanded the range of visual cultures of cinema to be analyzed beyond studio and national cinemas, but has also advocated new critical models of history that emphasize contiguities over continuities, and contexts over texts. Examples of areas that have been mined in this research area have included African American cinemas and other minoritized practices, amateur film, exploitation films, industrial and educational films, and regional exhibition practices. In fact, US government archival policy now identifies films that do not have a corporate home as "orphaned films," with special initiatives for acquisition, preservation, and access to these materials.[3]

Our conceptual models, then, for creating the live performance of *Within Our Gates Revisited and Remixed* derived from an intellectual and creative interest in addressing these two emerging, intersecting debates of critical historiography and the new film history about how to consider an embodied and pleasurable reevaluation and reanimation of the archive based on conceptualizations of spatiality, contingency, and contiguities. In this way, the project was not subservient to the textual operations of the film, with the music amplifying emotional readings positioned by the narrative or formal structure. Instead, the film was reformulated as an open archive into which other musical, historical, and aesthetic ideas could be built. These were meant to complicate the film through spoken word and music that summoned and evoked more polyvocalities: postcolonial theory advocating agency and a decentering of white models; the production and exhibition history of this African American independent film dealing with censorship; the race riots of the late teens and 1920s in the United States during the Great Migration of Blacks from the South to the North; and vernacular folk tales and music to voice the quotidian.[4]

The project sought to reconceptualize silent film as a performative act that was constantly changing. It positioned the film as a living organism reacting to a dynamic ecology of historical contexts. It sought to create a more fluid network of conceptual and historical ideas that was influenced by theories of circulatory cultural practices and recombinant media. As many digital theorists have argued, digitality suggests that visual culture is always mobile and changeable, endlessly reproducible and open to multiple reconfigurations. The notions of mobility and changeability challenge film theory's traditional orientation to close analysis of a fixed text. They also challenge cultural studies assumptions about resistance located in subversive readings of mass-mediated cultural practices and discourses.[5]

Although the project relied heavily on film theory to analyze the structure and aesthetics of the film and drew on cultural studies models to research the history of spectatorship as well as the use of music in black silent cinema, these models did not drive the project. Rather, they contributed to deciphering the problem of how to narrate the film differently and how to create a different kind of social exhibition space that was racialized and gendered differently. Many digital theorists have pointed to the idea that the divide between the digital and the analog constitutes an imaginary state, projecting false binary oppositions based on technologies. For these theorists, more traditional analog forms have been loaded into the computer where divisions between media forms and platforms are no longer distinctive. Our project operated in dialogue with these emerging ideas about digitality as both new and old in several ways. First, it mobilized ideas about mutability, changeability, and lack of fixity as a model for developing various musical and spoken-word elements. Secondly, we formulated a working conception that the film itself was a series of hyperlinks offering pathways to other historical and musical nodes, thereby allowing the film to open up into African American history and contemporary discourses on the war on terror and the USA PATRIOT Act. Thus, rather than moving in toward exposition and enhancement of the film's textual and narrative structures, we used the film to move outward toward multiple historical and political contexts. Thirdly, we created an opening prologue that featured a digital remix of images of African Americans in cinema accompanied by live djembe drumming and dancing to visually intervene into the false binaries between the analog and the digital, history and the present, silence and spoken word.

Within Our Gates Revisited and Remixed was a historical first for Ithaca College: a commission to a local composer to score and accompany a silent film in a live performance. Founded in 1892 as a music conservatory, Ithaca College houses a preeminent and nationally recognized School of Music. It also has the well-known Roy H. Park School of Communications, which includes a film school that has existed since the late 1960s. As a comprehensive college that mixes the liberal arts with professional schools such as Music, Communications, Health Sciences and Human Performance, and Business, Ithaca College is not the typical liberal arts small college. Humanities and Sciences is one school among six schools and divisions. However, for most of its history, the college has de facto erected high barriers between each of the schools, figuring them as unique universes and communities.

In the early 2000s, a new Institutional Plan was instituted under President Peggy Williams that determined that the insularity of the schools was not stimulating intellectual and creative growth and had created a campus with high walls and unproductive divisions. To remedy this situation, the Institutional Plan advanced interdisciplinary and joint projects across schools, providing new incentives and financial resources to stimulate projects that crossed between the different schools, divisions, and departments. *Within Our Gates Revisited and Remixed*, then, was produced within the context of a larger institutional plan that supported work between and across schools that would have been inhibited by lack of administrative support and resources only a few years before.

Despite two internationally recognized arts programs in music and cinema, Ithaca College had never undertaken the idea of scoring a silent film. The project evolved from a joint partnership with the Office of Multicultural Affairs on campus, with whom a curatorial collective called Cinema on the Edge comprised of a group of faculty in Cinema and Television /Radio had programmed film and video screenings for Black History Month for over five years. In the fall of 2003, the assistant director of the Office of Multicultural Affairs, Stephanie Adams, suggested that the February 2004 program focus on African American music. She wondered if there perhaps might be a way to engage in less predictable film programming, something beyond screening a social realist documentary on some aspect of black history with a panel of faculty experts leading the postscreening discussion.

Adams wondered if our curatorial group could imagine some kind of film event that would include music but also invoke history in a way that would mobilize and engage an audience of college students in a new, less predictable way. The student groups present at the meeting decided to focus on hip-hop culture. Our group came up with the idea of scoring a Micheaux film with live music to create an immersive, surprising, and historical multimedia event, a spectacle of film, music, and spoken word. The Office of Multicultural Affairs, the School of Music, the Roy H. Park School of Communications, the Office of the Provost, and the Division of Interdisciplinary and International Studies provided funding for the project and for the commission to composer Fe Nunn. Without collaboration across schools and disciplines, the project not only would never have been funded at the level required to mount such a large project, but would also not have evolved the way it did into a multimedia performance reconceptualizing how to think about the relationship between music, spoken word, multiple histories, and the image.

Within Our Gates Revisited and Remixed worked to establish a collaboration between local musicians in Ithaca, New York—a community widely recognized as a vibrant center for a wide range of music—and the academic community. Fe Nunn, an alumni of Ithaca College, was commissioned to work with the team. Nunn is a songwriter and composer who lives in Ithaca. He has written music for television and radio commercials as well as for film. He composed and performed the original score for the award-winning documentary *Passin It On* (directed by Simon Tarr and a collaborative team of Ithaca College students in 2002). As a pianist, he specializes in jazz and avant garde musical forms. He started playing piano at the age of five, accompanying the commercials on TV. Nunn grew up in Buffalo, New York, during the powerhouse jazz era there in the 1960s, where he regularly heard John Coltrane, Roland Kirk, and Sonny Stitt perform live at the Blue Moon Club. He wrote the score for the All of Us Project, an initiative to involve the entire community in children's education. With Dr. Jeff Claus and Dr. Baruch Whitehead, he helped to launch the Community Unity Music Education Program, a new form of music school for young children in Ithaca. His CDs include *We Can Make It* (1999) and *Precious Moments* (2004, dedicated to Rashad Richardson). A fourth-grade teacher at Beverly J. Martin Elementary School in Ithaca at the time of the project, he was interested in how involvement in the performing arts could spur academic success. He has played with guitarist Mike Vitucci for over twenty-five years. Nunn's experience in avant garde jazz brought a perspective of group interaction, improvisation, and ensemble where musicians responded to each other's unique contributions, bringing their individual talents to the project.

The team was comprised of an interdisciplinary group of scholars and artists who brought different intellectual skills and aesthetic orientations to the project. One of our team members, Anna Siomopoulos, had just completed a dissertation on visual representation, history, and the 1930s, and had done extensive research on Micheaux. Drawing on her research, she suggested *Within Our Gates* as a possible project because of its history of censorship, its position as a historically important film in American film history, and its uncompromising view on black life in the 1920s. Another member of the team, Grace An, had been writing on postcolonial theories of cross-cultural visual representation. Both Siomopoulos and An were emerging film studies scholars.

John Hochheimer, a scholar of journalism and radio, possessed a vast knowledge of the history of African American musical forms. I was a film, video, and new media historian and theorist with an interest in critical historiography. Zachary Williams, a new faculty member from the Center for the Study of Culture, Race and Ethnicity, was a specialist in African American intellectual thought, a spoken-word artist, and a preacher. Finally, four academically based artists joined our team. Baruch Whitehead from the School of Music not only played classical oboe, but had experience in leading African American choirs. Simon Tarr, a filmmaker and digital artist, was interested in working with live VJing with computers in order to remix and reprocess archival images of the history of African Americans in film. Filmmaking professors Changhee Chun and Meg Jamieson provided the theatrical lighting, which they mounted to evoke the style of Chinese New Year red lanterns in homage to the fact that the performance coincided with that holiday.

The goal of this project was to create a new way to read *Within Our Gates* critically, to refuse the arbitrary divide between the past and the present, between the analog and the digital, through music and spoken word. Further, our group was a combination of academics, community-based musicians, media artists, and scholars who invoked the principles of improvisation from the Fluxus movement, an interdisciplinary collective founded on a flexible, fungible approach to art. We privileged group rather than individual interaction, aleatory elements in production and performance, and the remaking of public space to reanimate a historical film.

Siomopoulos prepared a packet of film history readings on Micheaux from recently published books and journal articles for the entire team. During rehearsals, Nunn suggested that everyone involved in the project participate in the performance in some way, contributing in their own voice. The scholars on the project drew on Siomopoulos's reading packet (which included chapters from recently published scholarly books on Micheaux as well as other critical analyses of black film exhibition) for the spoken-word script. In addition, they also conducted additional research into African American history during the post–Civil War and Great Migration periods. Thus, the spoken-word segments of the production evolved from the collaboration between jazz musicians and academics: the musicians provided musical interpretations of and interventions into the film while the academics provided analysis as well as historical and theoretical context with spoken word. In this constellation of forces, the music and words operated within a dialectical relationship. The music released the images from silence and the past. The scholarly readings torqued and inverted the meaning of the images. The spoken word script functioned as a distanciation strategy, to separate the film from its narrative limitations and pull it into larger theoretical, critical, and historical contexts.

This description of how the project emerged within the institutional context of a push for interdisciplinarity and a larger intellectual and artistic context of rethinking the politics of archival film exhibition in the digital age leaves several questions unanswered. In a constantly shape-shifting media ecology, screening films on a wall in two dimensions has been largely drained of social and aesthetic impact because of the proliferation of media platforms and media that migrates between and across forms and moves between private and public arenas. The entire practice of film exhibition, then, needs to be reconceptualized because images themselves are now more accessible than ever. This opens up possibilities for archivists, artists, and performers who have investigated ways to reinvent film exhibition through multimedia.

Through reading, intensive and repeated screenings of the film, and vigorous analytical discussion, our group concluded that the two-dimensional image lacks salience now that it is almost infinitely accessible and privatized within home viewing. The central dilemma for curators and programmers, therefore, is how to create a public space for exhibition that is unique from other forms of spectatorship and that positions a film not as a commodity that is endlessly repeatable, but as a one-off, special experience. Commercial cinematic practices in the twenty-first century have moved toward the production of visual and auditory spectacle, with IMAX projections, large screens, digital immersive surround sound, and raked stadium seating that transform theaters into entertainment experiences beyond the image itself. In the art and public media worlds, a similar movement emerged with the development of microcinemas, installation digital and video art that recaptures and reconfigures space, and an interest in performing live music with various forms of projection assembled with classic silent films, experimental works, found footage, or orphaned cinemas. *Within Our Gates Revisited and Remixed* aimed to enter into this question of the place and function of historical cinemas in a rapidly recalibrated exhibition context by creating a form of counterspectacle mobilized by intellectual and musical ideas rather than simply visuality, as typified in theories of cinematic spectacle.

Our project asked the following questions: How could we create a spectacle that did not rely solely on visually overwhelming the senses, but activated an embodied critical engagement in audiences? Why undertake a collaborative project combining academic research, critical theory and history, visual and musical creation, feature-length film scoring, lighting and performance on an archival film? Why open Black History Month with a dialectic between the past and the present, between analog and digital, between celluloid and live performance?

To answer these questions, one needs to consider the normative forms of cinema education at the university level and how a project like *Within Our Gates* could provide a different model of the creative enterprise. The major tendency in most film programs, at least on the undergraduate level, is to focus on production courses, with film studies positioned as peripheral to filmmaking. Moreover, distribution and exhibition, the most powerful economic sectors of the global entertainment industry, are rarely if ever addressed, whether in studio-based or critical-studies courses.

Indeed, a cursory overview of most film studies programs reveals an epistemological overemphasis on the text, whether the focus is on producing a new text or analyzing old ones, in production or in film studies. On one end, many film schools adopt an industrial model of production, with an emphasis on a division of labor, hierarchies, classical narrative structures, narrative transparency, and unity. Often dubbed "professional training," this model mimics the classical Hollywood studio system of the golden era from about 1920 to 1948. On the other end, a more individualistic, romantic notion of the artisanal filmmaker expressing unique subjectivities often infiltrates both experimental and documentary practices. However, other models of production exist, such as collaborative models, collectives, group projects—models derived from cinematic and visual culture practices outside the often US-centric commercial or art models.

Our team was interested in reconceptualizing the politics of exhibition in the digital era outside and beyond these two modes of hierarchical production and artisanal work. Several contingencies contributed to exploring the idea of a collaborative ensemble based on a different model for making creative work and with possibilities to alter the relationship between production, distribution and exhibition. During my sabbatical, I had an appointment as a visiting professor at Nanyang Technological University in Singapore, an internationally recognized engineering school. In the School of Communication and Information, where I was appointed to teach, course projects and final-year projects were done in groups, not individually, as is the case in most American film schools. I observed the emphasis on collaboration, team building, generation of ideas, and quality of product that this structure enabled. I also observed that faculty were involved in a variety of joint research projects and research groups, not only doing their own individual research but also working on collaborative scholarly teams with colleagues. This model of horizontal structure, of course, is congruent with the way the new economy and new media organizations are structured to promote innovation and invention. I observed firsthand how deemphasizing the individual pushed ideas farther and faster, often with more rigor and vivacity. It refocused the work on ideas and concepts. I was struck by how much this model differed from my own academic experience in the United States. In fact, it was the exact opposite. Needless to say, this model of working with others who have different academic ranks across traditional hierarchies and come informed by different experiences in a collaborative project inspired me to think about how to enact a similar think-tank model at my home institution back in Ithaca, New York.

While on sabbatical and working on another book project, I became interested in models for collaboration that employed a more horizontal structure and that could deal with an ethics of representation of difference. David MacDougall's writings elaborating a critical ethnography that moved beyond the separation between maker and others, especially in his influential book *Transcultural Cinema*, provided ways to think about the collaborative process.[6] MacDougall, a filmmaker with many decades of experience working in Australia, Asia, and Africa, advances that filmmaking is not about speaking about, but speaking alongside and with. He argues that the filmmaking and the creative process is not about making a representation or an image, but about entering into a relationship where both parties engage within a liminal zone, and change from the encounter. Thus, the ethics of representation is not so much about the image, but about the process of performative acts of engagement with others to produce a common knowledge that is always an indeterminate exploration. For MacDougall, culture, and, by extension, the act of creation, is a continual process of interpretation, reinvention, and multivocality. This act of creation always involves crossing into liminal zones of difference requiring acknowledgement, collaboration, and participation in an encounter. It elaborates a convergence and conversation across difference and across cultures.

MacDougall's ideas were important in thinking through the racialized and gendered issues of *Within Our Gates*. Our team was mixed race, including African Americans, Asian Americans, Mexican Americans, and European Americans. We were dealing with a newly anointed classic film of African American independent cinema that approached difficult race issues of black education, segregation, the black middle class, lynching, and rape. This collaborative model has many cultural iterations beyond the academy in jazz, folk music, and ideas about cultural hybridity and cultural flows. It provoked a way to think through how to remake and reimagine making a project beyond the politics of representation toward a politics of reanimation through collaboration.

The team formed two ensembles to analyze and actualize these concepts and debates from critical historiography, the new film history, digital theory, and collaborative ethnography as a way to embody our theories of rejecting the idea of individual authorship and historical reanimation. The Body and Soul Ensemble was a collaborative team of Ithaca College faculty from Journalism, Television/Radio, Cinema, Music, and the Center for the Study of Culture, Race and Ethnicity dedicated to exorcising the false divides between theory and practice, history and the present, digital and analog, film on the wall and live performance. The ensemble deployed an improvisational, collaborative method of producing work that drew in and remixed many different modes, gestures, and forms, rejecting the idea of individual authorship. It configured cultural objects, visual culture, and histories as fluid and active, jettisoning notions of cultural practice as fixed. Deploying and remixing a range of old and new media technologies like cinema, computers, djembe drumming, lighting, and spoken word, the ensemble explored how marginalized histories could be mobilized to form new kinds of social spaces through embodiment and performance. Formed in 2003, the ensemble was named for the 1925 Micheaux film of the same name starring singer and social activist Paul Robeson. *Within Our Gates Revisited and Remixed* marked the ensemble's debut project.

A second ensemble, the Ida B. Wells Spoken Word Ensemble, was a collaborative research and performance group comprised of Ithaca College faculty from the departments of Cinema, Journalism, Television and Radio, and the Center for the Study of Culture, Race and Ethnicity. Formed in 2004, the group explored how cultural objects like early cinema could be voiced differently in a dialectic with the present through the layering of historical and theoretical source material. The ensemble employed Paul Gilroy's position on the political necessity of polyphonic forms as well as ideas from critical historiography advocating a historical practice based on contiguities rather than continuities. Through spoken-word performance, the group sought to mobilize historical research and critical theory as embodied in interactive dialogues between visual culture, critical analysis, and audiences. Named for the black feminist journalist who exposed the horrors of lynching, the Ida B. Wells Spoken Word Ensemble made its debut as a collective live performance team at *Within Our Gates Revisited and Remixed*.

Through this collaborative process, which was not without conflict, argument, and debate about how to work through the project, our team analyzed different approaches to the use of music for silent films. Based on our research into black exhibition practices in Chicago during the 1920s and also our research into how silent films are typically rescored to promote and enhance the narrative in order to emphasize emotional identification, we developed the idea of "blackening" the film through jazz and hip-hop. We also decided that the music would not function as subservient to the filmic text or narrative, but as an equal dialectical critical element to complicate the reading of the film for spectators. We sought to create a spectatorial liminal mode of interaction through a strategy of polyvocality. We also sought to animate theoretical notions of the instabilities of the text by destabilizing the text through music, spoken word, and multiple voices. Silent film was never truly silent. In fact, it was loud, interactive, improvisational, collective, and topical. It was always accompanied by live music, either a solo piano, an organ, a full orchestra, or a small trio. For some spectators, the music and live performance were more important than the screen images because the music was live and referenced the location of the theater in a given city or town.

In the first half of the last century, commercial movies houses were segregated. African Americans were often confined to the balcony so they did not interact with white spectators. However, black cinemas emerged in cities of the Great Migration like Chicago, Detroit, and New York where moviegoing was not about sitting quietly in your seat. Instead, it was about participating in the jazz, blues, and improvisations of extraordinarily gifted musicians who knew how to work the house and create a black cultural oasis. It was also about talking back to the screen to participate in or to comment on the film. The performance of *Within Our Gates* at Ithaca College evoked the improvisational immersive experience of black theaters on the South Side of Chicago in the 1920s. In these venues, black music drove the film and spectators' engagement of it through counterpoint, references, explosive solos, and audience participation, inverting the Hollywood film music conventions of supporting the pathos of the narrative.

D. W. Griffith changed film language and film form in *The Birth of a Nation* (1915). He also produced a film that celebrated the Ku Klux Klan and racism, invoking white fears about African Americans, black male sexuality, and imagined threats to white women. The NAACP organized protests about the depictions of African Americans in this film at theaters around the country. Five years later, as a retort to *The Birth of a Nation*, African American independent filmmaker Oscar Micheaux produced *Within Our Gates*. The film combines an unflinching portrayal of the gross violations perpetrated by whites against blacks with a determined call for black idealism. Repeatedly recut by censors who deemed the harrowing sequences of lynching and attempted rape too incendiary in the wake of the Chicago race riots of 1919, few saw Micheaux's film as he intended it. Lost for seventy years, *Within Our Gates* was rediscovered at the Filmoteca Espanola in Madrid and restored by the Library of Congress in 1993. The music and spoken word in the *Within Our Gates Revisited and Remixed* project reinvented the relationship between film and history by taking the backstory and foregrounding it, transforming the complex historical context into a more polyvocal text.

A powerful and enlightening cultural document and landmark film, *Within Our Gates* is no less relevant today than it was in 1920. It resonates and reverberates with racial profiling, defunding of education, diaspora, the war on terror. This special Ithaca College screening featured a large collaborative team of faculty historians, sociologists, film theorists, media and film historians, filmmakers, and local musicians joined together to perform a collective exorcism on this history by catapulting its ideas and forms into a conversation with the present.

The world premiere of this newly composed and arranged score for *Within Our Gates* featured live music and spoken-word performances to create a Fluxus- and jazz-inspired happening. Its structure revolved around polyvocalities to enliven and embolden a dialogue on race. Cultural and technological ingredients including African drumming; dance performance; digital and analog; digital loops; a light show; live VJ mixing of images from black cultural and political history; lynching and liberation; music and spoken word; piano, oboe, drum, and saxophone; the movie screen; and rape and resistance were layered to circulate and recirculate through history and the present.

Notes

1. For discussions of how music in classical Hollywood narrative films supports the narrative rather than interferes with or intervenes into it, see Kathryn Kalinak, *Settling the Score: Music and the Classical Hollywood Film* (Madison: University of Wisconsin Press, 1992).

2. For examples of critical historiography, see Jacques Derrida, *Archive Fever* (Chicago: University of Chicago Press, 1995); Keith Jenkins, ed., *The Postmodern History Reader* (London: Routledge, 1997); Howard Marchitello, *What Happens to History: The Renewal of Ethics in Contemporary Thought* (New York: Routledge, 2001); Ranajit Guha, *History at the Limit of World-History* (New York: Columbia University Press, 2002).

3. For discussion of the impact of orphan film policy in the United States on archival acquisition, see Patricia R. Zimmermann and Karen I. Ishizuka, *Mining the Home Movie: Excavations in Histories and Memories* (Berkeley: University of California Press, 2007).

4. For an extended scholarly analysis of Oscar Micheaux, see Pearl Bowser and Louise Spence, *Writing Himself into History: Oscar Michaeux, His Silent Films and His Audiences* (New Brunswick: Rutgers University Press, 2002).

5. For discussions of these ideas of networks and the mutability of the digital, see Sean Cubitt, *Digital Aesthetics* (London: Sage Publications, 1998); Critical Art Ensemble, *Electronic Civil Disobedience and other Unpopular Ideas* (Brooklyn, NY: Autonomedia, 1996); Peter Lunenfeld, *The Digital Dialectic: New Essays on New Media* (Cambridge, MA: MIT Press, 1999); Lev Manovich, *The Language of New Media* (Cambridge, MA: MIT Press, 2001).

6. David MacDougall, *Transcultural Cinema* (Princeton, NJ: Princeton University Press, 1998).

Figure 16.1. Image from Swipe performance and installation at the Beall Center for Art and Technology, Irvine, CA (2004). Credit: Preemptive Media (Beatriz da Costa, Jamie Schulte, and Brooke Singer).

16

LIVE!

Reconnecting the Histories of Live Multimedia Performance*

New Environments, Different Histories

The materiality of the archive—texts, artifacts, and documents—drives film and media history, which takes evidentiary traces of the past and quilts them together to form connections, explanations, and patterns. For professional academic film historians, archival records are never complete or totalized. Archival

---

* Since the early 1980s, I have intermittently attended conferences mounted by the National Alliance for Media Arts and Culture (NAMAC), now known as The Alliance. NAMAC/The Alliance is a media arts organization that connects a heterogeneous group of people involved in independent media arts ranging from exhibitors and distributors, to granting organizations, to practitioners, to media policy advocates for conferences that explore new developments, ongoing challenges, and underrecognized histories and legacies. These conferences surged with a vitality and urgency about independent media practice and documentary in particular that combined aesthetics, history, the future, politics, policy, and practice in ways that energized my thinking. The congregating of different kinds of people from different parts of independent media arts ecologies, particularly in documentary and experimental modes, pushed me to think in new ways.

This essay was originally commissioned by NAMAC for a special report called *Hidden Histories*, coedited by Helen De Michiel and Kathy High. They were feminist media artists whom I had originally met through the Robert Flaherty Film Seminar in the late 1980s, and with whom I have maintained friendships and collegiality for decades. They asked me to write for this project, and I elected to write about live multimedia performance for several reasons. First, it connected with the silent film/live music productions I was creating and producing, and second, I was interested in how live multimedia expanded the juncture between documentary and new technology. Helen and Kathy were rigorous editors who brought practitioners' sensibilities about clarity of structure and modes of address to my writing, constantly asking what I meant and how I might state it so it would be more compelling. They insisted that the stakes were high; the need to recapture lost histories of independent media was pressing as new technologies emerged.

This piece was written as a foray into creative nonfiction journalism, with many interviews with the subjects who shared their processes but with limited scholarly endnotes. Helen and Kathy also modeled a form of feminist collaborative media practice in their editing that propelled this piece to a more lyrical place than the one I started from. This essay was published in Helen De Michiel and Kathy High, eds., *Hidden Histories* (San Francisco: National Alliance for Media Arts and Culture, 2005), 19–32.

absences—not enough early cinema saved or amateur films waiting to be recovered—often loom larger than the subject of study itself. Lost films, deteriorating images, abandoned records, gaps, fissures, and silences mark our media arts histories. The political urgency of the archive can be mapped into these gaps and fissures: the structuring out of the marginal and the inchoate, the chaotic and the untamable, practices that refuse the rules and therefore reveal the most about the disruptions of historical processes.[1]

Since the early 1980s, film and media history (often referred to as the "new film history") has moved from the analysis of existing evidence to the recovery of lost archival objects and categories that expand the archive and ask us to reconsider what it privileges and marginalizes. The past is never inert or nostalgic, but always interacts with the present and the future, looking backward and forward simultaneously in infinite recombinations and mutations. The questions we ask of film history should not be reduced to what happened when. Rather, the past demands questions of how and why: questions of significance rather than linear progression and causality. Contemporary historiographic theory rejects the idea of the causal chain and instead has adopted the conceptual model of the collage, where different temporalities and categories of evidence realign and redistribute into new combinations to provoke new explanatory models and new connections.[2]

The image occupies the center of most film historical work, defining the contours and scope of media historiography. In this context, a live multimedia performance presents a complex historiographic problem because it is not located solely in the realm of the image. First, it is virtually absent from most film and media histories, most likely because it is ephemeral, fleeting, rarely documented—an archival impossibility. Second, its multiple artistic and political practices disperse across and then fold into histories defined by somewhat more unified fields such as avant-garde cinema, contemporary experimental music, digital media, fine art, hip-hop, performance art, theater, and video art. Third, it presents a practice that is not time-based, but spatialized and environmental, a different set of historiographic locations and concerns defined more by participant ethnographies and oral histories rather than by archival documents, artifacts, and texts.

These historiographic conundrums and unified categories may have contributed to the absence of live multimedia performance from our histories of media. Or maybe our histories of media have focused too much on fixed textual practices and recovered documents, thereby overlooking a range of performative political interventions that figure mediation as fluid, moving, malleable interactions with audiences and performers.[3] A preliminary excavation of live multimedia performance reveals the possibility of shifting the ground of media histories from the image to constructed interactive environments and to an infiltration of different spaces that emphasize not individual artistry but collaboration.[4]

In a period where people feel isolated and where media is both miniaturized and domesticated in the home, the hidden history of live multimedia performance provides a way to reconsider media tactics. As an immersive experience based on conceptual ideas and visceral pleasures, the multiplication of formats, images, interfaces, and music to create new social spaces moves our thinking about media histories away from a dependency on the image alone. As the dominant commercialized practices of digitality desensitize, disconnect, disembody, and isolate, the layered histories of live multimedia performance remind us that gatherings of people still matter, that total immersive experiences predate the internet, and that embodied sensuous interaction constitutes a key but underrecognized part of political engagement. This new historiography repositions media history from documents and images to spaces and environments.

Convergences

"When you do live media events, it's all about convergence," explains Anne Bray, executive director of L.A. Freewaves, a nonprofit organization that exhibits independent media in different venues around Los Angeles in their biennial L.A. Freewaves Festival. "However, this is not convergence defined by technologies, but by live bodies in real space. You need three elements for success: food and drink, a live element with media, and programming where people know there will be lots of people to talk to."[5] This brave new world obliterates distinctions between production, distribution, exhibition, technologies, performers, and audience. Legacy ways of framing cinema or media as a fixed, inert object on a flat screen retreat when images are no longer conceived as permanent.

In the history of live multimedia performance, two of the more important figures are Laurie Anderson and Steina Vasulka. However, they represent only a very small part of a sprawling, historically significant area of media practice that configures relationships between images, music, people, spaces, and technologies.

Bray, an artist who has organized and curated L.A. Freewaves since 1989, is a maverick in an expanding group of curators, media artists, film historians, musicians, festival directors, and archivists who are moving beyond immobilized audiences staring at the fixed image on the flat screen into live multimedia performances where many vectors become activated.

These multimedia performances with music are embodied, fluid, interactive, mobile, and multiple. Large audiences pack bars, concert halls, the internet, galleries, public spaces, streets, and theaters in numbers that frequently exceed traditional sit-in-the audience-watch-the-screen exhibition. Live multimedia performance unfolds over a long, multilayered history that has evaded most histories of media art, falling into the liminal zone between media, music, and theater. "There's been a big change in curatorial circles in the 1990s," observes long-time live performance media artist, composer, and violinist Tony Conrad, a veteran of both Fluxus and Happenings in the 1960s and 1970s. "Social action and the margins of art practice are infiltrating the galleries with utopian concepts of networking."[6]

Live multimedia performance also has a long legacy of radical political engagement in recharging social spaces. In the 1920s in Europe, Dada and surrealist artists deployed live performance with film and music to disrupt bourgeois romantic conventions. Dadaists explored nonmatrixed performing, with lectures, readings, sound poems, and dances. They brought facets of everyday life to the stage. Surrealists like Luis Bunuel and Salvador Dalí screened *Un Chien Andalou* (1929) accompanied by tango records playing on a phonograph—with the needle randomly dropped onto the record. Since the mid 1990s, according to VJ/DJ/digital artist Art Jones, a former member of Not Channel Zero, a collective of African American and Latino political media activists, live remixes constitute "perhaps one of the only areas not coopted by the commercial media."[7]

For Jones, live remix performances tap into a general cultural malaise of isolation that propels a craving for fun and direct pleasurable social interaction. "Live remixes are deployed in the service of topical ideas like the war in Iraq and the presidential election, delivering politics to larger social activities and gatherings," explains Jones. He further notes that live performance inverts how the field conceptualizes political media: rather than making a topical film and then working to attract an audience to receive the message, artists and collectives instead bring the work to the audiences and respond to them—live.[8]

Archives

A Japanese woman *benshi* (a performer who narrates silent films) in a kimono enacts vocal contortions. A pianist plays loud atonal music mixed with glissandos and then veers into melodramatic romantic melodies. On stage, a male narrator with a radio-groomed voice speaks into another microphone. He explains the process of the projection and live performance of silent film before the coming of sound. Another woman in a black dress and white face makeup ventriloquizes all the characters in the film in Spanish with rapid-fire succession, changing pitch and tone.

On a screen suspended on stage behind these performers, *El Automotival Gris*, a 1915 Mexican serial reedited in the 1930s into a disjointed feature, is projected. According to film programmer Jesse Lerner, it is one of the few surviving films from Mexican silent cinema. Based on a real case during the Mexican revolution, criminals, exploiting the general state of anarchy, acquired army uniforms. They then posed as officers, tied up civilians, and stole jewels.

Disruptive subtitles and intertitles of the words "meow, meow, woof, woof" and "bow wow" in a variety of fonts superimpose over a fight scene. Later, musical notes roll over the bottom of the screen under the action, with live singing from the woman at the microphone. During a chicken fight scene, the three performers vocalize abstract sounds, and the pianist plucks the inside strings of the piano. During the execution scene, a piece of actual documentary rather than narrative fiction, the performers remain silent.

It's the closing night of the 2005 Flaherty Film Seminar. And after a week of watching complex experimental and documentary fare from around the world on the flat screen, the Teatro de Ciertos Habitantes troupe's performance unsettles the Flaherty participants. Some love the audacity of the performance for its multicultural remix in three languages. Others find the performance unresolved and at loose ends. At the makeshift bar in the Claremont College dorm, Flaherty devotees down Merlot in red plastic beer cups, arguing about the politics of reactivating archival film.

Internationally, thanks to the labor-intensive work of film historians debunking myths about silent film through intensive primary research, silent film entered into a resurgence in the 1990s. Archives undertaking restorations worked to get these films programmed in public at film festivals and museums. "The job of a film archive is to take old film and make it new," argues Chris Horak, director of the UCLA Film & Television Archive in Los Angeles. Festivals ranging from the famed Pordenone Silent Film Festival in Italy to the Telluride and Virginia Film Festivals feature silent film restorations with live music. "This phenomenon of the popularity of silent archival film with live music is related to the fact that the archives have been doing restorations. We now have good quality material. In the 1970s, you would see a bad looking 35mm or 16mm print. Now, with preservation work, the image quality is also very high," explains Horak.[9]

"What people like about it is the performance aspect—it brings a different quality to a screening. With a full orchestra or a small ensemble or a pianist improvising, every performance is different," Horak continues. "The live performance gives viewing the archival film an immediacy you don't get otherwise. So many media experiences are mediated—live performance with archival material makes it much more direct and personal."[10] The one-time-only spectacle of silent film with live music provides a direct and unique experience with enormous payoffs for archives, the driving forces behind these performances. Through these exhibitions, archives can demonstrate their outreach and impact for restoration projects, which helps to secure future funding for lesser-known works.

Ensembles specializing in live silent film music, like the Alloy Orchestra with their new scores for classics such as *Man with a Movie Camera* (1929), *Metropolis* (1927), and Buster Keaton comedies and Club Foot Orchestra's work on *Nosferatu* (1922) both demonstrate how contemporary music can galvanize an audience to interact with films from another era, rearticulating the past of the artifact with the contemporary present of the live performance. Alloy Orchestra's pounding, loud, multilayered percussion, for example, underscores the relationship between machines and constructivist art in *Man with a Movie Camera*. However, in the often-contentious circles of academic film history and film archives, contemporary scores frequently generate controversy between those who argue for an authentic past and those who see the present and the past in a more dialectical relationship.

Some scholars and archivists contend that live performance should replicate the original performance, using only music contemporaneous with the period of the films. However, Horak, himself a well-known film historian and founding editor of *The Moving Image*, the journal of the Association of Moving Image Archivists (AMIA), engages a more generous and heterogeneous position: "To say you have to do it as 1924 is somewhat problematic. We don't live in 1924. You cannot reproduce the act of reception of 1924. The technology is different: we are no longer using a carbon arc hand-cranked projection, no longer using nitrate, so there is much less silver. The whole physicality of cinema is no longer 1924, so why not change the music too? Film is a living thing, and film reception is living too."[11]

Rick Altman, one of the groundbreaking scholars of film sound studies, concurs. He notes that with the new accompaniments of live music, archival film feels alive. His exquisitely detailed and important book *Silent Film Sound* (2004) elaborates the heterogeneity of early-cinema sound practices, dependent upon historical time period, technology, place, region, and location. After spending nearly a decade researching silent film in obscure trade journals, catalogs, and local newspapers, Altman has developed an antipathy toward archival film performances that promote the authenticity of their live musical accompaniment; they are often historically inaccurate, he contends. For instance, pianists frequently use music from the late teens and 1920s to accompany films from an earlier period.

Spurred by his work in primary sources often ignored by film scholars, Altman formed his own early-cinema performance troupe in 1998 called The Living Nickelodeon with film studies colleagues from the University of Iowa. The Living Nickelodeon brings a pre-feature-film experience to audiences through live performances. Early exhibition extensively used the illustrated song slide, projected lantern slides that used an image for each line in a song, often performed live.[12] In these instances, film was often not the main attraction, and was frequently shown without accompaniment. Ballyhoo, the clamorous patter used to lure audiences into theaters, was frequently done outside the theater or in the back of the house.

Altman explains that the pianist was often hired to accompany the soprano for the song slides—not for the film. With shows where audiences robustly sing along at the Chicago Art Institute, the Museum of Modern Art, the Bologna Film Festival, and the Louvre, The Living Nickelodeon has one purpose, according to Altman. "We want to show things going on that historians have ignored—the participatory nature of early cinema. Our audiences say they never truly understood the period before our performances."[13]

The Madcat Women's Festival has adopted a strategy opposite to Altman's, opting to reinvigorate neglected works of silent cinema with new music. Curator Ariella Ben-Dov has programmed the work of early women silent film directors like Alice Guy-Blaché, Cleo Madison, and Lois Weber—often ignored in film histories—with instrumental contemporary alternative music from bands like The Secrets of Family Happiness. Ben-Dov points out that she never uses a piano or a string quartet, but instead hires bands from San Francisco who will create performances that ignite the viewer to "look at the films in new ways." For Ben-Dov, the experiential immediacy of the live music with early women's cinema merges two different audiences—one from film, one from music.[14]

However, film historians and film archives frame only one side of the story of live performance and archival film. Electronic composers like Paul Lehrman drive historical reclamation projects in surprising ways, uncovering lost histories by excavating first through music rather than through the images alone. Bruce Posner, who curated the *Unseen Cinema* project on early experimental film, approached Lerhman about working on the music for Fernand Leger's *Ballet Mécanique* (1924), a canonical film in avant-garde film history. George Antheil, an American expatriate Futurist composer living in Paris in the 1920s, had created a score that was never performed with the original film.

According to Lerhman, the Antheil score constitutes a "relentless piece of visual and aural assault," requiring up to sixteen player pianos, percussion, and additional piano with more than 632 time changes. "It's a monstrous noise engine, and very difficult for a conductor to keep under control," notes Lehrman. "It's really a large machine piece, using player pianos, xylophones, bass drums for making machine, rather than melodic sounds."[15] Lerhman's new score, compiled on a MIDI file running the player pianos from standard sequencers, has been performed live with *Ballet Mechanique* eleven or twelve times internationally. Even though many cover their ears during the performance, "the audience always goes nuts," observes Lehrman. The performance engulfs the spectator in loud physicalized percussive sounds that penetrate the body and catapult new readings of the original film as an aggressive, pounding montage.[16]

Fluxus and Happenings

"In the 1960s, artists and performers went for what is simple," muses media artist Tony Conrad. Two kinds of live media performance coexisted during this period: Fluxus, dedicated to a post–John Cage demolition of the role of the composer in Western music and heavily imbedded in conceptual art, and multimedia happenings embracing what Conrad calls a "holistic scene" where exotic style, gay sexuality, improvisation, and politics unleashed a bawdy heterogeneity.[17] Fluxus live performance events with musicians like La Monte Young counterposed the visual excesses of an experimental filmmaker like Jack Smith. Conrad traveled between both poles, as did Andy Warhol, who merged both styles of performance in films like *Empire* (1964) and *Chelsea Girls* (1966).

For Conrad, although Fluxus events and happenings deployed media with live musical performances, both operated outside the media community; they were more closely allied to the art scene. One was Apollonian, the other Dionysian. Conrad cites Andy Warhol's Velvet Underground events as well as light shows and liquid projections made by pouring oil on a transparent projector screen at happenings as precursors to the media community's involvement. In San Francisco, live multimedia performance and light shows often included illegal drugs. Because film projection was difficult and video projection almost nonexistent during this period, artists employed transparency projectors and slides to create cheap visual effects.

In his 1972 live performance piece *Ten Years Alive on the Infinite Plain*, Conrad mounted four projections. He played live microtonal music during the performance on his amplified violin, building complexity out of simplicity with sustained minimalism. Subsequent film, media, and music curators have been particularly attracted to reviving this piece, drawn to its minimalist and improvisational performance style. It screened in Dortmund, Germany, and Dundee, Scotland, in 2004.

Expanded cinema, a term immortalized in the Gene Youngblood book of the same name, has been revived in the new millennium. Quite different from Fluxus, which juxtaposed minimalism with the quotidian, expanded cinema probed the interstitial areas between new technologies by mixing sound and image together to generate metaimagery. As outlined by Gene Youngblood in 1970, intermedia, another term for expanded cinema, engaged a different set of temporal and spatial coordinates than traditional film on a wall. Emerging out of shadow shows, expositions, and experimental theater practices, it foregrounded communal experiences, multiple projections, and sensory stimulation. Rather than focusing exclusively on the image, it explored and experimented with producing new environments for images. Intermedia also described interdisciplinary artistic practices that combined art forms such as film and theater with different genres.[18] The connection between live VJ remixing and expanded cinema is more than conjecture: it constitutes a historical trajectory that scholars are only beginning to understand as a complex fluid environment of media practice. Experimental filmmaker Ken Jacobs's various *Nervous System* (1996–ongoing) projects, for example, revive imaging technologies from the early cinema era to manipulate the image through projection: slowing it down, speeding it up, stalling it, repeating images.

"Younger curators and programmers have a renewed interest in expanded cinema," says Conrad. "A whole new generation is interested in what it means to loosen up the relationships between sound and image, to play improvisationally with the image in new ways."[19] The flat-on-the-wall screening room form of traditional exhibition, where the image is presented to the audience as unchanged and unchangeable, has given way to multiple screens, live manipulation of images and sound, and endless spatial variations in clubs, galleries, plasma screens, and lobbies. The construct of the immobilized spectator facing the screen has transformed into an embodied, moving, interacting, communicative spectator. Conrad contends that the hidden histories of live multimedia performance in the 1960s provide models, inspiration, and motivation for a new generation of multimedia performance artists to "blow out the stoppages and differentiations between different media and fields." For Conrad, "boundaries are some of the most obvious things to whack away at."[20] In the context of this reemergence of live multimedia performance, whacking away at boundaries materializes in concrete ways, where new concerns emerge beyond the formal elements of the image: the reinvention of the space of exhibition, the relationship of the spectators to the screens, the embodiment of performer and spectator, and the ephemeral nature of the practice.

However, live multimedia performance was not the exclusive domain of men with machines in the 1960s and early 1970s. Filmmaker Shirley Clarke formed the "Tee Pee Video Space Troupe," which included Dee Dee Halleck, David Cort, Perry Teasdale, Skip Blumberg, Wendy Clarke, and even Agnes Varda in the early 1970s at the Chelsea Hotel in New York. "It was like a think tank to play with live video as a form of performance," recalls Halleck, who ruminates that her experience with collaborative live video performances had a direct influence on the formation of Paper Tiger Television in the early 1980s.[21]

Known in film history literature for her historically important films *Portrait of Jason* (1967), *The Connection* (1961), and *The Cool World* (1963), Clarke is often positioned as a filmmaker critical of the supposed transparency of cinema verité. Her experiments with live performance are less recognized, although they have been influential across a wide range of independent media practices.

Clarke saw in video technology possibilities not offered by film: instant feedback, interactivity, performativity, collective action, and group bonding. "She was trying to push the tech to the edge," remembers Halleck. "It never worked, it was always populist, and the ideas were exciting. Shirley called it her playpen—video was to be played with like a game."[22] For Clarke, video technology functioned as a nodal point to create new kinds of embodied and live artistic communal practices. Clarke experimented with rethinking the means of production through technology: she deployed video as a sketchbook, a social activator, and a conjuring device for group interaction. Halleck notes that Clarke, trained as a dancer, envisioned her group of video performers as merging individual artistic expression (the traditional domain of the fine arts) with social interaction (the domain of performance and social activist work). This experiment in mixing two different artistic modalities through the interface of live video sometimes worked, sometimes failed, but was always centered on group dynamics and interaction. For example, one day the troupe shot various images of dawn in New York City: stoplights, birds, gates, stores opening. When they returned from their individual shoots, they stacked video monitors on the roof of the Chelsea Hotel and played back their various tapes on these monitors with the sun rising over New York City as the backdrop. Clarke created a bonding ritual through connecting the work of individual artists through the multiple monitors, supplying mimosas for the group to drink as they watched their pieces resonate and reverberate with each other.[23]

Experimental Television Center: Epicenter of Live

The experimental fusion of collaborative work, new technologies, performance, and real-time mediated imaging form the core of a history of live performance multimedia. The Experimental Television Center (ETC) in Owego, New York, founded in 1971 by Ralph Hocking as an outgrowth of his Binghamton University–based media access center, functioned as one of the epicenters of live video performance. "Performance-based works were some of the earliest media art created at the Center with the image-processing tools we made available through the Residency Program," explains Sherry Miller Hocking, assistant director of ETC.[24]

Woodstock Community Video in upstate New York presented the first Woodstock Video Expovision in August 1975, over a five-day period. Screening tapes of fifty New York state video makers, it featured a video synthesizer demonstration, an electronic media performance with dance, a video environment by Media Bus, and a panel discussion with Gerd Stern of Intermedia Systems, Barbara London of the Museum of Modern Art, and John Godfrey of WNET's Experimental TV Lab.

Couple 513 was a live video and dance performance mounted at the Everson Museum of Art in May 21–23, 1976. Lois Welk and Arnie Zane of the American Dance Asylum performed, while Meryl Blackman, Peer Bode, and the Experimental Television Center manipulated the live video. *Movements for Video Dance and Music,* with Peer Bode, Meryl Blackman, Bill Jones, and Arnie Neames was a 1976 performance at the Herbert F. Johnson Museum at Cornell University in Ithaca, produced with support from the Experimental Television Center.

"The tools available at the Center as well as the medium amplified the real-time nature of the medium. This first generation of video artists understood that the technology engendered intimacy and immediacy—in the creative actions of the maker, and the presentations to the viewer," Hocking noted.[25] The technology also promoted interactivity—performers as well as artists could affect the image/sound in real time. Hocking believes that this first generation of media artists was drawn to live performance multimedia because of interdisciplinary combustion. Most of these early media artists arrived at video via dance, music, and theater as well as the sciences. As a result, they imported tropes and forms from other disciplines into video. ETC, inaugurating an over thirty-year tradition of artists' audacity and innovation through pushing the limits of technology, invited these artists to use image processing tools to explore the performative aspects of video.[26]

In the 1970s, these artists experimented with analog synthesizers. By the 1980s, image processing tools migrated to digital technologies. Music collaborations were also extensive. In the 2000s, the ETC Residency Program supported the work of new media artists such as LoVid, Amoeba Technology, Benton C Bainbridge, and the Synaesthesiologists who investigated digital electronic imaging tools in live performances.

Clubs

The reversal of media flows and expectations by changing the sites of exhibition inflects live multimedia performance conceptually. Not only is the media art content programmed, but live media practices reconfigure the physical space of exhibition. For instance, the backyard of the El Rio Bar in San Francisco's Mission District has been a popular draw for experimental films by women set to live music at the Madcat Film Festival, whose mission is to bring avant-garde film to a range of audiences. Ariella Ben-Dov sees live music performances with archival and experimental film as a powerful and effective way to "make work somewhat more accessible to contemporary audiences who may not have an understanding of it."[27]

One of MadCat's innovations, *SSHH: Silent Films to Live Music* curates silent avant-garde films thematically, then contacts filmmakers to secure permission for a one-time-only ephemeral event. While some filmmakers are apprehensive, most are excited by this proposal and agree. Local musicians create music in dialogue with the images. These shows never encounter problems filling the two-hundred-seat venue. "Live music is a definite draw," says Ben-Dov, who is interested in exhibiting experimental film in alternative spaces.[28]

In 1994, a woman who owned a hip-hop label asked media artist Art Jones to do a live remix at The Knitting Factory in New York City. Jones had been hanging out at the Nuyorican Poets Café, where he witnessed the power of improvisational performance for political discourse. Armed with two VCRs, two monitors, and a Radio Shack AB Switcher, Jones did his first remix with videotapes while a spoken-word performer used a microphone. The performance combined media, hip-hop music, and spoken word. Also in 1994, DJ Spooky (Paul Miller) did a live remix at Woodstock '94. From there, Jones started mixing in bars and clubs with video decks, and then, later, with mini-DV decks. He moved into computers for live remixing in 2001.[29]

Inspired by site-specific happenings of the 1960s and 1970s, Jones saw that remixing offered the possibility of breaking media arts out to a different audience through combining music, visual artists, and video projectors. Jones points out that Robert Whitman's expanded cinema with multiple projectors and sound, Ken Jacobs's projections, Andy Warhol's Velvet Underground, and psychedelia served as predecessors of laptop remixers in clubs. At Woodstock '94, a group of kids, whom Jones affectionately heralds as "the lost tribe of Macintosh" talked to each other with their laptops, generating a communal spirit that Jones contends represents the radical potential of live multimedia performance.[30] For Jones, live remixes with sophisticated software running on paper-thin laptops constitutes a resolutely anticorporate ephemeral media environment designed to "intervene into the colonization of consciousness." Compared to traditional film schools and art schools, which often emphasize a romanticized view of individual artistry and self-expression, live remixing requires collaborative engagement as well as a "different way of engaging the spectator."[31]

"It's a way to intervene into the quiet contemplation of the object," says Jones. The central theoretical problem posed by live remixes revolves around the question of how the spectator can be engaged in a more compelling, embodied, and immersive way. Jones created remixes on the war in Iraq, cyberwarfare, and empire alone and in collaborative teams.[32] In contrast, some VJs simply generate video wallpaper without political content for clubs, creating screen after screen of abstract beautiful images with no connection to political or social relations, a practice that Jones assesses as ignoring the potential for dialogue with the audience/participants. With computers, images and sounds can be subdivided, live cameras can be added, more improvisation can erupt, and VJ/DJs can be more responsive to spectators, creating a more encompassing environment.

Concert Halls

Three layers of scaffolding surround the audience. A film is projected on three separate scrims. Musicians are positioned on different levels of the scaffolding. Images, live music, and constructed space engulf the spectator. It's Bill Morrison's *Decasia* (2002), a fifty-five-minute archival film epic exploring spirituality, loss, ineffability, and renewal, with a score by experimental music composer Michael Gordon, a member of Bang on a Can, performed live at Carnegie Hall.

The film and the complex multilayered score present a compelling exploration of decomposition and decay. Just out of art school in the late 1980s, Morrison joined the Bridge Theater, an experimental collective, as the group's only filmmaker. In the 1990s, he began a series of collaborations with musicians from Bang on the Can, an influential contemporary music group.[33] An experimental filmmaker trained as a painter who exorcises latent forms and meanings submerged in archival fragments, Morrison's artistic process subverts narrative structures in archival film to release the same emotional drive as music. He works closely with the film archive and museum communities as he searches for images to use in his art.

It is the changes in exhibition of the works that excite Morrison, for each new situation opens up different experiences, interpretations, and possibilities. With the increasing difficulty of projecting film properly, especially in ill-equipped concert halls, Morrison has moved into producing films for inclusion in enhanced CDs for musicians like David Lang (*How to Pray*) and Julia Wolf and Michael Gordon (*Light Is Calling*). Musicians are confronting the problem of how to market their works in the changing economic context of digital downloading. Experimental films add a new element, potentially mitigating the declining value of the CD. Morrison has worked on projections for experimental operas such as John Adams's *The Death of Klinghofer* (2003) for the Brooklyn Academy of Art and for dual-screen installations like *Outerborough* (2005) which uses archival footage of the Brooklyn Bridge, commissioned by the Museum of Modern Art.

Interfaces

Beyond material places and environments reconstructed for and by live media performances, interfaces and networks present another frontier for live multimedia performance. Although the term interface sounds like it came from the script of *The Matrix Reloaded* (2003), it refers to the junctures where hardware and software meet users. Interface includes everything from using a mouse to voice activating your cell phone to dial your mom. For those trained to think of media arts as solely about the image, terms like network-based art, transmission arts, and locative media might sound like technogeeks let loose in Best Buy doing word shuffles with a thesaurus to trance music.

However, these areas of live performance are deeply political and interventionist forms of public education about technologies. These new practices hone in on using performance to make visible technologies that are deliberately rendered invisible by corporate power structures and imbedded in our daily life—a tactic that resonates with oppositional media practices from the 1960s and 1970s. Except in this iteration, the move from invisibility to visibility is no longer about images and representations, but about technological systems covertly invading our daily lives. Embedded technologies like E-Z Pass scanners, invisible surveillance in stores, and machine/body interfaces like ATMs and nanotechnologies are foregrounded, live and in real time. This work poses complicated problems for film/media arts historiography because it is even more ephemeral than DJ/VJ remixes and live music with archival films: it is not about an artifact but about actions and events to expose technologies.

Performance artist, activist, and digital culture agitator Ricardo Dominguez summons the idea of the "performative matrix" in his work with the technoculture activist group Critical Art Ensemble and his projects on the Zapatistas. For him, the "performative matrix creates a site of confusion for powers that be, a gesture that is a minor simulation outside of dominant core influences."[34]

The "performative matrix" is quite simple, an updating and revitalizing of intermedia. The matrix combines internet actions and embodied performances to change how people think about terms like "infowar" and the Zapatistas. If intermedia zeroed in on the sensual and nonlinear, the performative matrix focuses on the semantic, trying to alter definitions and reconfigure concepts. According to Dominguez, these projects converge art, politics, and science to create a provisional zone or space for the marginal by disturbing dominant powers like the US government.[35]

In his work with Critical Art Ensemble throughout the 1980s and 1990s, Dominguez developed ideas about how to "allow political agency through hallucinatory space," inspired by his activist political work in the antinuclear movement in Nevada, the Bread and Puppet Theater, Teatro Campesino, Act-Up, and the history of agit-prop.[36] Critical Art Ensemble developed these ideas in two groundbreaking books, *Electronic Civil Disobedience and Other Unpopular Ideas* (1998) and *Electronic Disturbance* (2000). Despite a long-term, continuing interest in cyberculture, Dominguez insists that the performative matrix does not need to rely on machines, but on "machines for engineering concepts."[37] The performative matrix, then, operates as conceptual theater that uses whatever means are necessary—the internet, live performance, science—to shift ideas about how power infiltrates and operates within our culture.

Cofounder of the Electronic Disturbance Theater, Dominguez has led many virtual sit-ins on websites as a gesture to bring attention to the antiglobalization movement. A 1998 project to support the Zapatista movement in Chiapas, Mexico, deployed the refresh/reload button on computers to flood the web sites of the Pentagon, the Federal Communications Commission, and the School of the Americas. The action prompted the Pentagon and the House Arms Committee to change the doctrines of infowar to include electronic civil disobedience. Later, this same virtual sit-in process was deployed during the World Economic Forum in NYC in 2002, using the Dreamweaver software developed by media pranksters The Yes Men.

Free103point9 collective also works the frontier beyond the image. They use sound and radio frequencies to create different listening environments that encourage spectators to interact with machines in communal ways. Their goal: to develop the artistic and political possibilities of live transmission art with underused technologies like radio, ham radio, walkie talkies, FM/AM radio, cell phones, and light. Transmission art is defined as any work that uses technologies that transfer and move sound. The Free103point9 group emerged out of two audio movements: the microradio (formerly known as pirate radio) movement for FM low-power radio under 100 watts with radio barn raisings in communities and radio artists interested in sound experimentation with pioneers such as the audio collage collective Negativland.

Tom Roe, one of the members of the collective, explains that transmission arts involve live performance, physical embodiment, and a variety of sound technologies. In a project called *Radio 4x4*, four musicians each play into their own FM transmitter: "20-60 radios are spread out through a space and used as a public address system," Roe elaborates.[38] Each radio has a different speaker and different sound qualities, encouraging audience movement around the room. Free103point9 also produces live shows through online radio webcasting three to four times a week.

Wi-Fi, mobile phone cameras, and RFID are ubiquitous, invisible, and often—at least for the average cable TV-surfing, iPhone-listening person—incomprehensible. Wi-Fi refers to wireless fidelity, the technology that enables you to connect to a local area network at an access point to check your email while on the road. RFID is an acronym for radio frequency identification, tags that track everything from library books, to Walmart shipments of goods, to your car passing through toll booths without plopping in quarters. The Preemptive Media Collective (PM) reengineers your thinking about mobile digital technologies imbedded in our everyday environment. PM's art practice works to not only help spectators to see these invisible technologies that track our lives and our data, but to demystify them.

Locative media represents a newly emerging zone in performative multimedia. Locative media constitutes a new global independent media movement interested in the convergence between digital domains and geographic spaces. It anchors the digital, often viewed as placeless, in geographic space. Artists marshal portable networked computing devices like GPS, mobile phones, RFID, and wearable technologies to map space and intervene into data streams. Locative media practices focus on horizontal, user-led, and collaborative projects to interrupt and interrogate powerful systems of observation and control.

In live performances and real-time actions, the PM art, technology, and activist collective dislodges, disturbs, and redesigns new media technologies that are often ignored, like the bar codes on driver's licenses or radio frequency information devices used for E-Z Pass on highways. At the forefront of the "locative media movement," Preemptive Media repositions highly specialized technologies within the democratizing discourse of amateurism, which refutes technology as inaccessible, remote, and too complicated and instead argues for accessibility for everyone. The locative media movement has gathered steam and attention since 9/11 and the 2001 Patriot Act, which authorized unprecedented data mining, invasions of privacy, wiretapping, and internet surveillance.

Preemptive Media Collective's *ZAPPED!* (2005) foregrounds radio frequency identification tags (RFID), first used by the British military during World War II and then to track wild animals in the 1960s. In the last twenty years, RFID has been utilized for electronic tolls like E-Z Pass, for pets, prisoners, dance clubs, children, the Department of Defense, and Walmart, the largest profit-making enterprise in the world. The Spring Independent School district in the Houston area used RFID tags on elementary students to track their school bus rides. The *ZAPPED!* Project features workshops for kids and adults on altering the remote wireless detection chips. Phrases like "Help me! I'm a consumer!" "This is GOD. You have sinned. Be prepared for eternal damnation!" and "Don't hire me—I'm a felon" are inserted on the chips to pop up on scanners in stores. Instead of prices, these phrases appear. The RFID School Kit consists of a lunchbox and a keychain detector to locate RFID hotspots. Roaches with clandestine RFID tags taped to their backs are hidden in the lunchbox and then released in Walmart storage areas by activists sporting the blue Walmart vests, purchased on eBay.

Some theorists have questioned whether locative media is actually just another name for sabotage, civil disobedience, and illegal hacking. However, Preemptive Media's work replaces these negations with epistemological revelations: their reverse engineering strategies of altering technologies like RFID make visible these imbedded invisible technologies as a form of public education and political consciousness raising.

Reclamation and Reinvention

Neoliberal moves toward privatizing social life and transnational corporate media consolidations erect almost impenetrable barriers to collective action. Inviting spaces where audiences can engage and participate in critical media practices seem remote and unattainable. These hard-to-uncover histories of live performance multimedia—with and without music—may offer strategies and tactics to revise and to rebuild ephemeral micro-public spaces that elude the proprietary, consumerist domains of corporate media. Live multimedia environments redefine media space as engaging the senses and the body in a dynamic, aleatory system of collective affect and shared fun experiences. It is my hope that these hidden histories of live multimedia performance can mobilize that most elusive but necessary ingredient of any radical media practice: a hopeful, embodied gathering of committed people that disengages isolation and disturbs the universe.

Notes

1. For examples of theoretical historiography that question the notion of a meaning that can be fully recovered and argue instead for an idea that the past is created as a text constructed through structures of evidence, see Alun Munslow, *Deconstructing History* (London: Routledge, 1997); Robert F. Berkhofer Jr., *Beyond the Great Story: History as Text and Discourse* (Cambridge, MA: Harvard University Press, 1995); and Howard Marchitello, ed., *What Happens to History: The Renewal of Ethics in Contemporary Thought* (New York: Routledge, 2001).

2. For analysis of this rejection of causality and linearity in favor of a more polyphonic and heteroglossic historical strategy of explanation, especially in subaltern historiography, see

Philip Rosen, *Change Mummified: Cinema, Historicity, Theory* (Minneapolis: University of Minnesota Press, 2001), Vinayak Chaturvedi, ed., *Mapping Subaltern Studies and the Postcolonial* (London: Verso, 2000); Dipesh Chakrabarty, *Provincializing Europe: Postcolonial Thought and Historical Difference* (Princeton, NJ: Princeton University Press, 2000).

   3. For discussion of performance as an art form based on disappearance, with a permeable and fluid set of meanings between the body real and the psychic real, see Peggy Phelan, *Unmarked: The Politics of Performance* (New York: Routledge, 1993).

   4. For an analysis and explanation of what he terms a collaborative, multivocal ethnography, see David MacDougall, *Transcultural Cinema* (Princeton, NJ: Princeton University Press, 1998).

   5. Anne Bray, interview with the author, May 17, 2005.
   6. Tony Conrad, interview with the author, April 21, 2005.
   7. Art Jones, interview with the author, May 30, 2005.
   8. Jones interview.
   9. Jan-Christopher Horak, interview with the author, June 8, 2005.
   10. Horak interview.
   11. Horak interview.
   12. Rick Altman, *Silent Film Sound* (New York: Columbia University Press, 2004), 181–201.
   13. Rick Altman, interview with the author, May 21, 2005.
   14. Ariella Ben-Dov, interview with the author, April 23, 2005.
   15. Paul Lehrman, interview with the author, May 3, 2005.
   16. Lehrman interview.
   17. Conrad interview.
   18. For a full historical discussion of these practices, see Gene Youngblood, *Expanded Cinema* (New York: Dutton: 1970), 70–151, 300–391.
   19. Conrad interview.
   20. Conrad interview.
   21. DeeDee Halleck, interview with the author, June 28, 2005.
   22. Halleck interview.
   23. Halleck interview.
   24. Sherry Miller Hocking, interview with the author, April 4, 2005.
   25. Miller Hocking interview.
   26. Miller Hocking interview.
   27. Ben-Dov interview.
   28. Ben-Dov interview.
   29. Jones interview.
   30. Jones interview.
   31. Jones interview.
   32. Jones interview.
   33. Bill Morrison, interview with the author, June 20, 2005.
   34. Ricardo Dominguez, interview with the author, April 13, 2005.
   35. Dominguez interview.
   36. Dominguez interview.
   37. Dominguez interview.
   38. Tom Roe, interview with the author, June 25, 2005.

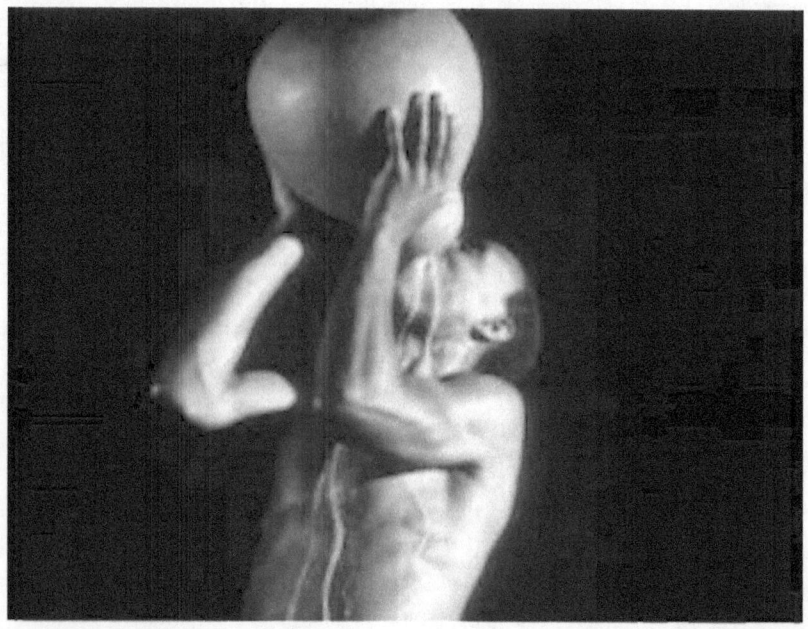

Figure 17.1. *Twilight City* (Black Audio Film Collective, UK, 1989). Courtesy Reece Auguiste/Black Audio Film Collective.

17

TOWARD A THEORY OF PARTICIPATORY NEW MEDIA DOCUMENTARY*

Disclaimer and Warning

Disclaimer: I will not present a manifesto on participatory new media documentary.

This unresolved, still-forming new territory excites me. But its complexity, vastness, global reach, and technological affordances are also intimidating.

My argument is simple. A diverse documentary ecology thrives beyond the character-driven, narrative arc, the genre-infused feature film, the heavily resourced and corporatized interactive documentary, and the documentary infusion in galleries. We are living in one of the most exciting periods of documentary: the documentary turn in the biennales, the participatory turn, the digital turn, the postcolonial turn, and the anthropocene turn churn up our theories and histories.

---

* This essay emerged from a collaborative effort with media artists Reece Auguiste, Aggie Ebrahimi, and Helen De Michiel to mount a panel on "Collaborative Documentary Practices" at Visible Evidence XXIII at Montana State University in Bozeman, Montana, in August 2016. In preparation for our panel, we did several group conference calls to discuss the histories and practices of collaborative and collective media production. Reece, Aggie, and Helen had all worked in these modes, which rejected the idea of the single auteur that dominated cinema studies. To emphasize the importance of reclaiming and reinvigorating the histories and practices of collaborative and collective work, Aggie put all our PowerPoints into one system so that the presentations were visually unified. We passed out a handout about working principles of collaborative media production to the audience, which was a summary of our conversations preparing for the panel. Helen's, Reece's, and my papers were later revised and published in the online version of *Afterimage* in spring 2017 as a "Dossier on Collaborative Documentary Practices: Histories, Theories, Practices," with each of our pieces rolled out at the beginning of the month starting in February. My piece was also published in *Afterimage: The Journal of Media Arts and Cultural Criticism* online at http://vsw.org/afterimage/2017/05/15/dossier-on-collaborative-documentary-practice-histories-theories-practices/.

This essay is dedicated to John Hess (1939–2015), who, with Chuck Kleinhans and Julia Lesage, founded the collective that has produced *Jump Cut: A Review of Contemporary Cinema* for over four decades.

Amidst these complex turnings, our ideas previously known as theories and our practices previously known as production have been dropped into a Cuisinart and pulverized into new essences. Because of that, I offer a very tentative, modest, provisional argument for small-scale, local, sustainable, modestly resourced, long-time-frame collaborative projects often ignored by festivals, museums, new media convenings, and scholars.

Warning: This paper invokes the utopian imaginary, the unresolved realm of participatory new media collaborative documentary built on collaboration, collectivity, engagement, politics, and process. And yes, it is idealized, romanticized, fantasized. But it can expand our arsenal.

A traffic jam of new technologies, affordances, and political challenges push us to reexamine documentary. As theorist Okwui Enwezor observes, "Artistic and intellectual collectives tend to emerge during moments of crisis."[1]

Histories: Incomplete, Fragmented, Crooked Stories

No longer a fixed object, documentary is moving to iterative, shape-shifting forms. With multiple screens and transmedia structures, it continues a parallel documentary history that displaces the auteur, character development, and story arcs. These parallel histories recalibrate documentary with a more place-based, political practice of collaboration, collectivity, and community. They tell what postcolonial historiographers call crooked stories, an incomplete, fragmented process.

A dialectic surrounds participatory new media documentary; it is both new and old. Let me share some navigational historical signposts. *Nanook of the North* (1922) can be read as a collaborative project. Flaherty worked with the Inuit who provided input, film developing, feedback, and food, a position elaborated by Jay Ruby and David MacDougall.

In the 1920s, Dziga Vertov's *Kinoks* in the Soviet Union provide another example of collective political practice, as Josh Malistky and Yuri Tsivian have argued. In the 1930s, Worker's Film and Photo Leagues in the United States and elsewhere chronicled labor unrest rendered invisible by news blackouts, according to Russell Campbell. Latin American third-cinema documentary practices of the 1960s offer another lineage for participatory and collaborative new media.

New media collaborative documentary is also linked to community media in Challenge for Change (Canada), elaborated by Tom Waugh, Ezra Winton, and Michael Baker, in film collectives like Newsreel as researched by Bill Nichols, as well as Appalshop and Kartemquin films (US) in the 1970s. The Black Audio Film Collective (UK) in the 1980s and 1990s threaded together collective practice, interventionist representation, and postcolonial histories, as Reece Auguiste has shown. In the 1980s, community-based video initiatives like Paper Tiger Television, ACT UP, Guerilla Girls, and Scribe Video (US) developed.

Indigenous-generated projects such as Video in the Villages (Brazil) and other first-nations initiatives told stories from below. Colective Cina Ojo (Chile) and Sistema Radio Venceremos (El Salvador) presented influential practices of collective production.

In the 1990s, antiglobalization movements propelled collective practices, with indymedia.org and Big Noise Films (US) aggregating media, as well as WITNESS, an NGO mobilizing the power of cameras and communities for advocacy. By the late 1990s, the international digital storytelling movement of user-generated stories confronting social issues, identity, or trauma extended participatory practices.

In the 2000s, collaborative practices multiplied. They constitute an important subset of i-Docs; they define distributed social media in antiregime actions in Brazil, Burma, Cambodia, Egypt, Hong Kong, Iran, and Tunisia; and they inform global citizen journalism. These histories of community-based, collective documentary practices revolve on cooperative praxis, crooked stories, and iterative use value. Decentering the text, the auteur, and the artisan, participatory new media projects continue these historical trajectories.

Theories: Micro, Migratory, Multiple

Participatory new media projects are defined by horizontal, place-based production. They emphasize process and ongoing recalibrations. They often operate in a nonconfrontational modality, creating space for multiple dialogues on conflictual issues rather than a singular, deductive exposition. Their political argument resides in their design, a mosaic model as advanced by Helen De Michiel.

These collaborative new media projects engage conflictual, unresolved politics at the microlevel. They supplement larger-scale political struggles. They open dialogic spaces built from multiplicities that political, social, environmental conflicts largely overshadow. Deploying a migratory strategy across many interfaces, they traverse the digital, the analog, and the embodied.

Recent media scholarship has analyzed this transmedia media ecology where media travel across film, social media, gaming, and product tie-ins. Through long-tail marketing and affective consumer relationships with corporate-produced storyworlds, this transnational sector expands media product shelf life. For Henry Jenkins, this multiplatformed universe depends on participatory audience engagement through sharing, appropriation, remixing, user generation, and fan culture narratives. Jenkins calls this spreadable media.

Art historians Grant Kester and Claire Bishop offer a different notion of participation that mobilizes collective encounters in socially engaged community arts practices. In the last decade, participatory relational aesthetics have designed projects to instigate collective action around contradictory, unresolved issues such as housing, democracy, or the environment. These dialogic practices mobilize interdisciplinarity, materiality, and embodied encounters. They are place-based rather than abstract, involving participants from different social sectors.

Participatory new media documentary operates within a more porous, open structure that I call "permeable media." Permeable media instigates engagements with the social and the political. These small-scale new media participatory documentary practices permeate into and through commercial media, communities, governments, and nongovernmental organizations. Rather than the entrapment of spectators in corporate storyworlds, permeable practices activate mutation, the micro, and story mosaics, infusing different institutional locations and platforms.

In permeable media, infiltration and seepage replace confrontation and binaries. These transitory public spaces are not Jurgen Habermas's idealized public sphere, but the dynamic places of Tim Cresswell, where people and an environment create meaning at the nexus of intersecting flows. Permeable new media produce convenings and microcommunities, a generative process with multiple foci and tactics.

Meg McLagan and Yates McKee reject political media as static objects of representation and deconstruction. Instead, they argue for the processual aspects of the activist imaginary, defined by networks of affordances, production, distribution, exhibition, material sites, and circulation across proliferating platforms. McLagan and McKee term this nexus "image complexes."[2] The participatory new media documentary image complex entails the mobility of images; the micro; place; mutability across platforms, contexts, communities; and permeability.

Case Studies

EngageMedia is an environmental and human rights social media portal and collaborative project engaging the Asia Pacific region. It features heterogeneous short videos spanning amateur user-generated, activist, advocacy, nongovernmental organizations (NGO) training pieces, public health videos, youth activist works, professionally produced news, and experimental works. EngageMedia negotiates specifically Indonesian contradictions between accessible consumer-grade media technologies, social media openings, and highly regulated commercial media. It addresses the need for distribution of works produced across Indonesia developed out of anti-Suharto oppositional politics during *Reformasi* in the late 1990s.

EngageMedia exemplifies permeable, migratory, malleable, collaborative new media. As a portal, it aggregates user-generated social media about Asian Pacific environmental and social justice issues. Dubbed the "YouTube for Southeast Asian Activists," EngageMedia assembles genres, topics, and countries to map the underside of the massive economic development redefining the Asia Pacific. EngageMedia focuses not on the national but on microterritories as transnational.

EngageMedia's Migrant Workers Stories exemplifies a collaborative image complex. Testimonies are gathered in short, shareable videos produced by migrants and circulated through transnational labor networks. The International

Labor Organization of the United Nations estimates that over 4.3 million Indonesians are overseas migrants in the Middle East and Asia; 75 percent are women domestic workers. To counter Indonesian governmental migrant narratives, EngageMedia initiated the Migrant Worker Stories project in 2012. It collaborated with migrant worker advocacy organizations in Indonesia and Malaysia to launch capacity-building workshops in Kuala Lumpur and West Java, training migrants to tell their own stories with cheap video and mobile phones. EngageMedia also collaborated with Citizen Journalists Malaysia, an initiative from Malaysiakini, a highly successful alternative news website countering government and corporate news monopolies. EngageMedia operates not only as a video aggregator but also as a partnership and organizational aggregator, countering ASEAN regional, state-focused trade hegemony.

The Quipu Project (Maria Court/Rosemarie Lerner, Peru) is a migratory participatory new media project traversing the digital, analog, and embodied. It addresses an unresolved political conflict in Peru: rural Quechua-speaking women endured unconsented sterilization in the 1990s under President Fujimori.

This project aggregates indigenous women's voices in remote villages without access to the internet in order to create a testimonial archive for political action and justice. To protect the women's anonymity and to work around the lack of digital capacity, the designers set up a toll-free number. Women were given mobile phones to tell their story anonymously in a phone call.

The project collects the stories on a website, protecting the women's anonymity. It operates on the participation of the women, who are reached through small gatherings in collaboration with Amnesty International and local women's groups. The project depends on a participatory double helix across organizations and across rural women's communities. Through stories shared via phone, the project generates a testimonial cartography.

The project aggregates testimonies rather than identities. The stories transform into mobilizing agents, impelling more meetings of women and political demonstrations. The project is based on the Quipu, an Andean circular necklace constructed of strands knotted to a circle. Also called talking knots, they were record-keeping devices. The Quipu functions as a metaphor for the participatory process and structures the project design across analog, digital, and embodied forms of engagement, a circulation of stories, women, gatherings.

In Ukraine, after President Victor Yanukovich rejected joining the European Union in fall 2013, there were mass protests, and the Maidan Revolution was born, called the Revolution of Dignity. More than 800,000 took to the streets of Kyiv and occupied Maidan Square to protest the EU decision and government corruption and to advocate for civil society. International news organizations converged in Kyiv, covering the spectacle of mass demonstrations, occupations, and shootings where a hundred people were killed. Documentary film directors of Ukrainian heritage also arrived, producing epic, feature-length films such as *Maidan*

(2014) by Sergey Loznitsa and *Winter on Fire* (2015) by Evgeny Afineevsky. Ukrainian activist filmmakers criticized these films and international news coverage for their focus on the spectacles of massive demonstrations, street actions, violence, shootings, and burnings.

During the Maidan, the Babylon '13 collective countered these representations with on-the-ground stories, featuring small, everyday acts like cooking and conversation. The filmmakers first gathered in the fall of 2013 in the basement café of a famous Soviet-built cinema. The one hundred filmmakers of the Babylon '13 collective reflect a wide range of ages and technical acumen, from professionals to amateurs, from broadcast TV reporters to ordinary citizens with cellphones. A famous 1929 soviet film about the 1871 Paris Commune where revolutionaries were shot inspired the name Babylon; 13 derived from the year of the Maidan revolution. The Babylon '13 Collective produced these videos specifically for sharing among activists across Ukraine, a micro archive from below. These short videos countered Russian information wars arguing that the CIA and the US government operatives instigated the Maidan. They were designed for shares on Facebook, a platform used more than email in Ukraine, rather than for festivals or broadcast.

The works of Babylon '13 are not signed; some have English subtitles. Posted on the Babylon '13 YouTube channel, these shorts document the Maidan with its diversity of ages and classes, elaborating a more complex portrait than international news. After the Maidan ended in February 2014, fighting broke out in the eastern region of Donbass, a predominantly Russian-speaking area that sought independence from Ukraine, with indirect Russian support. Then, Russia occupied Crimea. Babylon '13 filmmakers covered Donbass and Crimea. They chronicled soldiers' stories about the crowdsourced war, where citizens donate money and food, and about the more than one million internally displaced people. The filmmakers explored environmental destruction in Ukraine linked to oligarch corruption. Babylon '13's urgent, anonymous short form microdocumentaries map war, occupation, and political transition from multiple viewpoints, a participatory new cartography.

Some Constituents of Participatory and Collaborative New Media Documentary

- Collaboration
- Engagement
- Making Place
- Micro
- Multiple
- New Cartographies
- Participation
- Permeable
- Unresolved conflicts

Notes

1. Okwui Enwezor, "Coalition Building: Black Audio Collective and Transnational Post-Colonialism," in *The Ghosts of Songs: The Film Art of the Black Audio Film Collective*, eds. Kodwo Eshun and Anjelika Saga (Liverpool, UK: Liverpool University Press, 2007), 122.

2. Meg McLagan and Yates McKee, "Introduction," in *Sensible Politics: The Visual Culture of Nongovernmental Activism*, eds. Meg McLagan and Yates McKee (Brooklyn: Zone Books, 2012), 12.

PART IV
SPECULATIVE ENGINEERING

Figure 18.1. *Vacaciones en Necochea* (Cattaneo, Argentina, 1970s). Image courtesy of Andrés Levinson and Museo del Cine Pablo Ducros Hicken, Buenos Aires, Argentina.

18

HOME MOVIE AXIOMS*

1. Hollywood films are the home movies of global capital.
2. Home movies provide a site to perform exorcisms on the international crisis to recover public memory and signal a return to the real, the referent, the body.
3. Home movies present facts that are fictions and fictions that are facts.
4. Home movies are not empirical evidence. Rather, they stage psychic tracings, disturbances, dreamscapes, phantasms, colliding registers, and contiguities.
5. Home movies are neither images nor representations. Instead, they are mediations of fragmentary, incomplete symptoms of the breakage of the psyche, the breakage of the text, and the breakage of social and political relations.
6. Home movies are inscribed by and in continual conversation and movement with historical and psychic traumas.

---

* Home movie axioms emerged from the convergences between archives, history, museums, public life, and theory beyond the academic. I started to write about home movies and film history in 1977 while a graduate student at the University of Wisconsin. At the time, the new film history was emerging, turning to archives and other primary source material to trace the economics, aesthetics, and operations of the Hollywood film industry and other international cinemas. Scholars were beginning to employ more rigorous historical and economic methodologies than had previously been the case when film history relied largely on interviews with studio heads and film executives. An unexplored territory, home movies presented a way to look at the intersections of technology, history, marginalized cinematic practices, the everyday, and democratic communication. I ended up not only doing my PhD dissertation on the history of amateur film in the United States, but subsequently writing two books on amateur film, *Reel Families: A Social History of Amateur Film* (Bloomington: Indiana University Press, 1995) and, coedited with Karen Ishizuka, *Mining the Home Movie: Excavations in Histories and Memories* (Berkeley: University of California Press, 2007).

By the late 1990s, different festivals, museums, archives, and organizations both within the United States and internationally started to invite me to lecture. I was asked to speak about amateur film and home movies at venues apart from academic conferences as diverse as the American Moving Image Archivist Association in Toronto; Le Centre national de l'audiovisuel in Luxembourg; the University of Cork; Concordia University; Cornell University; the Fédération Internationale des Archives du Film in Cartagena, Columbia; the Getty Research Institute; Hampshire College; the University of Iowa; JAAGA in Bangalore, India; the University of Minnesota; MIT; Nanyang Technological University, Singapore; Oregon State University; the Royal Netherlands Institute of Southeast Asia and Caribbean Studies in Leiden; the University of

7. Home movies constitute microhistories that serve as intersections between local, regional, national, and global movements and fluidities.
8. Home movies narrate the nation differently and in difference(s).
9. Home movies exceed linear causal historical explanation. They necessitate the continual formation of an archive of contiguities and collage that opens to the future.
10. Home movies require multilinearities and multispatialities. A home movie is never singular. It is multiple in all vectors.
11. To work with home movies is to mine and to excavate and to reclaim visual artifacts from the quotidian in specificity.
12. Home movies are always disparate and incomplete objects that are also imaginaries. They necessitate a retheorization of film history into a more polyvocal and contrapuntal model.
13. Home movies are an unseen cinema of public memories and historical traumas, visual artifacts that define and also defy the fixities of object status.
14. Public memory is that which moves beyond the private to the collective and the political. It speaks beyond the self in compound knowledge with others in a constantly moving dialectic between the past and the future. Home movies, as the seen and the unseen, hold the possibilities of public memory.
15. Home movies require a shift from the temporal to spatial.

Sunderland in the UK; SUNY Purchase; the Wales Film Archive; and the Wolfson Media Center in Miami.

At these events, I was asked to speak to a more public and more interdisciplinary audience beyond film historians, and to make a case for the significance of amateur film. Since my work on amateur film had focused on American film history, I found I needed to extrapolate theories and historiographic models that could be useful beyond the US context as new caches of amateur films emerged and as archives around the globe began to reclaim their visual heritage in everyday cinemas. I also found that these venues were asking me for specific arguments they could use to secure funds or justify expansion of their collections. They wanted arguments about how to regard amateur films, why they were significant, and what they offered as history that differed from other cinematic artifacts. These programmers and archivists at these venues asked me for a simple handout to supplement my books on amateur film.

As a result, the axioms I discuss here first saw the light of day as handouts for various invited talks, and were constantly adapted as I encountered different constituencies, countries, and histories. In 2001, Dan Streible, who runs the Orphan Film Symposium, invited me to present my work at Orphans of the Storm II: Documenting the 20th Century, that year's symposium at the University of South Carolina. My colleague Jake Homiak, from the Human Studies Film Archive at the Smithsonian, where I had done research for *Reel Families* was going to attend, and I worked with him to bring together a group of films from that archive to present at the symposium. My Ithaca College colleague Simon Tarr was going to the conference as well, and so was archivist Jan-Christopher Horak, director of the UCLA Film & Television Archive, so I enlisted them to help make the films from the Smithsonian come alive. I rewrote the axioms and asked Chris to read them with me, alternating, while Simon remixed the images with a rudimentary computer system. I also hired an African drummer from the area to enter the back of the theater drumming while the films screened, and to drum underneath our recitations as a way to create a more arresting context for these films and bring these theories to life. I have used these axioms in multiple ways: as performance scripts with music, as hand-outs, and as ideas that can be adapted in different national contexts for amateur film archival collection.

16. Home movies engage a historiographic mapping process of the incomplete and fragmentary archives of an imagined past.
17. Home movies function as psychic vectors. As texts and histories without closure, they overflow with dynamic contradictions. Home movies are not fixed objects.
18. Home movies are condensations, imaginaries, and dreamscapes that are fluid and changing as they interact with other discursive, political, and social formations.
19. Home movies speak through their gaps, fissures, silences, vacancies, and elisions. To understand the signification system of home movies and their historiographic meaning, it is necessary to move from the causal and the linear to the multilinear, the contiguous, and the polyphonic.
20. All home movies and amateur films represent acts of death, loss, trauma, decay, and mourning. Their ghosts call out to us to be made real, to be remembered, and to be named.

Figure 19.1. *Subatlantic* video still (Ursula Biemann, Switzerland, 2015). Courtesy of the artist.

19

SPECULATIONS ON ENVIRONMENTAL SENSUALITIES AND ECO-DOCUMENTARIES*

1. Environmental and ecological thinking requires reimagining and reconceptualizing the environment.
2. Thinking differently about the environment and sustainability necessitates immersion within interconnected, fluid, and global contexts. It means redefining the environmental beyond the confining materialities of air, land, and sea.
3. Thinking differently about the environment and sustainability suggests considering embodied, heterogeneous, intersecting, political, social, and transnational practices.
4. Thinking differently about the environment and sustainability suggests the need to catapult across and beyond art forms, borders, ethnicities, formats, genres, nations, and nature.

---

* In 2004, I was appointed the codirector, with Thomas Shevory from the Ithaca College Department of Politics, of the Finger Lakes Environmental Film Festival (FLEFF). When funding from Cornell University ceased in 2003, the director of the festival, Christopher Riley, approached Ithaca College. Our then-provost, Peter Bardaglio, saw sustainability and environmental issues as areas of national visibility and impact, given the growth of environmental studies and sciences on our campus as well as many environmental initiatives in the Finger Lakes region.

The college sought to augment its position in environmental arenas, asking us to reinvent the festival so that it would be more interdisciplinary, more international, and engage all the schools at Ithaca College. We conceived a more expansive definition of the terms environmental and sustainability. We revised the festival from a film festival into a multiarts and multidisciplinary festival that included film, video, installation, fine art, new media, scholars, lectures, silent film/live music commissions, roundtables, workshops, labs, forums, and meet-ups. We partnered with the local art cinema, Cinemapolis, to show a heterogeneous group of international feature-length films in documentary, narrative, and experimental genres, and worked with scores of faculty to show films and host guests in their classes.

In full disclosure, I had never been particularly interested in environmental issues, either politically or intellectually. I supported environmental justice movements but had focused most of my scholarly work on political issues in documentary. When I was appointed codirector, I was secretly relieved to collaborate with Tom, who had written many books on environmental issues,

5. Sustainable development and the environment flow as active, collaborative, and interdependent ecosystems.
6. Nature is often privileged as an edenic ideal, a pastoral fantasy, and a romanticized projection of desire into the unassailable, uncontaminated, and uncontrolled domain of science.
7. Nature is often represented as neutral and is oversimplified; as a result, questions of power are repressed.
8. Nature is often confined, ineffable, overpowering, remote, safe, and tame. It is often figured in reductionist terms.
9. False dichotomies are established between the argumentative and the empirical, the human and the natural, the social and the scientific, the United States and the globe.
10. An ecological/environmental way of thinking entails constantly moving vectors of aesthetic innovation; access to health care, clean water, and housing; class; equality; freedom; gender; nation; race; sexualities; and social justice.
11. Environments and ecologies signify a complicated nexus of the aesthetic, economic, natural, physical, political, social, and technological.
12. An ecological way of thinking demands tracing these complex interactions in order to understand them—and act on them.
13. Ecology means understanding how things, people, and ideas are interconnected.
14. Ecology/environment means considering how the senses and communities operate within larger aesthetic, biological, political, and social matrices.
15. The concepts of ecology and the environmental are deeply subversive because they dislodge categories that are presumed to be stable. Ecological and environmental thinking mines and explores the conflicts and intersections between the human and the natural.

---

taught environmental politics, and understood it all much more deeply than I did. On the advice of several outside consultants who programmed major festivals, such as Ruth Bradley, Gretjen Clausing, Richard Herskowitz, and Shannon Kelley, we immediately decided to program FLEFF around particular themes.

A few years later, in 2008, Dale Hudson, who had been at Ithaca College when we took over FLEFF and has worked as one of our curators from the very beginning, was teaching at Amherst College. Amherst was looking to develop environmental studies, so Dale invited the two of us to give a lecture on FLEFF and to show some experimental media work we had programmed. For this presentation, Tom and I did not want to read a lecture, because we felt that festivals should create space for interaction and engagement with audiences.

I volunteered to go through the four festival catalog essays and many grants we had written together to see if I could pull out phrases that might map our ideas about the nexus of environment and media, partially driven by a consistent question we encountered after revamping the festival: how is this an environmental film festival? We considered our programming a success if it prompted this question, as we worked to move beyond any typical or predictable way of thinking about the environment and media. The presentation we did at Amherst was called "Environmental Sensualities" and featured a version of what later evolved into the following speculations on PowerPoint slides interspersed with experimental films, video, and new media from our festival.

16. UNESCO's initiative on sustainable development has redefined and expanded environmental issues to explore the international interconnection between air, cultural heritage, disease, diversity, education, food, health, genocide, the land, technology, war, and water.
17. Environmental sensualities means reconnecting to more collective and emancipated forms of production for the creation of a public commons.
18. Environmental sensualities imagine locations differently. They are composed with many intersecting layers in constant motion. They are collaborative, material, and relational.
19. Environments constitute in-between zones where we actively engage with, manipulate, and negotiate external forces.
20. In the liminal zones between bodies as active, sensing agents and the environment and the natural world as complex systems in flux, openings emerge. These pathways invent new aesthetic, biological, political, and social spaces through hearing, seeing, tasting, and touching.
21. Rather than hierarchies, environmental sensualities suggest clusters, layers, and networks—horizontal, continually forming relationships.
22. Environments are systems comprising changes, fluidities, incessant interactions, movements, and transversals.
23. Environments are only sustainable if they are complex, heterogeneous, multiple, and sensual.
24. Disturbances and debates can relocate us into a new interstitial imaginary zone that can open up the possibility of joining together to build a contentious and energized public commons.
25. It is urgent and necessary to think and act differently about the ecological, the environmental, and the sustainable in new ways: new forms, new interfaces, new public commons.

Figure 20.1. *The Shore Line* (Elizabeth Miller, Canada, and many international collaborators, 2018). Design credit: Helios Design Labs.

20

SPECULATIONS ON REVERSE ENGINEERING

*Algorithms for Recombinant Documentaries across Platforms**

1. Reverse engineering identifies the system's components and their interrelationships and then rebuilds that system at another level of abstraction. Reverse engineering dismantles technologies to understand how their parts articulate. It cracks codes and discovers contradictions as a starting place to invent unique forms, always emphasizing building something new out of the old. It offers a strategy of reversals and reversing to open up the potentials of documentary.
2. A point of contradiction in critical historiography as it applies to documentary practices is narrative versus structure. Instead of the restrictions of linear continuity, the notion of contiguities, of artifacts and ideas and images side by side, resonating with each other, allows us to speculate on new systems. Contiguities suggests reconfiguration of both narrative and structure within a larger set of coordinates that through their juxtapositions, contradictions, and layerings create new meanings and interpretations, new futures.
3. Reverse engineering and the archive it mobilizes are always open and recombinant, active rather than static, evolving, not fixed. Reverse engineering opens to the future.

---

* I developed these speculations on reverse engineering in order to have a simple, easy-to-read handout for audiences at public invited talks where I discussed amateur film, archives, documentary, and new media as well as models of critical historiography derived from poststructural and postcolonial theory both in the US and internationally. I culled these speculations from my writing and notes and initially devised them to prep myself for questions-and-answer sessions or for more interactive workshops, as a sort of cheat sheet of major concepts to help me articulate them in a compelling, clear way. I found that students appreciated handouts on theories both in hard copy and digitally, so inspired by their response, I wanted audiences at conferences, museums, and universities to have a takeaway that was more concrete than just the ephemeral spoken word. These particular speculations also function as a concluding chapter for this volume, as they bring together ideas about engineering, histories, historiography, platforms, reversals, and speculative thinking. They also work with concepts of analog, archives, digital, documentary, and platforms.

4. Archival objects and tools are not static. They should not be sacralized, monumentalized, or fossilized. Artifacts—rather than archival objects—are provisional and fluid rather than fixed. They are mobilized to create a collaborative performative space for the imagination of new histories and new futures. New tools must always be produced.
5. The archival process is to name the unburied dead. This naming creates a liminal zone between that which is alive and that which is phantasmatic, ghostly, apparitional. Reverse engineering is always imbedded in the transnational relationships of war and genocide, illness and famine, environmental destruction and extraction, exploitation and oppression.
6. Witnessing and testimonial, image and artifact, together, as parts of documentary practice, move and work through repetition to create memory that is collective and always forming and reforming, collaged and reconfigured.
7. The point of the digital archive and reverse engineering is to fight the anesthesia and amnesia of transnational capital that is ultimately authoritarian without change or mutation. The digital archive and documentary across platforms fight back with synesthesia and polyphony.
8. It is necessary to ignite and mobilize the digital archive and documentary toward collective public memory through creating networked models of hybrid and multiple temporalities.
9. Histories and stories and documentaries are always told and retold differently, moving from the speaker to the listener, from the state to the everyday, from the interface to the body, from the virtuoso to the amateur.
10. Temporality in the digital archive and in documentary is plural. There is no longer one progression, but many. Contiguities become more revealing than continuities.
11. There is no divide between the digital and the analog, between documentary and experimental modes, between the visual and the aural, between history and the future, between theory and practice, between object and subject, between the artifact and the spaces it creates. All work in a dialogic, morphing interface.
12. All images and all sounds form an archival surround. In the digital age, we live in the archival interface and operate constantly within this archival surround. We must enter into and reactivate it in recombinant ways that entail swarm tactics, cells, provisional claiming of spaces for historiographic, semiotic, and political interventions, and a conceptualization of documentary across platforms.
13. An archive is not a place. It is, rather, a theater of operations that spans the analog and digital. It stages political interventions into the image/sound surround and engages provisional rewirings of historical imaginaries.
14. Reverse engineering is never singular or unified: it is relentlessly polyphonic, polyversal, polyvocal. As documentary operates across platforms, these different kinds of multiplicities animate it.

15. The digital archive and reverse engineering of documentary refuses the nineteenth-century romanticism of the individual, the precious artifact, the subjective form, the linear narrative.
16. The digital archive and the reverse engineering of documentary employ an algorithm of collaboration that imagines and materializes new contiguities to produce new archives and multiple platforms and reversals.
17. In the digital age and the archival surround, one screen is problematic and archaic. The task is to make many screens and many spaces through recombinant archives of contiguities and documentaries across many platforms.
18. The digital archive is recombinant. The digital archive is contiguous. The digital archive is fluid. The digital archive is polyphonic. Therefore, documentary across platforms will mobilize recombinant, contiguous, fluid, and polyphonic practices.
19. Reverse engineering is a conceptual algorithm that is productive, changing, and mobilizing. It is not a technology but a theoretical process aimed toward action and customization.
20. The archive and documentary function as a process and not a product. They are never finished and always revised, at multiple nodal points in production, distribution, exhibition, and reception Recombinant documentaries across platforms serve as an interface between histories and memories, artifacts and imaginaries, the real and the phantasmatic, history and the future, technology and the body. It is these interfaces and interstices that produce a documentary practice across platforms.

ACKNOWLEDGMENTS

OVER THE LAST TWO DECADES, MANY PEOPLE, PLACES, and politics inspired the ideas in *Documentary across Platforms* and galvanized the writing and revising of these twenty essays. Analyses, conceptualizations, critiques, and theoretical models do not materialize in isolation from the world; they require conversations, debates, and solidarities that clarify and embolden new thinking. Not only do these essays chronicle twenty years of writing in different styles for different venues and different audiences, they also represent the impact of many different communities that insisted on the urgency of engaging politically and thinking alternatively about documentary in all its forms, modes, and platforms. My debts, therefore, are vast.

Some of these essays grew out of conference papers where my initial tentative ideas unfolded at meetings of the Asian Media and Communications International Centre, the Association for Comparative Literature, the Documentary Now Conference, the Flow Conference on Television Studies, the iDocs Symposium, the International Cultural Studies Association, the Orphan Film Symposium, the Society for Cinema and Media Studies, the University Film and Video Association, the Visible Evidence Conference on Documentary, and the What Is Documentary Conference.

Attendance at these conferences and the time to write this book were made possible by generous research support from a variety of grants from Ithaca College, such as Provost Small Grants for Academic Research, Reassigned Time Grants, and several Summer Research Grants. Multiple grants from the Roy H. Park School of Communications at the college, such as the James B. Pendleton Grants, supported editorial and photographic assistance, research assistants, and travel across the United States and the world to attend conferences. I am grateful to my students and colleagues at Ithaca College, where I tested many of the book's ideas in courses housed in the All-College Honors Program; the Department of Media Arts, Sciences, and Studies and the Documentary Studies and Production Program in the Roy H. Park School of Communications; and the Division of Interdisciplinary and International Studies, now disbanded, but formative and rewarding for so many scholars at Ithaca College.

Other essays in this book emerged from invited talks, where new topics pushed me to consider new aesthetic, political, technological, and theoretical recalibrations of documentary. I thank colleagues at the following US academic institutions for their kind invitation to share my work and their generosity and collegiality in hosting me. I am grateful to Amherst College, Brown University, Colgate University, Cornell University, Dartmouth College, Elmira College, Hamilton College, Hampshire College, Hobart and William Smith Colleges, Massachusetts Institute of Technology, Oregon State University, St. Mary's College of Maryland, Southern Illinois University, State University of New York–Purchase, Syracuse University, University of California–San Diego, University of Illinois, University of Iowa, University of Michigan, University of Minnesota, University of New Hampshire, University of Oregon, University of Rochester, University of Southern California, University of Washington, and Yale University.

I would also like to express my gratitude to the universities outside of the United States for invitations to share my work and to learn from their robust sense of scholarly community across borders: Carleton University (Canada), Concordia University (Canada), Dubreka Arts Institute (Guinea), Hong Kong Baptist University, University of Bristol (UK), Institutes Superieur de Information et Communication (Guinea), University of Leiden (The Netherlands), Quangdong University of Foreign Studies (China), Middlesex University (UK), Mohyla University (Ukraine), Nanyang Technological University (Singapore), National University of Singapore, New York University–Abu Dhabi (United Arab Emirates), Sun Yat-Sen University (China), University of Cork (Ireland), University of Hong Kong, University of Sunderland (UK), University of Toronto (Canada), and York University (Canada).

I thank the magnanimous, amicable, and visionary arts administrators, archivists, curators, and programmers of various festivals and archives where I was invited to share my thinking with audiences and communities beyond the academy. In the United States, these organizations include The Alliance, the Association of Moving Image Archivists, the Athens International Film Festival, Cinema Pacific Film Festival, Getty Research Institute, Houston Cinema Arts Film Festival, the Human Studies Film Archive of the Smithsonian Institution, the Lynn and Louis Wolfson II Florida Moving Image Archives, Miami International Film Festival, Minneapolis International Film Festival, National Alliance for Media Arts and Culture, Northeast Historic Film, Orphan Film Symposium, Pacific Film Archive, Robert Flaherty Film Seminar, Rose Goldsen Archive of New Media Art at Cornell University, Sundance Film Festival, Virginia Film Festival, and the White River Indie Film Festival.

I want to thank the organizations beyond the United States whose invitations brought me into critical dialogues and compelling debates: Bangalore Film Society (India), Le Centre National de l'audiovisuel (Luxembourg), Community Organization Development Forum (China), Fédération Internationale des Archives du Film, iDocs Symposium (UK), JAAGA Space for New Media (India), Morelia International Film Festival (Mexico), Nigerian Film Institute, Oberhausen Film Festival (Germany), Substation (Singapore), and World Association of

Newspaper Publishers for the Asia Pacific Region (Singapore/Hong Kong). In addition, I thank three organizations that have put me and my work out into the world beyond the United States: the American Film Showcase of the US State Department, which appointed me as a Film Envoy for Documentary for many years; the Fulbright Association, where I serve as a Fulbright Specialist; and the Wee Kim Wee School of Communications at Nanyang Technological University in Singapore, where I did two life-changing stints, the second as the endowed Shaw Professor of New Media.

Research, theorizing, and writing on documentary means entering a space beyond archives, artifacts, and libraries, a zone where activists, artists, collectives, groups, and individual makers remind one that this work constitutes rigorous theorization that requires courage, fortitude, and an unwillingness to cease. For their insights and for sharing their work with me, I want to express my appreciation and respect to the artists and makers who move deftly across platforms and who spoke with me and shared the work that informed these essays: Robby Aceto, Enrico Aditjondro, Reece Auguiste, Ursula Biemann, Maureen Bradley, Anne Bray, Dana Claxton, Tony Cokes, Tony Conrad, Maria Court, Ricardo Dominguez, Renate Ferro, Elson Fróes, DeeDee Halleck, Mark Hosler, Art Jones, Philip Mallory Jones, Michael Kienitz, Paul Lehrman, Rosemarie Lerner, Andres Levinson, Les LeVeque, Andrew Lowenthal, Louis Massiah, Elizabeth Miller, Allyson Mitchell, Naeem Mohaeimen, Bill Morrison, Fe Nunn, Daniel Reeves, Rick Rowley, Brooke Singer, Jacquie Soohen, Ellen Spiro, Simon Tarr, and b.h. yael. Collectives and organizations also contribute to this vibrant zone that expands documentary and my thinking in the essays in this book such as The Alliance, Artisan D'Angkor (Cambodia), Babylon '13 (Ukraine), Big Noise Films, Code Pink, Deep Dish TV, EngageMedia (Indonesia), Experimental TV Center, Finger Lakes Environmental Film Festival, Human Rights Watch, Human Studies Film Archive of the Smithsonian Institution, Museo del Cine Pablo Ducros Hicken Buenos Aires (Argentina), National Alliance for Media Arts and Culture, Northeast Historic Film, Paper Tiger TV, Scribe Video Center, and WITNESS.

Ithaca College is a small four-year college in upstate New York, but its embodiment of intellectual camaraderie makes it feel much larger. Colleagues have supported me in weathering the neoliberal hurricanes blowing into higher education, reminding me that ideas need community and communities cannot function without ideas.

Since 2004, I have served as codirector of the Finger Lakes Environmental Film Festival (FLEFF) at Ithaca College, an interdisciplinary, multiarts festival now over two decades old that explores sustainability across the arts, music, film, video, new media, literary work, research, policy, and activism. I am indebted to Tom Shevory, who serves with me as codirector, for taking me on a journey into thinking differently about the environment, and for being a comrade in this endeavor where nothing ever stays the same. I also thank the executive producer of FLEFF, Tanya Saunders, who in her other job serves as assistant provost for International Programs and Extended Studies. My research, thinking, and writing have been honed by FLEFF because at the festival, artists, makers, new works, robust discussions, and unresolved ideas nourish and challenge me. The FLEFF team is expansive both in terms of people and in spirit at Ithaca College and beyond with members in other countries and at other institutions, an interdisciplinary crew of artists, musicians, writers, and scholars who remind me that collaboration is one of the most powerful paths toward new ways of thinking and analyzing. I would like to especially thank core team members Barbara Adams, Janet Galvan, Jairo Geronymo, Dale Hudson, Deborah Martin, Ann Michel, David Ost, Claudia Costa Pederson, Karen Rodriguez, Philip Wilde, and Mary Zebell for collaborating to make FLEFF what it is.

Upstate New York has a long history of independent media arts in documentary and experimental media, and in experiments with technology. The region also has many colleges and universities with innovative programs in film and media. The independent media arts ecology in upstate New York is a diverse ecosystem that constantly renews me. It includes many people whose brilliant minds and uninhibited passion for media analysis, making, and programming make me feel part of something larger than myself, and remind me that ideas are in people, not institutions: Matt Fee, Renate Ferro, Vincent Grenier, Roger Hallas, Scott MacDonald, Timothy Murray, Lisa Patti, Leah Shafer.

The field of documentary studies functions as a battalion of like-minded souls who believe that all forms of media can create space for necessary debates that map out a preliminary route to resistance to authoritarianism, power, the ravages of transnational capital, and war. For showing me that being fierce intellectually and politically is the only option, I want to acknowledge Judith Ashton, Helen De Michiel, John Hess, Jan-Christopher Horak, Chuck Kleinhans, Julia Lesage, Brenda Longfellow, Elizabeth Miller, Dorit Naaman, Bill Nichols, B. Ruby Rich, Mandy Rose, Sharon Lin Tay, Gail Vanstone, Thomas Waugh, and Brian Winston. I also thank Alexandra Juhasz and Brian Winston for their sharp reader's reports of the initial manuscript, which helped to shape it into something a bit more pointed and, I hope, more persuasive.

Gina Marchetti has been my friend and ally since we were graduate students enrolled in different PhD programs in the late 1970s. Together, we have weathered many different schools of film theory, many pitched battles about the politics of film and media, and many conferences across the globe over our decades of friendship. For six years in the late 1990s, she team taught introduction to film aesthetics and analysis with me at Ithaca College, where we instituted a model of extreme heterogeneity across genres, countries, and forms—and spent many delightful hours of "booth time" in the Park Auditorium, analyzing the films, talking film studies, and figuring out how to best teach that week's topic. Gina convinced me to take the position in Singapore, as she had taught there before me. I am especially grateful and honored that she wrote the elegantly organized, deeply considered, and beautifully written foreword to this book.

I owe a very special and deep thanks to two people who helped to bring these essays and their accompanying images into a new and, I hope, somewhat improved form for this book. First, I thank the incomparable Jane Banks for her meticulous line editing and copyediting to help to update and sharpen the prose, bring it into conformity with *The Chicago Manual of Style*, and provide counterfactual arguments and coaching on clarity of expression throughout. I feel so lucky to count her as a friend and colleague in the field of communications for four decades, and now, as a line and structural editor with an acumen few possess. Second, I thank Hend Alawadhi, my research assistant, who worked for months to help find the images that illustrate the essays in this book and collaborated with the various artists and organizations to secure permissions for publication. An emerging documentary scholar, Hend brought an artistic eye and a meticulous research sensibility to this work of selecting and procuring the images that appear in this book.

Books are endeavors one executes alone, sitting in a study, searching in libraries, and pounding away at a computer. But every writer needs special people who remind one of the worlds beyond the screens. Stewart Auyash's love as well as his passion for a world made better and more equitable through ferocious collective engagement fortifies and inspires me to trudge forward when faced with big winds and white-capped waters. Sean Zimmermann Auyash constantly reminds me that love is a muscle that moves us to a better place and helps us to question any and all assumptions with vigilance.

INDEX

Page numbers in italics refer to illustrations

Abu Ghraib, 18, 142–143
Aceto, Robby, 166
ACT UP, 232
Adams, Barbara, 6
Adams, John: *Death of Klinghofer, The* (2003), 225
Adams, Stephanie, 202–203
Afghan Explorer, 22–23
Afghanistan War, 19, 34, 125; and blasting war, 105–111
Afineevsky, Evgeny, 77, 236
Afterimage (journal), 8, 9
Agamben, Giorgio, 91
agitprop, ix, xii
Airport Insecurity, 136, 144, 145, 146
Algeri, Dion, 121
Alic, Fikret, 102n59
Allen, Paul, 122
All My Babies (George Stoney, 1953), 39
Alloy Orchestra, 166, 217–218
Al Qaeda, 109, 110, 125, 126
Alston, Angela, 130
Altman, Rick, 218–219
American Civil Liberties Union (ACLU), 109, 110, 124, 126
American Independence Film Festival, 75, 78–79
An, Grace, 204
Angola, 108–109
Ankersmit, F. K., 145
Antheil, George, 219
Antz (1998), 126
Apocalypse Now (Francis Ford Coppola, 1979), 75, 86
Appadurai, Arjun, 138
Appalshop, 39, 232
ardent space, 33–34
Arnheim, Rudolph, 180
Ashcroft, John, 109
Association of Moving Image Archivists (AMIA), 9, 176n5, 218

Association of Southeast Asian Nations (ASEAN), 161, 235
Atom Films, 122, 125
Auguiste, Reece, 232

Babushkas of Chernobyl, The (Holly Morris and Anne Bogart, 2015), 80
Babylon '13 Collective, 79, 236; *#Babylon '13 Cinema of A Civil Protest*, 70
Bahru, Johor, 21, 153
Baker, Michael, 232
Baldwin, Craig, xii; *Sonic Outlaws*, 191
Ballet Mécanique (Fernand Leger, 1924), 219
Baudrillard, Jean, 90
Beglov, Volodymyr, 72
Being John Malkovich (1999), 110
Bellour, Raymond, 49
Ben-Dov, Ariella, 219, 223
Benedict XVI, Pope, 137
benshi (performer who narrates silent films), 216
Bergin, Dan, 129
Berkhofer, Robert F., Jr., 140–141, 146, 170, 174
Berkowitz, Bruce, 19
Berlin: Symphony of a Metropolis (Walter Ruttman, 1927), 39
Bernstein, Daniel, 98
Bernstein, Karen, 129
Biemann, Ursula, 244
Big Noise Film Collective, 120, 233
Bin Laden, Osama, 18, 107, 111, 125–127
Bin Laden Nowhere to Run, Nowhere to Hide, 127, 128
Biondi, Frank, 122
Birth of a Nation, The (D. W. Griffith, 1920), 183, 209
Bishop, Claire, 233
Bistransky, Shari, 75
Black Audio Film Collective, 232; *Twilight City* (1989), 230
Blackman, Meryl, 222

259

Blair, Tony, 185
Blau, Andrew, 17
Blumberg, Skip, 221
Bode, Peer, 222
Bollywood, 19, 21
Boltanski, Christian, 94
Bolter, Jay David, 26–27n27, 95, 126
Bosnia, 89–91, 102n59
Bourriaud, Nicolas, xiii, 169
Bradley, Maureen, 30; *Birthday Suit Management* (2001), 30; *What I Remember* (1998), 32–33
Bray, Anne, 215
broadband internet, 110, 121, 124, 125, 129, 161
Brooks, James, 122
Buddhas, Cambodian, 150, 152–162; and DVD pirates, 153–55; and economic exchange, 155–156; and *Lara Croft Tomb Raider* (2001), 159; and psychic economies of global circulation of craft, 157–158; shopping for, 159–160, 161–162
Buffalo Bone China (1997), 28
Bunuel, Luis, 216
Bush, George W., 106–109, 111, 125, 127, 142–143, 160, 182, 185, 195
Bush in 30 Seconds (Moveon.org), 17

cable access movement, 39
calibration, narrative, 91–93, 96, 99. See also recalibration
Cambodia, xii, xiii, 24–25, 150, 151–162; adoption in, 152–153, 156–157, 159; Angkor Wat, 159–160, 161; Buddhas, 150, 151–152, 154–155, 157–162; economic exchange in, 155–156; genocide and crafts in, 156–157; Khmer Rouge, 156–158, 161–162, 166; *Killing Fields, The* (Roland Joffe, 1984), 158; and *Lara Croft Tomb Raider* (2001), 159; least-developed country (LDC) classification, 152; and media piracy, 153–155; psychic economies of global circulation of craft in, 157–158; *S21: The Khmer Rouge Killing Machine* (Rithy Panh, 2003), xiii, 24, 158; sex slave industry in, 154–155; Siem Reap, 157, 159, 161–162; textile sweatshops in, 155; and Vietnam War, 157, 162; Yale Cambodian Genocide Project, 24–25
Campion, Jane, 120

Capra, Frank, 126
Card, Andrew, 107
Carr, Edward Hallet, 107
Carr, John, 129
Carr, Lena, 129
Carruth, Cathy, 44
Celebration, The (Thomas Vinterberg), 119
cellular convergences, 138
Center for Digital Democracy, 124, 133n25
Central New York Programmers Group, 8
Challenge for Change, 232
Challenger explosion, 92
Chakrabarty, Dipesh, 145–146
Chatterjee, Partha, 141
Cheney, Dick, 107
Chernobyl nuclear power plant disaster, 73–74, 79, 80
Chernomyrdin, Viktor, 92
Chirac, Jacques, 92
Chun, Changhee, 204
Chuprina, Alexandra, 79
Cinemapolis, 7
cinephilia, 169–70, 176
Clark, Ramsey, 98
Clark, Wesley, 84, 92
Clarke, Shirley, 221–222; *Connection, The* (1961), 221; *Cool World, The* (1963), 221; *Portrait of Jason* (1967), 221; "Tee Pee Video Space Troupe," 221
Clarke, Wendy, 221
Claxton, Dana, 30; *Anwolek/Regatta City* (2005), 32; *Buffalo Bone China* (1997), 28, 31–32; *Hope* (2007), 30; *I Want to Know Why* (1994), 31–32
Clinton, Bill, 86, 88, 92–93
club live performances, 223–224
Code Pink, xii, 140
cognitive mapping, xi
Cokes, Tony, 142–146; *Evil 8: Unseen* (2004), 134
Colectivo Cina Ojo, 233
Collage as Cultural Practice Symposium (University of Iowa), 194
colonial imaginary, 154
Columbine shooting, 86–88
computer and video games, 21, 88, 110, 153; *Airport Insecurity*, 136, 144, 145, 146; *Counter Strike*, 18; *Deep Focus* report on, 17;

digital skins, 111; and reverse engineering, 18; *Tomb Raider,* 159; and US military, 17–18, 86–87; *Velvet Strike,* 18
computer-assisted design and manufacturing (CAD CAM), 22–23
concert halls, 224–225
Conrad, Tony, 215–216, 219–221; *Ten Years Alive on the Infinite Plain* (1972), 220
convergences, 215–216; cellular convergences, 138
Coppola, Francis Ford, 75
copyright industries, 19–20
Cornell Cinema, 8, 48, 166
Cort, David, 221
Couple 513, 222
Creative Commons, 191
Cresswell, Tim, 234
Crouching Tiger, Hidden Dragon (2000), 119
Csíkszentmihályi, Chris, 22–23
Cuatro Estaciones Porteñas (The Four Seasons of Buenos Aires, 2007), 174–175
Cuevas, Ximena, 195
cultural studies, 5, 167, 201
cyberspace, 84, 89, 122–123, 128

Dalí, Salvador, 216
Dancer in the Dark (Lars Von Triers, 2000), 118
Davis, Sammy, Jr., 174
Deep Dish Television, 140, 144, 146
Deep Focus: A Report on the Future of Independent Media, 17, 139
Deleuze, Gilles, ix, 180, 183–185
De Michiel, Helen, 233
Department of Homeland Security, 109, 111
deployments, digital, 115–131; Flash animation, 127–128; targets of, 131; types of, 119
Derrida, Jacques, xii, 48, 54–55, 85–86, 95, 183, 200
Die Hard (1998), 110
Digital Millennium Copyright Act (DMCA), 21
DisappearedinAmerica.org, 138, 146
Dismantling Empire: Live! (2003), 24
Dismantling War (Art Jones and Simon Tarr, 2005), 171
Disney, 19, 21, 122, 126, 194
Dominguez, Ricardo, 225–226

Dorfman, Ariel, 107
Dorme, Yves, 171
Dovzhenko, Alexander, xii
Dovzhenko Film Archive, 77, 79
Downey, Juan, 46
Downhill Battle, 20
Dyer, Richard, 88

Eberhart, Matt, 82, 99
eco-documentaries, 245–247
ecology: art-making, 52; definition of, 2; new media ecology, 1–2, 4–5, 15, 17, 18, 22, 23, 78, 135–136, 139, 142; and public domains, 135–136, 139, 142
Economist, 75
Eisenstein, Sergei, xii–xiii, 103n74, 146
Eisenstein, Zillah, 107
El Automotival Gris (1915), 216
Electronic Disturbance Theater, 226
El Salvador, 61, 63, 233
EngageMedia, 234–235; Migrant Worker Stories, 234–235
Enwezor, Okwui, 232
Etra, Bill, 16
Everson Museum (Syracuse University), 8
Everson Museum of Art (Syracuse University), 8, 222
Evil Series (Tony Cokes), 142–146
Experimental Television Center (Owego), 8, 222–223
Eyes on the Prize (1987 and 1990), 20

fair use, 189, 191, 193, 195
Fall of the House of Usher (1928), 8
Fall Roads Bus (Michael Kientiz, 1981), 58
Fallujah, 140, 144, 145, 146
Fanon, Frantz, 44–45
Farm: Zone 2, The (M. Vadimski [pseudonym], 2017), 74
Federal Communications Commission, 110, 124, 226
Feldman, Shoshana, 46
feminism, xi–xii, 5, 6, 30–34, 38, 47, 49, 50, 140, 151, 168, 208
Fierce: Women's Hot-Blooded Film/Video (McMaster Museum of Art), 29–34; *Afghanimation* (Allyson Mitchell, 2008), 34; *Birthday Suit Management* (Maureen

Fierce (cont.)
  Bradley, 2001), 30; *(of) Fences* (b.h. yael, 2001), 33–34; *Hope* (Dana Claxton, 2007), 30; *Hot Sandfilled Wind, A* (b.h. yael, 2006), 33; *I Want to Know Why* (Dana Claxton, 1994), 31–32; *Melty Kitty* (Allyson Mitchell, 2007), 31; *My Life in 5 Minutes* (Allyson Mitchell, 2000), 32; *Precious Little Tiny Love* (Allyson Mitchell, 2003), 31; *Trading the Future* (b.h. yael, 2008), 34; *What I Remember* (Maureen Bradley, 1998), 32–33
Figgis, Mike, 118, 122
Fight Club (1999), 110
Finger Lakes Environmental Film Festival, xii, 135, 165, 176n1, 245
Fiore, Mark, 126
Fisk, Robert, 106–107
Flaherty, Robert: *Nanook of the North* (1922), 39, 232
Flash animation, 10, 17, 116, 117, 120, 121–131
Florida Moving Image Archive (FMIA), 172–174
Flusser, Vilém , 91
Fluxus live performance events, 204, 210, 216, 219–222
Forbidden Planet (Fred Wilcox, 1956), 182, 183, 185
foreign-language films, 118
Forgács, Péter, 195
Framework (film journal), 9
Free103point9 collective, 226–227
Fróes, Elson, 98–99
Fukuyama, Francis, 90

Galan, Hector, 129
Ganesh, 189–190, 196
Garcia, Chad, 79
Gates, Bill, 182
Geneva World Summit on the Information Society (2003), 22
George, Paul, 173
George Eastman House Museum and Archive, 8
Geronymo, Jairo, 174–175
Gilroy, Paul, 208
Glass, Phillip, 191
Godard, Jean-Luc, 49
Godfrey, John, 222
Goenka, Tula, 8

Gone with the Wind (Victor Fleming, 1939), 183
Good Machine, 119
Gordon, Michael, 166, 224–225
Gore, Al, 88
Govil, Nitin, 19
Great Depression, xii, 98
Green, Michael, 193–194
Greenwald, Jeff, 159
Grierson, John, ix
Griffin, Susan, 49
Griffith, D. W., 183, 209
Grusin, Richard, 26–27n27, 95, 126
Guatemala, 61, 67–68, 107
Guattari, Félix, 184–185
Guha, Ranajit, 23, 141–142, 145, 170, 200
Gulf War, 44, 49, 85, 92, 94, 107, 109, 117, 131
Guy-Blaché, Alice, 219

Habermas, Jurgen, 234
Habib, Nadia, 33
Hall, Stuart, 44–45
Hallas, Roger, 8
Halleck, Dee Dee, 221
Hampton, Henry, 20
handicrafts, 10, 53, 153–155, 162; Cambodian, 155, 157–158; *vyshyvka* (Ukrainian decorative embroidery), 80
Hand That Holds Up All This Falling, The (Daniel Reeves, 1997), 50–55; *Color Digital Paintings*, 53; *Eingang: The Way In* (1990), 50, 51–52, 55; *Gas Masque* (1997), 53; *Homage to the Lovers of Pompeii* (1997), 53; *Lines of Lamentation* (1997), 51, 54–55; *Manos para la muerte* (1997), 53–54
happenings, 168, 216, 219–222
Haynes, Todd, 120
Heemskerk, Joan, 103n70
Henderson, Cynthia, 166
Herbert F. Johnson Museum of Art (Cornell University), 8, 222
historiography, 199–201, 204, 207–208: postcolonial, 167, 232; and public domains, 140–142; and reverse engineering, 2–5, 16, 23; subaltern, 23, 141–142, 146, 170
Hitchcock, Alfred: *Spellbound* (1945), 181, 184; *Vertigo* (1958), 181, 183–185
Hitler, Adolf, 73
Hochheimer, John, 204

Hocking, Ralph, 222
Hocking, Sherry Miller, 222
Holocaust, 49, 91, 94–95, 97, 102n59
home digital projection, 123
home movie archive live, 165–176; and polyphony, 175–176; and rational aesthetics, 168–169; and space, 171–174
home movie axioms, 241–243
Horak, Chris, 217–218
Hosler, Mark, 194
How Stuff Is Made (web project), 16
Hozic, Aida, 87, 90, 122–123, 160
Hudson, Dale, 8
Human Rights Watch, 84, 95–96
Human Studies Film Archives (HSFA), 165, 171, 174
Hun Sen, 152
Hussein, Saddam, 107
Hyman, Judy, 165

Ice Storm, The (1997), 119
Ignatieff, Michael, 84
independent film, redefining, 115–117; and film exhibition (retail), 120–124; and Flash animation, 124–128; and fluid exchanges among economic sectors, 117–120; and streaming technologies, 128–131; targets of, 131
Independent Television Service (ITVS), 120, 129–130
India: computer-assisted design and manufacturing (CAD CAM), 22
Indie Lab, 74, 77–79
industry studies, 5
Institute for Creative Technologies (University of Southern California), 19
intellectual property piracy, xi, 3, 17, 19–22, 98, 110, 136, 142, 153–155
intellectual property rights, 19–21, 136, 153, 160, 168, 185–186, 189–190, 195–196
interfaces, 182, 225–228
International Action Center, 97–98
In the Fields (Andril Lytvynenko, 2014), 76
Iraq War, 61, 107–108; and activist media, 143; and collaborative knowledges, 140; and digital communication, 19; Iraqjournal.org, 111, 130–131; and public domains, 137, 140, 143; and remixes, 185, 216, 224; and reverse engineering, 17–19

Jackson, Jesse, 101n26
Jacobs, Ken, 224; *Nervous System* (1996–ongoing), 220
Jameson, Fredric, xi
Jamieson, Meg, 204
Jenkins, Henry, 233
Jennings, Humphrey, 75
Jeremijenko, Natalie, 16
Joffe, Roland, 158
Joint Vision 2020 (US Department of Defense vision statement), 17
Jones, Art, xii, 24, 171, 216, 223–224
Jones, Bill, 222
Jones, David, 16
Jones, Philip Mallory, 8; *Sporting Life* (2016), 16

Kartemquin, 39, 232
Katz, Leandro, 195
Kester, Grant, 168–169, 233
Kiarostami, Abbas, 108
Kienitz, Michael: career of, 59–60, 61–62; childhood in works of, 63–64; dislocation in works of, 60–61; gaze in works of, 67–68; incongruities and contiguities in work of, 64–65; and maps of omission, 61–62; and noncombatants, 60, 66–67; photographs taken in El Salvador, 63; photographs taken in Guatemala, 67–68; photographs taken in Lebanon, 66–67; photographs taken in Nicaragua, 65–66, 67; photographs taken in Northern Ireland, 58, 61, 65, 68; photographs taken in Pakistan, 59, 61, 108, 137–138; photographs taken in the United States, 64; power in work of, 65–66; *Small Arms-Children of Conflict*, xiv, 58, 59–69; and trauma, 62–63, 66, 68; and Vietnam War, 59–60, 61. *See also Small Arms-Children of Conflict* (Michael Kienitz)
Konscious, 129, 130
Kosovo War, 83–97; and archive of contiguities, 85–86; *Autopsia das Utopias* (Autopsy the Utopias) (Elson Froes, 1999), 98–99; jodi.org, 97, 103n70; and narrative calibration, 91–93, 96, 99; NATO bombings of, 83–95, 97–99; and pocho.com, 101n26; Weakblood website, 98–99; *Wordwar* (Matt Eberhart, 1999), 82, 99
Koyaanisqatsi (Godrey Reggio,1982), 39

Kracauer, Siegfried, 180
Kroker, Arthur, 84, 87, 96
Kroker, Marilouise, 84, 87, 96
Ku Klux Klan, 64, 209
Kyung Sun Yu, 129

L.A. Freewaves, 215
Lang, David, 226
Lange, Dorothea, 94–95
La Riva, Gloria, 98
Last Broadcast, The (1998), 120
Laurie Anderson, Laurie, 215
Lawrence of Arabia (David Lean, 1962), 184
Lean, David, 184
Lebanon, 61, 66–67, 106
Lee, Ang, 120
Lee, Kevin, 130
Lee, Spike, 122
Leger, Fernand, 219
Lehrman, Paul, 219
LeVeque, Les, xii, *178*, 179–187; *2 Spellbound* (1999), 181, 185; *4 Vertigo* (2000), 181, 184–185; *6xTheHillsAreAliveWithTheSoundOfMusic*, 185; *Backwards Birth of a Nation* (2000), 184; charged space in works of, 183–184; *Dramatically Repeating Lawrence of Arabia* (2004), *178*, 181–182, 184; hallucinations in works of, 184–185; interfaces in works of, 182; materialities and operation in works of, 180–182; *Notes from the Underground* (2003), 182; *Song from the Cultural Revolution, A* (1998), 182; *Strained Andromeda Strain* (2002), 185; tensional zones in work of, 186–187
Levinson, Andrés, 240
Lévy, Pierre, 84–85
Lifton, Robert Jay, 45, 85
Liss, Andrea, 94
Listen to Britain (Humphrey Jennings and Stewart McAllister, 1942), 75
Littleton, Colorado (Columbine), shooting, 86–88
live performance, 213–228; archives, 216–219; clubs, 223–224; concert halls, 224–225; convergences, 215–216; Experimental Television Center, 222–223; Fluxus and happenings, 219–222; and interfaces, 225–228

Living Nickelodeon, The, 218
Locarno Film Festival, 108
London, Barbara, 222
Loznitsa, Sergey, 236
Lucas, George, 123
Lucasfilm, 122
Lukács, Georg, x, xi
Lynch, David, 122
Lytvynenko, Andril, 76

MacDonald, Scott, 8
MacDougall, David, 24, 145, 207, 232
Madblast, 125, 126–127
Madcat Women's Festival, 219, 223
Madison, Cleo, 219
Magical History Film and Video Bus Tour, 172–174
Maidan (Sergey Loznitsa and Chad Garcia, 2014), 77, 78–79
Makhmalbaf, Mohsen: *Kandahar* (2001), xiv, 104, 106, 108, 111; "Limbs of No Body," 105
Malaysia, 10, 21–22, 138, 153–155, 160, 235
Mandell, Joan, 129
Marks, Laura U., 8
Marxism, 5
masculinity, 92–93, 184
Massiah, Louis, *36*, *114*, 129
Materre, Michelle, 8
Matrix, The (1999), 86, 87–88, 153
Matrix Reloaded, The (2003), 225
Matrix Revolution, The (2003), 21
McAllister, Stewart, 75
McKee, Yates, 234
McLagan, Meg, 234
Media Buffalo, 8
media concentration and consolidation, 110, 124, 146, 228
Memescapes (Ann Michel and Phil Wilde, 2007), 165–166
Menanteau, Veronik, 99
Mendes, Sam, 120
Metropolis (1927), 217
Meyer, Jeffrey, 174–175
Micheaux, Oscar: film history readings on, 204–205; production of *Within Our Gates* in response to *The Birth of a Nation*, 209; *Within Our Gates* (1920), xii, *198*, 199–210. *See also Within Our Gates: Revisited and Remixed*

Michel, Ann, 165–166
Mickey Mouse, 192, 196
microradio (pirate radio), 22, 226
microterritories, 32–33
Miller, Elizabeth, 248
Milosevic, Slobodan, 86, 93, 97
Minority Report (2002), 119
Mitchell, Allyson, 30; *Afghanimation* (2008), 34; *Melty Kitty* (2007), 31; *My Life in 5 Minutes* (2000), 32; *Precious Little Tiny Love* (2003), 31
Mohaiemen, Naeem, 138
montage, xii, xiii, 33, 45–47, 51, 53, 74, 89, 98–99, 143, 146, 172, 187, 219
Montreal Free Trade of the Americas, 33–34
Moorman, Charlotte, 8
Morrison, Bill, 166, 224–225; *Decasia* (2002), 224
Moss, Jesse, 75, 79
Motion Picture Association (MPA), 19–21, 153; Operation Eradicate, 21
Moveon.org, 17
Murray, Timothy, 8
Mykolyshn, Oleksandra, 79

National Alliance for Media Arts and Culture (NAMAC), 9, 17, 139; *Deep Focus: A Report on the Future of Independent Media*, 17, 139
Nation Erupts, The (1992), 24
NATO Targets (International Action Center, 1999), 97–98
Nazism, 64, 72, 76, 86, 91, 94–95
Neames, Arnie, 222
Negativland, xii, 189–196; *Dispepsi* (1997), 191; *Escape from Noise* (1987), 191; *Gimme the Mermaid*, 190, 194; *Helter Stupid* (1989), 191; *No Business* (2005), 188, 189–196; sampling license development, 191; and transnational media corporations (TMCs), 189–190, 192, 194–195; *U2* (1991), 191
new film history, 5, 199, 200–201, 207, 214
Newsreel, xii, 39, 130, 232
New York Film Festival, 108
New York State Council on the Arts (NYSCA), 7–8
Nicaragua, 61, 65–66, 67
Nichols, Bill, 96, 232
9/11 Moment, A, 114, 129–130; *Flag* (Louis Massiah), 129; *Quintera Yazzie* (Lena Carr), 129; *Scout Leader* (Joan Mandell), 129; *This Is Not a John Wayne Movie* (Ellen Spiro and Karen Bernstein), 129
Nixon, Richard, 157
Northeast Historic Film, 7
Northern Ireland, 58, 61, 65, 68
Northern Lights (1978), 118
Nosferatu (1922), 217
Not Channel Zero Video Collective, 24; *X 1/2: The Legacy of Malcolm X* (1993), 24
nuclear disaster, 73–74, 79, 80
nuclear war, 44
Nunn, Fe, 199, 203, 204

online festivals, 121–122
Orekhova, Marina, 80
orphaned films, 200
Outerborough (2005), 225

Paesmans, Dirk, 103n70
Paik, Nam June, 8
Panh, Rithy, xiii, 24, 158
Paper Tiger Television, xii–xiii, 39, 221, 232, 255
participatory new media documentary, 231–236; Babylon '13, 236; case studies, 234–236; and community media, 232–233; constituents of, 236; and histories, 232–233; microlevel, 233; Migrant Worker Stories (EngageMedia), 234–235; migratory strategies, 233; permeable media, 234; Quipu Project, 235
Patterson, Orlando, 88
Pederson, Claudia, 8
performance, live. *See* live performance
performance art, 107, 191, 194, 214, 221
performative matrix, 225–226
permeable media, 234
Piazzolla, Astor, 174–175
pirate radio (microradio), 22, 226
Pollard, Sam, 129
polyphonies, 31–32
Posner, Bruce, 219
postcolonialism, 4, 11, 48, 50, 204; postcolonial historiography, 167, 232; postcolonial studies, 38; postcolonial turn, 231
Powell, Colin, 107, 108, 110, 127
Powell, Michael, 110
Preemptive Media Collective, 227–228; *ZAPPED!* (2005), 227–228

Prelude to War (Frank Capra, 1942), 126
Prometheus Radio Project v. the FCC, 22
Propp, Vladimir, 93
psychoanalysis, 5, 85, 89, 93, 127, 180–184
public domains, 135–146; and alternatives to panic, 142–144; collaborative antiwar works, 140; and collaborative histories, 145–146; Creative Commons, 191; definition of, 135–136; and historiography, 140–142; and Negativland, 190–193; and new media ecologies, 138–139; and production of panic, 137–138; and transformative history, 144–145
Putin, Vladimir, 74–75

Quotations from Chairman Mao Tse-Tung (1967), 182

Rashid, Ahmed, 108
recalibration, 3, 5, 10, 124; and participatory new media projects, 232, 233; and subaltern historiography, 23; and war, 91–93, 95, 96, 99
Reclaim the Media, 133n25
Reeves, Daniel, xiv, 43–55; *Ganapati: Spirit of the Bush* (1986), 44, 47; *Hand That Holds Up All This Falling, The* (1997), 50–55; *Perdu*, 53; *Sabda* (1984), 44; *Smothering Dreams* (1981), 43–44, 51; *Sombra a Sombra* (1988), 44, 46; *Try to Live to See This* (1988), 52–53; *White Television, The* (1977 and 1997), 51. See also *Hand That Holds Up All This Falling, The* (Daniel Reeves, 1997)
Reeves, Keanu, 21
refugees: Afghan, 34, 108; Cambodian, 157, 159; Haitian, 173; Iraqi, 140; and Kosovo War, 83, 87–88, 90–96; and Vietnam War, 157
Reggio, Godrey, 39
Reid, Anna, 73
reverse engineering, xi, xiii; and algorithm of collaboration, 251; and computer games, 17–18; and historiography, 2–5, 16, 23; and Iraq War, 17–19; and tools, 16; and antiwar computer games, 18; and archival objects, tools, and artifacts, 250; and the archival process of naming unburied dead, 250; and archival surround, 250; and contiguities, 249, 250; definition of, 249; in India and Cambodia, 22–25; by LeVeque, Les, 180; and listeners, 250; in Malaysia and Geneva, 19–22; and memory, 250; and openness, 249; as polyphonic, polyversal, and polyvocal, 250; by Preemptive Media, 228; as process rather than product, 251; as productive, changing, and mobilizing, 251; and public domains, 137; purpose of, 250; and recombinant, contiguous, fluid, and polyphonic practices, 251; and repetition, 250; and romanticism, 251; and speakers, 250; speculations on, 249–251; and temporality, 250; and transnational capital, 250; and Vietnam War, 16
Revolution in Military Affairs (RMA), 17, 84, 110, 111
RFID (radio frequency identification), 139, 227
Richner, Beat, 152–153
Ridge, Tom, 109
Robert Flaherty Film Seminars, xii, 7–8, 48; 2005 Film Seminar (fiftieth anniversary), 217; "Explorations in Memory and Modernity," 8–9
Robeson, Paul, 208
Roe, Tom, 227
Rose Goldsen Archive of New Media Art, 8
Rosen, Philip, 107, 146, 170
Rosenblatt, Jay, 117
Roy, Arundhati, 107
Ruby, Jay, 232
Rumsfeld, Donald, 125
Russian Woodpecker, The (Chad Garcia, 2015), 79
Ruttman, Walter, 39

S21: The Khmer Rouge Killing Machine (2002), xiii, 24, 158
Sakwa, Richard, 74
Sarai, 19, 195
SARS (severe acute respiratory syndrome), 151, 153
Scahill, Jeremy, 111, 130
Schamus, James, 119
School of the Americas, 226
Scribe Video Center, xiii; *Documentary History Project for Youth*, 39; *Precious Places Project* (2005-ongoing), 36, 37–40;

Putting the Nice Back in the Town, 39; *To Badlands and Back Again* (2005), 37–38
Secrets of Family Happiness, The, 219
sensualities, 245–247
September 11, 2001, 18, 106–108, 117, 126–127; 9/11, 120; *9/11 and Beyond: Independent Voices*, 130; *9/11 Moment, A*, 114, 129–130; *Afghanistan: From Ground Zero to Ground Zero*, 130; *Invisible Girl*, 130; *New York Chinatown 9/11*, 130; *Underground Zero* (Jay Rosenblatt, 2002), 117. See also *9/11 Moment, A*
Serbia, 71, 84–90, 93, 97–98, 110
Shobak.org, 138, 144, 146
Shocking and Awful (Deep Dish Television), 140, 144, 146
Shore Line, The (Elizabeth Miller and international collaborators, 2018), *248*
Shtyka, Ella, 78
simulation technologies, 18, 19, 72, 86–87
single-channel work, 44–51, 54, 142
Siomopoulos, Anna, 204
Sistema Radio Venceremos, 233
Small Arms-Children of Conflict (Michael Kienitz): *Aftermath* (1982), 67; *Belfast Street* (1981), 65; *Break Time* (1981), 63; *Fall Roads Bus* (1981), 58, 68; *Flea Market Booth* (1978), 64; *Lads of the Murph* (1981), 65; *Little General, The* (1984), 59, 61; *Makeshift Morgue* (1982), 63; *Milltown Cemetery* (1981), 65; *Natural Causes* (1984), 63; *Nazi Youth* (1980), 64; *Playground* (1982), 67; *Push Cart* (1984), 66; *Scavenger* (1978), 65; *Search, The* (1984), 65–66; *Shoe Shiner* (1988), 68; *Wood for the Oven* (1988), 67–68
Smith, Jack, 219
Snyder, Timothy, 73
Somma, Thomas, 55
Sonnenfield, Barry, 122
Soohen, Jacquie, 111, 130
Sound of Music, The (Robert Wise, 1965), 183, 185
Spanish Civil War, 44, 46, 53
Spiderman (2002), 119
Spielberg, Steven, 123
Spiro, Ellen, 129
Sporting Life (2016), 14
Squeaky Wheel, 8

Stalin, Joseph, 73
Star Wars (George Lucas, 1977), 120, 122
Stern, Gerd, 222
Stokes, RaeJean, 71, 79
Stoney, George, 39
Strasser, Reiner, 98
subaltern historiography, 23, 141–142, 146, 170
Subatlantic (Ursula Biemann, 2015), 244
Sumar, Anna, 76
Sundance Film Festival, 120, 123, 139

Tadpole (Gary Winick), 119
Taliban, 106, 108, 125–127
Tarr, Simon, 24, 171, 203, 204
Taussig, Michael, 45
Teasdale, Perry, 221
Téno, Jean-Marie, 195
Termite TV Collective, 129
Terrorism, Information and Prevention System (TIPS), 109
This Is What Democracy Looks Like (2000), 120
Tiazhlov, Dmytro, 78, 79
Time Code (Mike Figgis, 1999), 118
Todorov, Tzvetan, 144, 169, 200
Toy Story (1995), 126
transnational media corporations (TMCs), 19–21, 25, 85, 99, 115–121, 138, 153, 159, 189–195
Trinh T. Minh-ha, 48, 50, 89
Tupelo, Mississipi, 64
Turan, Kenneth, 118

Ukraine, xii; *Babushkas of Chernobyl, The* (Holly Morris and Anne Bogart, 2015), 80; Babylon '13 Collective, *70*, 79, 236; chernozem (black soil), 71–73, 76, 78–80; Heavenly Hundred killings, 77–78; *Maidan* (Sergey Loznitsa, 2014), 77, 78–79; Maidan Nezalezhnosti (Independence Square), 77–79; recent history of, 72–73; *tusit* (strolling together in public), 80; *vyshyvka* (Ukrainian decorative embroidery), 80; *Winter on Fire: Ukraine's Fight for Freedom* (Evgeny Afineevsky, 2015), 77, 78, 236
Ukrainian Documentary New Wave, 78–79
Underground Zero (Jay Rosenblatt, 2002), 117
United States 2016 presidential election, 74
Unseen Cinema, 219

USA PATRIOT Act, 17, 105, 109, 202, 227
US Techniques of Genocide in Vietnam (1968), 16

Vacaciones en Necochea (1970s), 240
Valenti, Jack, 153
Vallejo, Cesar, 46
Varda, Agnes, 221
Vasulka, Steina, 16, 215
Vasulka, Woody, 16
Velvet Underground, 220, 224
Vertov, Dziga, xii, 47, 146; *Kinoks,* 232; *Man with a Movie Camera* (1929), 217
Vice News, 72
Video in the Villages, 233
Vietnam War, xiii, xiv, 16, 43, 44–45, 49, 51, 55, 59
Vinterberg, Thomas, 119
Virilio, Paul, 49, 89, 185
Visible Collective, 138
Von Triers, Lars, 118

Wag the Dog (1997), 86
War and Peace D Word Collaborative Project, 130
War at Home (1979), 118
Warhol, Andy, 220, 224
Wasko, Janet, 122
Waugh, Tom, 232
Weber, Lois, 219
Weibel, Peter, 89
Welk, Lois, 222
White, Hayden, 91, 92, 144, 200
Whitehead, Baruch, 204
Whitman, Robert, 223–224
Who Killed Vincent Chin? (Christine Choy and Renee Tajima, 1989), 96
Wieland, Joyce, 34
Wiesel, Elie, 94
Wilde, Phil, 165–166
Williams, Peggy, 202
Williams, Raymond: *Long Revolution, The,* xiii; *Keywords,* xiv
Williams, Zachary, 204
Wilson, Andrew, 74

Winter on Fire: Ukraine's Fight for Freedom (Evgeny Afineevsky, 2015), 77, 78, 236
Winton, Ezra, 232
Within Our Gates: Revisited and Remixed (Ithaca College, 2004), 199–210; "blackening" the film through jazz and hip-hop, 203, 208–209; and Body and Soul Ensemble, 199, 207–208; collaboration of musicians and academic community, 203–204; and collaborative ethnography, 199, 207–208; conceptual underpinnings of, 199–200; and critical historiography, 199–201, 204, 207–208; and digital culture theory, 199, 204, 207–208; film history readings for, 204–205; goal of, 204; and Ida B. Wells Spoken Word Ensemble, 199, 208; and new film history, 199, 200; racialized and gendered issues, 207–208; scoring of, 202–203
WITNESS, 233
Wolf, Julia, 226
Wolfowitz, Paul, 107
Woman in Black, A, 33
Women Direct Film and Video Series (Ithaca College), xii, 6–7
Women Make Movies, 7
Woodstock Community Video, 222
Workers' Film and Photo League, xii, 98

X 1/2: The Legacy of Malcolm X (Not Channel Zero, 1993), 24

yael, b.h., 30; *Hot Sandfilled Wind, A* (2006), 33; *(of) Fences* (2001), 33–34; *Trading the Future* (2008), 34
Yanukovich, Victor, 235
You Are on Indian Land (1969), 39
Young, La Monte, 219
Youngblood, Gene, 220
YouTube, x, 236

Zane, Arnie, 222
Zapatista (1999), 120
Zapatista movement (Mexico), 120, 225–226
Zen Buddhism, 46, 52
Žižek, Slavoj, 46, 89, 92–95, 108

PATRICIA R. ZIMMERMANN is Professor of Screen Studies at Ithaca College and codirector of the Finger Lakes Environmental Film Festival. She is author and editor of numerous titles, including *Reel Families: A Social History of Amateur Film* (Indiana University Press, 1995); (with Dale Hudson) *Thinking Through Digital Media: Transnational Environments and Locative Places* (Palgrave Macmillan, 2015); (with Scott MacDonald) *The Flaherty: Decades in the Cause of Independent Film* (Indiana University Press, 2017); and (with Helen De Michiel) *Open Space New Media Documentary: A Toolkit for Theory and Practice* (Routledge, 2018).

www.ingramcontent.com/pod-product-compliance
Lightning Source LLC
Chambersburg PA
CBHW021805220426
43662CB00006B/182